Daily Wisdom
for Women

2014 Devotional Collection

Daily Wisdom
for Women

BARBOUR
PUBLISHING

2014 Devotional Collection

Daily Wisdom

for Women

Introduction

Experience an intimate connection to your heavenly
Father with the *Daily Wisdom for Women* devotional
collection. Featuring a powerful devotional reading
and prayer for every day of 2014, this beautiful volume
provides inspiration and encouragement for your soul.
Enhance your spiritual journey with the refreshing
readings—and come to know just how deeply
and tenderly God loves you.

Do Over

*The LORD says, "Forget what happened before,
and do not think about the past. Look at the new thing
I am going to do. It is already happening. Don't you see it?
I will make a road in the desert and rivers in the dry land."*
ISAIAH 43:18–19 NCV

There is nothing quite as redemptive as a "do over." A popular psychologist encourages parents to offer children an opportunity for a "do over" when a behavior needs correcting. The parent states, "That was not acceptable behavior. Would you like a do over?" Almost without exception, the child gladly accepts a chance to make things right.

We get some "do overs" in life. New Year's is one of them. Without making a list of resolutions that you will forget about in a week, consider this: Where do you need a "do over"? Is there a relationship in your life that needs repair? Do your priorities need revision? If you haven't been eating healthy, should you alter your grocery list?

As you begin a new year, realize that no one is perfect. Take inventory, though, of the areas in your life that could benefit from a fresh start. Embrace the chance for a "do over"!

*Thank You, Lord, for a new year! Give me the discipline that it takes
to make necessary changes. I love You, Father. Amen.*

In His Presence

*Let us therefore come boldly unto the throne of grace, that we may
obtain mercy, and find grace to help in time of need.*
HEBREWS 4:16 KJV

Abigail was only three, but she knew that when she was at
Grandpoppa's house he made the best playmate ever. Sometimes she
only had to ask twice to get him to play tea party with her and several
of Grandmama's stuffed animals or special dolls. He was usually
pretty quick to turn on the sprinklers so Abigail could run through the
grassy yard in her bare feet. More than anything, she enjoyed crawling
up in his lap with her favorite book and presenting it to him to read.
If he ever got tired of the same old story, he never let on. Instead, he
read it each time with surprise and sincerity—like he'd never seen the
words before.

What a joy to know that, just like Abigail, we can come into the
presence of God and make our requests known to Him. Just like a
grandparent loves to see joy in his grandchild's eyes, God loves to give
us gifts and see us delight in time spent with Him. Whatever we have
need of, we can come in and sit down with our heavenly Father and
tell Him everything.

*Heavenly Father, thank You for always welcoming me into Your
presence. I have assurance that You know what I have need of and
that I can always rest in Your mercy and grace. Amen.*

Put on Love

And over all these virtues put on love,
which binds them all together in perfect unity.
COLOSSIANS 3:14 NIV

How many mornings have we stood in our closets, looking hopelessly at its overstuffed contents and thinking we have nothing to wear? What we're really thinking is that we have nothing to wear that makes us feel cute or pretty or sporty or professional—or whatever look we're going for that day. We want to look attractive. We want others to be drawn to us. And sometimes, no matter how many blouses we have to choose from, nothing feels right.

But there is one accessory we all have available to us that always fits. It always looks right, is always appropriate, and always makes us more attractive to others. When we wear it, we are beautiful, no matter how faded or dated our wardrobes may be. When we wear it, we become more popular, more sought after, more admired.

What is that accessory, you ask, and where can you buy it?

It's love, and you can't buy it anywhere. But it's free, and it's always available through the Holy Spirit. When we call on Him to help us love others, He cloaks us in a beautiful covering that draws people to us and makes us perfectly lovely in every way.

Dear Father, as I get dressed each day, help me to remember the most important accessory I can wear is Your love. Amen.

A Twig to Rest On

*This is what the LORD says: "Stand at the crossroads and look;
ask for the ancient paths, ask where the good way is,
and walk in it, a nd you will find rest for your souls."*
JEREMIAH 6:16 NIV

The day was so long and stressful that Tracey didn't get out to her
front porch until late at night to water her flowers. Recent days had
been so unusually hot and dry in the Midwest, draining both Tracey
and her once-luscious hanging petunia baskets into a weary state.

She breathed a calming sigh to be out in the cool of the evening,
hearing a few last birds coo while the crickets took the next singing
shift. But as she reached up to water one thirsty pot, something
fluttered furiously out through the stream of water. Frightened,
Tracey jumped back and tried to determine what it was. The small
creature flew directly into a rose of sharon bush next to the porch,
where Tracey could now see it was a baby sparrow. *Maybe it's injured*,
she thought, as it fell asleep on the tiny twig, swaying with the gentle
breeze of the night.

In the morning she found the bird still resting in the same place
and slowly approached it. The sparrow flew off with strength into the
sunshine.

*Lord, thank You for giving me the rest I need along the journey. Just
like You do for the tiny sparrow, so much more You do for me. Amen.*

Promises of God

*"For the LORD your God is living among you. He is a mighty savior.
He will take delight in you with gladness. With his love, he will
calm all your fears. He will rejoice over you with joyful songs."*
ZEPHANIAH 3:17 NLT

Look at all the promises packed into this one verse of scripture!
God is with you. He is your mighty savior. He delights in you with
gladness. He calms your fears with His love. He rejoices over you
with joyful songs. Wow! What a bundle of hope is found here for the
believer. Like a mother attuned to her newborn baby's cries, so is your
heavenly Father's heart for you. He delights in being your Father. He
knows when the storms of life are raging all around you. He senses
your need to be held close and for fears to be calmed. It is in
those times that He is for you a Prince of Peace, a Comforter. He
rejoices over you with joyful songs. Can you imagine that God loves
you so much that you cause Him to sing? God sings over you. And
the songs He sings are joyful. He loves you with an unconditional,
everlasting love. Face this day knowing that your God is with you. He
calms you. And He sings over you. You are blessed to be a daughter of
the King.

*Father, thank You for loving me the way You do.
You are all I need. Amen.*

Working Hard

*Whatever you do, work at it with all your heart,
as working for the Lord, not for human masters.*
COLOSSIANS 3:23 NIV

Paul encouraged his readers to work hard, with all their hearts. Many of the new converts were enslaved to non-Christian masters. The tension between Christians and non-Christians increased when the non-Christian had the authority to lord it over the Christian.

But the wisdom in this verse applies to us today. We should always work hard, always give our best, even if we don't like our bosses. Ultimately, the quality of work we do reflects on our Father. If we're lazy or if our work is below standard, it has a negative impact on the Body of Christ. But when we meet our deadlines and our work exceeds expectations, we give others a positive impression of what it means to be a Christian.

If we want to get ahead in our jobs and we want to help build the kingdom of God, we must have impeccable reputations. One way to build a positive reputation is to be a hard worker. When we do our absolute best at any task, people notice. When we consistently deliver quality products and services, people notice. We honor God and we honor ourselves when we work hard at the tasks we've been given.

*Dear Father, I want to honor You with the work I do.
Help me to work hard, with all my heart. Amen.*

When Words Fail Me

Before a word is on my tongue you, LORD, know it completely.
PSALM 139:4 NIV

Pastor John's message on Sunday morning had been about prayer. After the service, Melissa, a young mother in the congregation, asked the pastor if they could speak privately.

"Pastor," she said, "I can't pray. Your prayers sound so beautiful. But when I pray, I sometimes have no words, and when I do they sound. . .well. . .stupid."

Her pastor smiled reassuringly. "Melissa, God doesn't care how eloquent your words are. He cares about what's in your heart. Without you telling Him, God already knows your thoughts and desires. When you pray, speak to Him as if you're talking with your loving Father."

Sometimes Christians feel so overwhelmed by their needs or by the greatness of God that they simply can't pray. When the words won't come, God helps to create them. Paul says in Romans 8:26, "And the Holy Spirit helps us in our weakness. For example, we don't know what God wants us to pray for. But the Holy Spirit prays for us with groanings that cannot be expressed in words" (NLT).

God hears your prayers even before you pray them. When you don't know what to say and the words won't come, you can simply ask God to help you by praying on your behalf.

*Dear God, I'm grateful today that in my silence You still hear me.
Amen.*

I Forgive You

*Smart people know how to hold their tongue;
their grandeur is to forgive and forget.*
PROVERBS 19:11 MSG

Great power comes in these three little words: *I forgive you.* Often they are hard to say, but they are powerful in their ability to heal our own hearts. Jesus taught His disciples to pray, "Forgive us our trespasses as we forgive those who trespass against us." He knew we needed to forgive others to be whole. When we are angry or hold a grudge against someone, our spirits are bound. The release that comes with extending forgiveness enables our spirits to commune with God more closely, and love swells within us.

How do you forgive? Begin with prayer. Recognize the humanity of the person who wronged you, and make a choice to forgive. Ask the Lord to help you forgive the person(s). Be honest, for the Lord sees your heart. Trust the Holy Spirit to guide you and cleanse you. Then step out and follow His leading in obedience.

By forgiving, we can move forward, knowing that God has good things in store for us. And the heaviness of spirit is lifted, and relief washes over us after we've forgiven. A new sense of hope and expectancy rises. *I forgive you.* Do you need to say those words today?

*Father, search my heart and show me areas where I might need
to forgive another. Help me let go and begin to heal. Amen.*

Bold Prayers

Joshua prayed to the LORD in front of all the people of Israel.
He said, "Let the sun stand still over Gibeon."
JOSHUA 10:12 NLT

Do you pray conservatively or audaciously? Joshua prayed audaciously—and the sun stood still. Hannah prayed audaciously—and God granted her a son. Daniel prayed audaciously—and the lions' mouths stayed closed all night. (Whew—what a relief to him!) Jesus prayed audaciously—and Lazarus rose from the dead.

What about you? Have you dared to pray a bold prayer, or are you content to ask God for easy things?

Jennie, her husband, and two boys decided to pray audaciously that God would help them adopt a little girl from Haiti. They had no extra money, and the fee to adopt came to over $15,000. Still, they felt led to start filling out the required paperwork and making plans.

About the time they had hoped to complete the process, the family was still woefully short on funds. But out of the blue, a distant relative called Jennie and said that her great-uncle (whom the family had only met once) had died and left an inheritance to Jennie. The next week, Jennie nearly fainted when she opened a certified mail envelope—and a check for $14,500 fell out.

Pray audaciously. You never know what God will do.

God, thank You for answering mightily when we pray with bold faith.
Amen.

Get Above It All

*Set your minds and keep them set on what is above (the higher
things), not on the things that are on the earth.*
COLOSSIANS 3:2 AMP

If you've ever taken a trip by airplane, you know with one glimpse from
the window at thirty thousand feet how the world seems small. With
your feet on the ground, you may feel small in a big world; and it's
easy for the challenges of life and the circumstances from day to day
to press in on you. But looking down from above the clouds, things can
become clear as you have the opportunity to get above it all.

Sometimes the most difficult challenges you face play out in your
head—where a struggle to control the outcome and work out the
details of life can consume you. Once removed—far away from the
details—you can see things from a higher perspective. Close your eyes
and push out the thoughts that try to grab you and keep you tied to
the things of the world.

Reach out to God and let your spirit soar. Give your concerns to
Him and let Him work out the details. Rest in Him and He'll carry you
above it all, every step of the way.

*God, You are far above any detail of life that concerns me. Help me
to trust You today for answers to those things that seem to bring me
down. I purposefully set my heart and mind on You today. Amen.*

Answer Me!

*Answer me when I call to you, my righteous God. Give me relief
from my distress; have mercy on me and hear my prayer.*
PSALM 4:1 NIV

Have you ever felt like God wasn't listening? We've all felt that from
time to time. David felt it when he slept in a cold, hard cave night
after night, while being pursued by Saul's men. He felt it when his
son Absalom turned against him. Time and again in his life, David felt
abandoned by God. And yet, David was called a man after God's own
heart.

No matter our maturity level, there will be times when we feel
abandoned by God. There will be times when our faith wavers and our
fortitude wanes. That's okay. It's normal.

But David didn't give up. He kept crying out to God, kept falling
to his knees in worship, kept storming God's presence with his pleas.
David knew God wouldn't hide His face for long, for he knew what we
might sometimes forget: God is love. He loves us without condition
and without limit. And He is never far from those He loves.

No matter how distant God may seem, we need to keep talking
to Him. Keep praying. Keep pouring out our hearts. We can know, as
David knew, that God will answer in His time.

*Dear Father, thank You for always hearing my prayers. Help me to
trust You, even when You seem distant. Amen.*

A Choice

*I'm singing joyful praise to GOD. I'm turning cartwheels of joy to my
Savior God. Counting on GOD's Rule to prevail, I take heart and gain
strength. I run like a deer. I feel like I'm king of the mountain!*
HABAKKUK 3:18–19 MSG

Many days, life seems like an uphill battle, where we are fighting
against the current, working hard to maintain our equilibrium.
Exhausted from the battle, we often throw up our hands in disgust
and want to quit. That's when we should realize we have a choice. We
can choose to surrender our burdens to the Lord!

What would happen if we followed the advice of the psalmist
and turned a cartwheel of joy in our hearts—regardless of the
circumstances—then leaned and trusted in His rule to prevail? Think
of the happiness and peace that could be ours with a total surrender
to God's care.

It's a decision to count on God's rule to triumph. And we must
realize His Word, His rule, never fails. Never. Then we must want to
stand on that Word. Taking a giant step, armed with scriptures and
praise and joy, we can surmount any obstacle put before us, running
like a deer, climbing the tall mountains. With God at our side, it's
possible to be king of the mountain.

*Dear Lord, I need Your help. Gently guide me so I might learn
to lean on You and become confident in Your care. Amen.*

The Lord Himself Goes before You

"The LORD himself goes before you and will be with you; he will never leave you nor forsake you. Do not be afraid; do not be discouraged."
DEUTERONOMY 31:8 NIV

How comforting and freeing when we allow God to go before us! Stop and consider that for a moment: you can relinquish control of your life and circumstances to the Lord himself. Relax! His shoulders are big enough to carry all of your burdens.

The issue that has your stomach in knots right now? Ask the Lord to go before you. The problem that makes you wish you could hide under the covers and sleep until it's all over? Trust that God Himself will never leave you and that He is working everything out.

Joshua 1:9 tells us to "be strong and courageous. Do not be afraid; do not be discouraged, for the LORD your God will be with you wherever you go." Be encouraged! Even when it feels like it, you are truly never alone. And never without access to God's power.

If you've trusted Christ as your Savior, the Spirit of God Himself is alive and well and working inside you at all times. What an astounding miracle! The Creator of the universe dwells within you and is available to encourage you and help you make right choices on a moment-by-moment basis.

Thank You, Lord, for the incredible gift of Your presence in each and every situation I face. Allow me to remember this and to call upon Your name as I go about each day. Amen.

Jonah's Prayer

*"When my life was ebbing away, I remembered you, LORD,
and my prayer rose to you, to your holy temple."*
JONAH 2:7 NIV

Jonah ran from God. He knew where God had directed him to go, but he refused. He thought he knew better than God. He trusted in his own ways over God's. Where did it get him? He ended up in the belly of a great fish for three days. This was not a punishment but rather a forced retreat! Jonah needed time to think and pray. He came to the end of himself and remembered his Sovereign God. He describes the depths to which he was cast. This was not just physical but emotional as well. Jonah had been in a deep struggle between God's call and his own will.

In verse 6 of his great prayer from the belly of the fish, we read these words: *"But you, LORD my God, brought my life up from the pit."* When Joseph reached a point of desperation, he realized that God was his only hope. Have you been there? Not in the belly of a great fish, but in a place where you are made keenly aware that it is time to turn back to God? God loves His children and always stands ready to receive us when we need a second chance.

*Father, like Jonah I sometimes think my own ways are
better than Yours. Help me to be mindful that Your ways
are always good and right. Amen.*

How Great Is Our God!

And I said, O Lord God of heaven, the great and terrible God,
Who keeps covenant, loving-kindness, and mercy for those
who love Him and keep His commandments. . .
NEHEMIAH 1:5 AMP

When Dorothy finally met the wizard she had been searching for in
The Wonderful Wizard of Oz, she was disappointed. The "Great and
Terrible" magician, who had promoted himself as an all-powerful
man with a short temper, turned out to be a normal person behind a
curtain—albeit one who was good at special effects.

Rest assured, when we finally meet God, we won't have the
same kind of letdown. The Bible notes God's inestimable qualities—
unconditional love, unending mercy, unimaginable strength—with
reverence. The New Testament authors also repeatedly wrote about
God's mercy and compassion, lest we despair of ever coming near Him.

Of course, we need to fear the holy Creator and Maker of all
things and strive to do His will, but as the One who formed us, God
knows that we will fail (and loves us anyway). His love is why He sent
Jesus to die on the cross.

Today, think about God's love, mercy, and strength as you go
about your day. When you face problems, ask Him to solve them,
instead of trying to fix them yourself. Repeatedly and reverently
surrender to Him—because He is great, but He's certainly not terrible.

Creator, Maker, Redeemer God—You are wonderful.
Thank You for Your wisdom, strength, and love. Amen.

Love and Marriage

Submit to one another out of reverence for Christ.
EPHESIANS 5:21 NIV

Young couples often approach marriage thinking that their love will survive anything. Then when the first trial tests their faith and endurance, their love crumbles.

Author and aviator Antoine de Saint-Exupéry wrote, "Love does not consist in gazing at each other but in looking outward together in the same direction." Such is the goal of a couple committed to Christ.

Admit it: marriage is work. Yet God unites two people for a common purpose—to lift one up when the other falls, to give instead of receive, to exercise the art of compromise and understanding. On the other hand, a loveless marriage is one based on self-absorption or selfishness on the part of one or both individuals.

The love that once attracted us to our spouse isn't the love that sustains our marriage. Rather, God's love prevails in the lives of the couple who choose to, in mutual submission, place Christ first.

The above scripture indicates that submission applies to both men and women, yet Paul goes on to exhort women to submit to their husbands—for as a woman submits or respects her husband, he, in turn, loves his wife (Ephesians 5:22–28).

The result? A man and woman united in faith, traveling in the same direction.

*Father, help me become the helpmate You intended.
Guide me to live a submissive life to You first and then my husband.
May we both follow Your lead, not our own. Amen.*

Have Thine Own Way

Know that the LORD is God. It is he who made us, and we are his;
we are his people, the sheep of his pasture.
PSALM 100:3 NIV

"Thou art the potter, I am the clay." Those are ringing words from the song "Have Thine Own Way" that stirs up emotions and a desire to allow God to mold us and make us in His image. But what a hard thing to do. We strive to create our own worlds, to make a plan, to fix it. However God asks us to allow Him free rein.

Sheep follow their shepherd and trust in him for provision. "As in his presence humbly I bow." Submissive to their masters, they quietly graze the hillsides knowing the shepherd knows best. What a wonderfully relaxing word picture: relying on God's guidance and timing, following His lead.

It is a simple prayer to ask Him to help us give up control, yet not a simple task. In obedience to His Word, we can bow our heads and ask for the Holy Spirit's direction and take our hands from the steering wheel. Then wait. Quietly on our hillsides, not chomping at the bit; hearts "yielded and still." We wait for the still, small voice. This day, resolve to listen and follow.

Lord, we humbly bow before You and ask for Your divine guidance.
Help us to follow Your plan with yielded hearts, ever ready to give
up control to You. Amen.

From Rotting

*[God will] bestow on them a crown of beauty instead of ashes,
the oil of joy instead of mourning, and a garment of praise instead
of a spirit of despair. They will be called oaks of righteousness,
a planting of the LORD for the display of his splendor.*
ISAIAH 61:3 NIV

Sometime in August, after weeks of busy work schedules by day (and sometimes night) and a bathroom tiling project by night (and into the wee morning hours), Mary walked down her front porch steps and took a deep breath.

When she looked around, she was shocked to realize how neglected her landscaping was. There were massive broad-leaf weeds taking over the ground. A closer look revealed that the "weeds" were actually pumpkin plants that last year's rotting pumpkin display had inadvertently provided.

She thought about ripping out the vines, since there wasn't much growing on them yet, but she decided to let what was alive and well continue to grow. Before long, three large, bright orange volunteer pumpkins had pushed past red (now barely visible) mums.

Mary started thinking how many things volunteer themselves right into her life—and end up being beautiful additions to her days.

*God, thank You for taking the rotten things of life
and turning them into bountiful blessings. Amen.*

Stop Pretending

Don't just pretend to love others. Really love them.
ROMANS 12:9 NLT

Many times in our lives we are hurt deeply by those closest to us. And because they are family members or people that we must maintain a relationship with, we pretend to love them by sweeping issues under the rug. We go through the motions of relating to them in peace while nursing bitterness in our hearts. Mother Teresa said, "If we really want to love we must learn how to forgive."

God wants our relationships to be real. He wants us to be real with Him and real with others. Pretending is being dishonest. He says in Matthew 15:7–8 that the religious leaders honored Him with their lips, but their hearts were far from Him. He calls them hypocrites.

Are you hypocritical in your close relationships? Are you pretending to love when you feel nothing even close?

Tell the Lord how you feel. Ask for His help to overcome your fear of sharing your heart and being real with Him and others. Learn how to forgive, and watch as the Lord transforms your relationships into something that honors Him.

Heavenly Father, help me overcome my fear of sharing my true feelings. Forgive me for pretending to love when my heart is not in it. I want to live in authentic relationship with You and with those I love. Amen.

Climbing Mountains

The LORD is my light and my salvation—whom shall I fear?
The LORD is the stronghold of my life—of whom shall I be afraid?
PSALM 27:1 NIV

The Meteora in Greece is a complex of monastic structures high atop a mountain. Access to the structures was deliberately difficult. Some of these "hanging monasteries" were accessible only by baskets lowered by ropes and winches, and to take a trip there required a leap of faith. An old story associated with the monasteries said that the ropes were only replaced "when the Lord let them break."

While the vast majority of us will probably never scale the mountain to visit these monasteries, we often feel that we have many steep mountains of our own to climb. Maybe it's too much month at the end of the money. Or, perhaps we are suffering with health or relationship troubles. Whatever the reason we are hurting, angry, or feeling despair or hopelessness, God is ready to help us, and we can place all our hope in He who is faithful. We can do that because we are connected to Him and have seen His faithfulness in the past.

Lord, I will stay strong in You and will take courage. I can trust and rest in You. Whatever I am feeling now, whatever emotions I have, I give them to You, for You are my hope and salvation. You are good all the time, of which I can be supremely confident. Amen.

Talk to Your Best Friend

*God is faithful, who has called you into fellowship with his Son,
Jesus Christ our Lord.*
1 CORINTHIANS 1:9 NIV

When do you pray? How often do you call on God? Where do you talk to Him?

Just as we converse with our spouse or best friend about what's happening in our lives, the Lord expects and anticipates conversations with us, too.

Yes, He knows all about us, but He desires our fellowship one-on-one. Jesus chose twelve disciples with whom to fellowship, teach, and carry His Gospel to every nation. They lived and ate with Jesus; they knew Him personally; they were His best friends. In the same manner, God gives us the divine privilege to know Him on a personal level through our relationship with Christ.

When, where, or how we talk to God is of little importance to the Savior. We can converse with the Lord while driving down the street, walking through the park, or standing at the kitchen sink. We can ask for His help in the seemingly insignificant or in bigger decisions. Our concerns are His concerns, too, and He desires for us to share our heartfelt thoughts with Him.

Fellowshipping with God is talking to our best Friend, knowing He understands and provides help and wisdom along life's journey. It's demonstrating our faith and trust in the One who knows us better than anyone.

*Lord, remind me to talk to You anytime, anywhere.
I know that as I pray, You will talk to me, too. Amen.*

Refuse to Quit

*And I will pray the Father, and he shall give you another Comforter,
that he may abide with you for ever; Even the Spirit of truth; whom
the world cannot receive, because it seeth him not, neither knoweth
him: but ye know him; for he dwelleth with you, and shall be in you.*
JOHN 14:16–17 KJV

There are days when it seems that nothing goes right and you
struggle just to put one foot in front of the other. The good news on
a day like that is the truth that you are not alone. Whatever obstacle
is in your way, you don't have to overcome it in your own power. God
is with you. Jesus sent the Comforter. The Holy Spirit is your present
help in any situation.

The Holy Spirit is the very Spirit of God Himself. He is with you
always, ready to care for and guide you. By faith you can rest and rely
on the Holy Spirit for strength, wisdom, and inspiration.

The next time you feel like giving up, refuse to quit. Ask the Holy
Spirit to intervene, to provide you with the strength and wisdom to
continue your journey.

*Jesus, You have sent the Comforter to me. I believe He is
with me always, providing what I need today to refuse to quit.
I take the next step in my journey knowing He is with me.
I can press on by faith today. Amen.*

Because I Love You

*Whoever spares the rod hates their children, but the one who loves
their children is careful to discipline them.*
PROVERBS 13:24 NIV

Julie saw the five-year-old's frame slump against the wall. Jeremy
had been sent to time out—again. It almost broke Julie's heart when
she had to discipline her son. She often wondered if she was doing
the right thing, if she had been too harsh or too quick in reacting. One
thing she did know, she loved her son deeply and wanted him to grow
up to be a responsible, confident person.

God's discipline has the same goals. Discipline administered by a
loving, forward-looking parent with a goal of helping the child become
all that he can become means that He loves us. His purpose for this
is so we can share in His holiness. Discipline is never enjoyable, for
either the person giving the discipline or the one on the receiving
end. But if we look at correction as a sign of His genuine love for us, it
will help us to change our behaviors out of love for ourselves and our
heavenly Father.

*Abba Father, thank You for loving me enough to show me the way to
go, even through Your discipline. Please encourage me not to think
this is punishment but a loving reaction to a wrong behavior.
I want to be holy and can only accomplish that with Your help
and guidance. In Jesus' name, I pray. Amen.*

Creating and Enjoying

Then God looked over all he had made,
and he saw that it was very good!
GENESIS 1:31 NLT

Mary had been working diligently on tiling her bathroom. It was a big project for her and required a lot of planning and thought to design it just right. There was the mortarboard that had to replace the old, moldy drywall, and the plumber had to frame in the tub for her. She measured, sawed, carried heavy boards, nailed, cut, glued, and grouted. Every night after work she labored carefully and fell into bed exhausted for nearly three weeks straight.

Finally it was done, and she loved it! She adorned it with new curtains and a few fresh towels. She found herself going in the bathroom just to be in that room, she was so pleased.

A few days later she found her son standing in the bathroom. "I like to come in here and just look at it, Mom; it's so nice. I can't imagine how good you must feel!"

Mary thought about it and smiled. "God made us like Him. You know, how He stood back and enjoyed His creation after He made it."

Lord God, thank You for allowing us to be creative and enjoy the work
of our hands. Most of all, thank You for making us and watching over
us every day because You love what You've made! Amen.

Difficult People

*"So be strong and courageous! Do not be afraid and do not panic
before them. For the LORD your God will personally go ahead of you.
He will neither fail you nor abandon you."*
DEUTERONOMY 31:6 NLT

Jennifer had been successful in her job at a large insurance company,
but a shift in management turned her dream job into a nightmare.
Jennifer and her new boss did not get along. Whatever she did, he
seemed displeased. He called her into his office and complained about
her work, and he stood at her desk and scolded her in front of her
coworkers. Sometimes Jennifer went home and cried.

She didn't know what to do. There were several options. She
could find another job; she could learn to put up with her boss's bad
behavior; or she could confront him in a godly way. As she searched
for answers through prayer and scripture, Jennifer decided to have a
talk with her boss. The idea frightened her. Her mind raced with the
consequences. She could lose her job! Still, it was what she needed to
do. Jennifer carefully prepared what she would say. She planned her
next steps if the conversation went badly, and she held tightly to the
promise that the Lord would lead her.

Are you dealing with a difficult person? Then do what Jennifer
did. Seek God's will. Act in faith knowing that He will support you.

*Lord, help me in my relationship with _____.
Show me what to do. Amen.*

Praying for the Persecutor

"You have heard that it was said, 'Love your neighbor and hate your enemy.' But I tell you, love your enemies and pray for those who persecute you, that you may be children of your Father in heaven."
MATTHEW 5:43–45 NIV

"I can't believe she threw me under the bus that way," Sherri told a friend at work. "My boss stood up in the meeting with the president and senior leadership and told everyone how I had botched the budget presentation." The truth was Sherri had done everything correctly. She had every right to hate her boss at that moment. Instead, she prayed for her. What allowed her to pray for her boss was a love that was inhumanly possible.

What situations have you been in where it would have been much easier (and perhaps more fulfilling) to lash out against someone who had wronged you? At those moments, we should ask the Holy Spirit to fill us with love so we can pray blessings over those who hate us. That is the love of Christ—to love each person, not because of her actions but because of her humanity.

Loving Father, please help me to pray for those who wrong me. Please fill me with Your agape love, so I can look past my personal hurt and ask for blessings. Only in this way can I truly exemplify the love You have for people. In Jesus' name, I pray. Amen.

Call Me

*"Call on me in the day of trouble;
I will deliver you, and you will honor me."*
PSALM 50:15 NIV

"Call me and we'll do lunch."

"Call me and we'll talk more."

"Call if you need anything."

How many times have we said those words or heard them in return? Those two little words, *call me*, which hold such significance, have become so commonplace we barely think about them.

But when God says He wants us to call Him, He means it. He must lean closer, bending His ear, waiting, longing for the sound of His name coming from our lips. He stands ready to deliver us from our troubles or at least carry us through them safely.

David called on God in his troubles. Some of those troubles were of David's own making, while others were out of his control. It's a good thing God doesn't distinguish between the troubles we deserve and those we don't deserve. As far as He's concerned, we're His children. He loves us, and He wants to help us any way He can.

While He doesn't always choose to fix things with a snap of His fingers, we can be assured that He will see us through to the other side of our troubles by a smoother path than we'd travel without Him. He's waiting to help us. All we have to do is call.

*Dear Father, I'm so glad I can call on You anytime,
with any kind of trouble. Amen.*

Encourage One Another

So encourage each other and build each other up,
just as you are already doing.
1 THESSALONIANS 5:11 NLT

Encouragement means literally to "put courage in." When you encourage someone, you are putting courage into his or her heart. Christ calls us to encourage one another. This does not mean just to offer compliments or utter overused phrases in times of trouble such as, "It will all be okay," or "I hope it all works out." Biblical encouragement means instilling in someone's heart the courage needed to face the world. The Greek root word translated "encourage" in the New Testament is *paracollatos*, the verb form of the noun *paraclete*. Paraclete means "to lay alongside." We are called to come alongside those in need and encourage them. Just as the Holy Spirit encourages our hearts, we are to affirm others. Try to focus your encouragement on the person and not anything he or she has done. Build him or her up. Speak words of truth into his or her life. Steer clear of empty compliments or forms of encouragement that rely on actions. Try, "I believe in you. God will be faithful to complete the good work He has begun," or "I really appreciate who you are."

When you need encouragement, does it sometimes seem that no one is there to offer it? Simply ask the Holy Spirit to draw near to you. He is your Comforter, sent by the Lord to strengthen and guide you.

Lord, I want to put courage into others' hearts. Amen.

Comfort for Comfort

*For this reason Jesus had to be made like his brothers and sisters
in every way so he could be their merciful and faithful high priest
in service to God. Then Jesus could die in their place to take
away their sins. And now he can help those who are tempted,
because he himself suffered and was tempted.*
HEBREWS 2:17–18 NCV

God chose to come to earth in human form to be made like us. To
understand what it's like to be human. To be able to fully take our
place and remove our sins. Because He was fully human while being
fully God, He can help. He can comfort. The Bible says that He
"comforts us in all our troubles, so that we can comfort those in any
trouble with the comfort we ourselves have received from God" (2
Corinthians 1:4 NIV).

It's so encouraging that Jesus was just like us! Our God is not
one who wants to remain as a distant high king, out of touch with the
commoners. He wants a very personal relationship with each one of
us. He lowered Himself to our level so that we could have personal
and continual access to Him. His glory knows no bounds, yet He
desires to be our Friend. Take great comfort in that.

And then when people around you are troubled, you can step
in. You can wrap your arms around someone else who needs a friend
because of what Jesus has done for you.

*Dear Jesus, thank You for the great gift of Your friendship.
Allow me the opportunity to be a friend and comfort to those
around me in need. Amen.*

Trials and Wisdom

*Consider it pure joy, my brothers and sisters, whenever you face
trials of many kinds, because you know that the testing of your faith
produces perseverance. Let perseverance finish its work so that you
may be mature and complete, not lacking anything. If any of you lacks
wisdom, you should ask God, who gives generously to all without
finding fault, and it will be given to you.*
JAMES 1:2–5 NIV

Trials and troubles are an everyday part of living here in a fallen
world. Pastor and author Max Lucado says, "Lower your expectations
of earth. This isn't heaven, so don't expect it to be."

Things won't be easy and simple until we get to heaven. So how
can we lift our chins and head into tomorrow without succumbing
to discouragement? We remember that God is good. We trust His
faithfulness. We ask for His presence and peace during each moment.
We pray for wisdom and believe that the God who holds the universe
in His hands is working every single trial and triumph together for our
good and for His glory.

This verse in James tells us that when we lack wisdom we should
simply ask God for it! We don't have to face our problems alone. We
don't have to worry that God will hold our past mistakes against us.
Be encouraged that the Lord will give you wisdom generously without
finding fault!

*Lord Jesus, please give me wisdom. So many troubles are
weighing me down. Help me give You all my burdens and
increase my faith and trust in You. Amen.*

Never Give Up

Then Jesus told his disciples a parable to show them
that they should always pray and not give up.
LUKE 18:1 NIV

Jesus told his disciples the story of a widow who pled her case to an unjust, uncompassionate judge. Though the judge didn't care about her, she kept bringing her case to him, again and again. He finally made sure she was treated justly, simply to be rid of her.

If an unmerciful judge can show mercy just to get rid of someone, how much more will our merciful God show mercy and grace and compassion? He loves us. He wants only good things for us.

This doesn't mean we need to utter countless, meaningless repetitions in order for God to act. We do, however, need to keep our faith. We need to walk in an attitude of constant prayer, knowing that God is as mindful of our needs as we are. He wants us to trust Him, and persistent prayer is one way we demonstrate that trust. When we pray, we show Him that we know He's the One with the answer.

His answers to our prayers may be delayed. They may not be the answers we want. But we must never give up on His goodness. We can trust His heart and know that in the bigger picture, His plans for us are always, always good.

Dear Father, thank You for listening and acting on my behalf.
I trust You, even when I don't understand. Amen.

Choose Love

"I give you a new command: Love each other. You must love each other as I have loved you. All people will know that you are my followers if you love each other."
JOHN 13:34–35 NCV

There are people in your life that you can't help but butt heads with—the ones that get under your skin, rub you the wrong way, and push your buttons at a moment's notice. They can cause an eruption of emotion within you just by entering the room—people you work with, go to church with, and, unfortunately, even those within your own family.

So, how do you keep the volcano from exploding and causing deep hurts in your relationships? Jesus gave a command to love; and because we love Him, we have the ability to live each day in His love.

The Bible says, "God's love has been poured out into our hearts through the Holy Spirit" (Romans 5:5 NIV). It's not your love but God's love that responds to those button-pushing moments. Imagine taking your irritations and dropping your emotional reaction into the sea of God's love that flows through your heart. It disappears in the flood, and then you can love out of His overflow of love for others.

Heavenly Father, remind me to take a deep breath and choose to love no matter the circumstances. Help me to love others as You do by living out of Your love and responding to them as You would. Amen.

Step by Step

*For we walk by faith [we regulate our lives and conduct
ourselves by our conviction or belief. . .with trust and holy fervor;
thus we walk] not by sight or appearance.*
2 CORINTHIANS 5:7 AMP

The experiences and circumstances of our lives can often lead us to
lose heart. The apostle Paul exhorts us to look away from this present
world and rely on God by faith. Webster's dictionary defines faith as a
firm belief and complete trust. Trusting, even when our faith is small,
is not an easy task. However, when we understand God is a God of
faith and He works in ways that faith, not feelings, can discern, we
will more easily trust Him.

Toddlers learn to walk by gripping hold of furniture or a parent's
hand. They release that grip and bobble, sometimes fall, but by nature
they stand once again and take another step. How they are cheered on
when to learning to walk! Step by wobbly step.

Today, grasp hold of God's Word and feel His presence. Hold
tightly and don't let your steps falter. He is beside you and will lead
you. Trusting and walking with Him is a process, much like the
toddler's. Remember to look up, and if you stumble, He's there to grab
hold.

*Dear heavenly Father, today I choose to clutch Your Hand
and feel Your presence as I trudge the pathways of my life.
I trust You are by my side. Amen.*

Pray Persistently

*Rejoice always, pray continually, give thanks in all circumstances;
for this is God's will for you in Christ Jesus.*
1 THESSALONIANS 5:16–18 NIV

The Gospel of Luke tells about a widow who had an ongoing dispute with an enemy. The woman was stubborn and determined to win, and she refused to give up her dispute until a judge ruled in her favor. Many times she went to the judge demanding, "Give me justice!"

This judge didn't care about God or people, and he certainly didn't care if the woman got justice, but he *did* care about himself. The widow was driving him crazy! So, to make her go away he ruled in her favor.

Jesus used this story to teach His followers about persistent prayer. He said, "Learn a lesson from this unjust judge. Even he rendered a just decision in the end. So don't you think God will surely give justice to his chosen people who cry out to him day and night?" (Luke 18:6–7 NLT).

When evil stalks Christians, they cry out, "Lord, deliver us!" Sometimes it feels like God is far away. But the widow's story reminds believers to be persistent in prayer and remain faithful that God will answer them. When Christians pray, it shows not only their faith in God but also their trust in His faithfulness toward them. In His time, the Lord will come and bring justice to His people.

*Dear God, help me to remain faithful and not grow weary in prayer.
Amen.*

Press On to Know Him

"Let us press on to know him. He will respond to us as surely as the arrival of dawn or the coming of rains in early spring."
HOSEA 6:3 NLT

Monica stood in the church entrance hall, determined to regain control of herself. Stepping into the building had triggered tears—lots of them. As the congregation inside the worship center sang, Monica took deep breaths and wiped her eyes.

Suddenly, Sharon, the congregation's ministry to women coordinator, rounded the corner. "Monica?" she asked. "What's wrong?" Sharon steered Monica toward a bench.

Monica struggled to put words to her emotions. "I just feel like God's not listening to my prayers."

"I feel like that sometimes," Sharon replied.

"You do?" Monica asked. As a new believer, she didn't know veteran Christians had doubts.

"Sure!" Sharon said, patting Monica's knee. "Just tell Him about it, even if you feel like your prayers are hitting the ceiling. He already knows how you're feeling anyway."

Monica smiled shyly. "I guess I could do that," she said. "Will it get better?"

"Sure it will," Sharon said. "God is faithful. I don't know how long you'll have to wait, but I do know that He is right here with us. Want me to pray for us?"

"Yes, please," Monica said. "I'd love it."

Father, give us faith to see, even in the dark. Grant us patience to wait on Your answers and friends to come alongside us in Your waiting.
Amen.

The Definition of Love

Love is patient and kind. Love is not jealous or boastful or proud or rude. It does not demand its own way. It is not irritable, and it keeps no record of being wronged. It does not rejoice about injustice but rejoices whenever the truth wins out. Love never gives up, never loses faith, is always hopeful, and endures through every circumstance.
1 CORINTHIANS 13:4–7 NLT

The refined, pristine, perfect definition of love is. . .well, let's explore. The above scripture gives us a bird's-eye view of what love truly embraces: patience and kindness and lack of pride, jealousy, or rudeness. Love isn't demanding nor is it irritable, and it keeps no record of wrongdoing. It rejoices in the truth and never quits or loses faith!

What Christian exemplifies all of those attributes all of the time? None. Now read today's verse again and substitute the word *love* with *God*. Ready? Next, read the verse as if God were talking to you personally. He never gives up on you, never loses faith in you; and His love never fails. Most of all, despite your imperfections and failures, He continues to love you.

C. S. Lewis said, "He loved us not because we were lovable, but because He is love." What is the true definition of love? God.

Heavenly Father, how can I express my love to You when Your standard of love is so high and mine is so imperfect? Help me to love as You love. Amen.

Into His Presence

*"Let us come before Him with thanksgiving
and extol Him with music and song."*
PSALM 95:2 NIV

If God is everywhere, how is it possible to come *into* His presence? While it's true that God is ever-present, His children are given a special invitation to draw near to Him. Yes, He may be at the banquet, but *we* can occupy the seat of honor right next to Him.

The way we draw near to God is through a beautiful, balanced combination of reverence and excitement. While our respect for God requires a measure of solemnity, God is no fuddy-duddy. He wants us to be happy and joyful in His presence. He longs to hear a simple, sincere, excited "thank-You" from His children, for all the things He's done in the past. He longs to see us sing and dance in His presence and tell Him how much we love Him.

When God feels distant, we can remember our special invitation to join Him in intimate conversation. He will welcome us into His arms when we fall before Him, give excited thanks, and sing joyful songs of love and praise.

*Dear Father, thank You for inviting me into Your presence. Sometimes I barge right in, spouting off my list of requests, and I forget to say "thank You." I forget to tell You how wonderful You are. Forgive me for that. Thank You, Father, for all You've done for me. I love You.
Amen.*

Obedient Love

And this is love: that we walk in obedience to his commands.
2 JOHN 1:6 NIV

When a friend's golden lab had puppies, Betty eagerly adopted one and named it Louie, after Louis Armstrong, the musician.

Louie grew big and quickly learned to sit, roll over, and lie down. He loved Betty and followed all of her commands—except when it came to going for walks. Louie had a mind of his own! As soon as Betty put the collar and leash on Louie and opened the front door, he rushed out, pulling Betty behind him. Neighbors watched as Louie coughed, gagged, and tugged at his collar while Betty trotted along behind him, grateful just to hang on.

In some ways, God's followers are a lot like Louie. They love the Lord and have no problem obeying some of His commands, but when it comes to others, they sprint on ahead and do exactly what they want.

Are you like Louie? Do you disobey God sometimes? He understands, and He loves you anyway.

*Heavenly Father, help me to love You even more
by obeying Your commands. Amen.*

Pray Instead of Plotting—or Fretting

*"Pray that the LORD your God will show us
what to do and where to go."*
JEREMIAH 42:3 NLT

Whether you're a mom, wife, employee, or friend, your list of "to do's" never seems to get done. Meanwhile, the house is a wreck; the relatives are bickering; the bills keep coming—and amid the cacophony, God seems conspicuously absent.

However bleak your situation seems, God hasn't forgotten you. Philippians 4:6–7 (NIV) says, "Do not be anxious about anything, but in every situation, by prayer and petition, with thanksgiving, present your requests to God. And the peace of God, which transcends all understanding, will guard your hearts and your minds in Christ Jesus."

Jeremiah 42:3 echoes this statement. It urges believers to pray for guidance instead of setting out with a preconceived notion of how the day (or month or decade) will turn out.

When you begin to worry that you don't have what it takes to meet life's demands, remember that you don't have to—because God does. Author and speaker Rebekah Montgomery says, "If God asks you to build an ark, He'll give you the measurements. If He asks you to get out of the boat and walk on water, He'll show you the technique. If He asks you to pray, He'll teach you how. If He asks you to love your neighbor, He'll give you love."

*Jesus, thank You for Your presence and the peace You so freely give.
Help me to pray before I worry, categorize, or strategize. Amen.*

He Makes All Things New

*Create in me a pure heart, O God, and renew a steadfast spirit
within me. Do not cast me from your presence or take your
Holy Spirit from me. Restore to me the joy of your salvation
and grant me a willing spirit, to sustain me.*
PSALM 51:10–12 NIV

King David committed adultery and had the woman's husband killed
in battle (see Psalm 51). Talk about guilt! Yet the Bible says David was
a man after God's own heart. David truly loved God, and being a king
with power, he messed up royally!

David had faith in God's goodness. He was truly repentant and
expected to be restored to God's presence. He could not stand to be
separated from God. He recognized that he must become clean again
through the power of forgiveness.

Perhaps there have been times when you felt distant from God
because of choices you made. There is no sin that is too big for God
to cover or too small to bother Him with. He is willing to forgive, and
He forgets when you ask Him. He expects you to do the same. If you
don't let forgiven sin go, it can become a tool for torture for the enemy
to use against you. God sent Jesus to the cross for you to restore you
to relationship with Him.

*Heavenly Father, thank You for sending Jesus to pay for my sins.
Forgive me and make me new. Fill me with Your presence today.
Amen.*

Good-bye and Hello

*So we do not give up. Our physical body is becoming older and
weaker, but our spirit inside us is made new every day. We have small
troubles for a while now, but they are helping us gain an eternal glory
that is much greater than the troubles. We set our eyes not on what
we see but on what we cannot see. What we see will last only a short
time, but what we cannot see will last forever.*
2 CORINTHIANS 4:16–18 NCV

One of the most difficult things in life is watching a loved one nearing
the end of their life. Maybe you know someone who is caring for such
a person right now. Those last miles in the earthly journey can be long
and hard.

The American author and clergyman Henry van Dyke offers
encouragement in his poem "Parable of Immortality." He compares
a person to a beautiful and strong ship spreading its sails in the
morning breeze and slowly sailing for the horizon. In time, she fades
into where the ocean meets the sky, and someone says, "There she
goes." But at that exact moment, those on the other side see her
appear on the horizon just as strong and powerful as when she began
her journey, and they shout joyfully, "Here she comes!"

Isn't it magnificent that God promises Christians eternal life? The
journey may be hard, but the destination is magnificent.

*Dear God, thank You for the assurance of eternal,
joyful life for all who believe in Jesus. Amen.*

Be Still and Learn

*His delight and desire are in the law of the Lord, and on His law
(the precepts, the instructions, the teachings of God) he habitually
meditates (ponders and studies) by day and by night.*
PSALM 1:2 AMP

Do you desire to know God better? To be strengthened by Him?
Spending time with the Lord in prayer and Bible reading are the best
ways to learn more about His mercy, His kindness, His love, and His
peace.

These disciplines are like water on a sponge. They help us
understand who God is and what He brings to our lives. In His
presence, we become aware of His blessings and the resources He has
provided to strengthen us for each day's battles. He will empower us
to fulfill His plan for our lives.

It does take discipline to spend time with the Lord, but that
simple discipline helps to keep our hope alive, providing light for
our paths. When the schedule seems to loom large or the weariness
of everyday living tempts you to neglect prayer and Bible study—
remember they are your lifeline. They keep you growing in your
relationship with the Lover of your soul.

*Heavenly Father, I want to know You more. I want to feel
Your presence. Teach me Thy ways that I may dwell in the
House of the Lord forever. Amen.*

Soaring

*But those who hope in the LORD will renew their strength.
They will soar on wings like eagles; they will run and
not grow weary, they will walk and not be faint.*
ISAIAH 40:31 NIV

The recently painted walls in the stairway are already marred with
dirty fingerprints from the kids. There is an indistinct odor coming
from the pantry and garbage can vicinity that is difficult to pinpoint.
An irreparable burn mark on the carpet begs for replacement but gets
a decorative area rug instead. Work and school call the family away
from the house as dust balls roll behind them like tiny tumbleweeds
toward the slamming door.

A quick after-school convening of the crew at the house brought
Sue to the front yard to grab the mail before running off to a cross-
country meet. Something caught her eye, and she looked up to see
an eagle soaring high above the neighborhood. It was a much-needed
pause.

On the way to the meet, Sue thought about the view that eagle
had, how quiet and together things must seem from that perspective.
She thought about how crazy and unkempt life gets so often, and yet,
when she trusts God in all of it, she has an unexpected strength.

*Lord God, thank You for helping us soar through even the low-lying
places in life, in Your strength. Amen.*

Into My Heart

*For it is by believing in your heart that you are made right with God,
and it is by confessing with your mouth that you are saved.*
ROMANS 10:10 NLT

A cold, February rain fell as she collected her crayons and construction paper and spread them on the kitchen table. Carefully, she traced around a red cardboard heart, a leftover Valentine's Day decoration recycled as a tool for her artwork. She colored in the heart-shaped outline using a bright-red crayon and then cut it out with blunt scissors. The tip of her tongue slipped through her pursed lips as she tried hard to cut on the line. Finally, she held the heart up and studied it. Something looked wrong. She plunged the scissor's blades into its center and created a gaping hole. There. Now she could show her mother.

"That's so pretty, honey," her mother said. "But why does the heart have a hole?"

"So Jesus can get inside!" she replied.

"Sweetie, Jesus doesn't need a hole to get in. When you believe that He loves you so much that He died for your sins, then He comes into your heart."

She thought awhile. "I believe that, Mommy," she said. "Do you believe it, too?"

"I do," her mother answered.

And on that rainy morning, cradled in her mother's arms, her little heart swelled with Christ's love.

*Dear Jesus, remind me today not only to believe in You
but also to share You with others. Amen.*

Real Love

*Beloved, let us love one another: for love is of God;
and every one that loveth is born of God, and knoweth God.
He that loveth not knoweth not God; for God is love.*
1 JOHN 4:7–8 KJV

The world is full of counterfeits, but God's Word reveals the truth
about love. The simple fact is that if we know God, we spend our lives
loving Him. And the greatest way that we can love Him is by loving
others. The apostle Paul tells us in 1 Corinthians that love is patient
and kind. We can live with that. But then he gets to the part about
not keeping a record of wrongs. . . Whoa, now that's a different story!
What about severe offenses? We are supposed to just forgive and
forget? What about our rights? Our boundaries? Isn't there a limit to
how much an individual can forgive? The world says yes, but Jesus
lived and taught the seventy times seven rule. Forgive again and
again. Love relentlessly. Love is so much more than Valentine candy
in a box one day a year. It endures. It stays the course. It keeps no
record of wrongs.

*Father, You love me with an unfailing love. You are incapable of
anything less. May I reflect Your love to the world around me and
to those who are closest in my life, especially to those who are close
enough to hurt me. Amen.*

When God's People Pray

Pray for the peace of Jerusalem: "May those who love you be secure."
PSALM 122:6 NIV

When it comes to making a difference in this world, sometimes it's easy to feel helpless. Wars are being fought on the other side of the world. People are starving, suffering, hurting. As much as we'd like to help, there's not much we can do, right?

Except, there is something we can do. It's the most powerful thing anyone can do—we can pray. God, in all His power, has invited us to come alongside Him. He's asked us to join Him in His work by praying for each other.

For centuries, God's people have been treated unfairly and unjustly. Yet we've survived, when other groups haven't. The reason we've survived when so many have sought to silence us is because we have something our enemies don't have. We have the power of God behind us.

When we pray, we call upon every resource available to us, as the children of God. We call upon His strength, His compassion, His ferocity, His mercy, His love, and His justice. We have the ability to extend God's reach to the other side of our town or the other side of the world, all because we pray.

*Dear Father, thank You for letting me join You in Your work.
Please bless the people who love You, wherever they are in this world.
Allow them to prosper according to their love for You. Amen.*

Love Multiplied

"For where two or three gather in my name, there am I with them."
MATTHEW 18:20 NIV

Sunday morning was cold and gray. Jackie would much rather have snuggled back under the covers instead of going to church. In fact, it was extremely tempting to sleep in. Jackie willed herself from the warm bed and got ready to leave. Within moments of entering the church, she was greeted by a couple of friends who invited her to sit with them during the service. The bleak, cloudy day was immediately transformed by the blessings of love and friendship.

Sometimes it seems that attending church is a burden instead of a blessing. God reminds us with today's verse that we are meeting more than other people. We are meeting *Him* there! Whenever two or more are gathered to worship Him, His presence is experienced in an awesome way. Not only is this a blessing, it is also a privilege. Many in the world are not able to worship freely.

Thank You, Father, for the gift of fellowship in a beautiful family of believers. Thank You also for the privilege to worship You freely. We feel You in our midst, even in the smallest of groups. What an encouragement to know how much You love us and how You are always with us. Amen.

Remain in His Love

"As the Father has loved me, so have I loved you. Now remain in my love. If you keep my commands, you will remain in my love, just as I have kept my Father's commands and remain in his love."
JOHN 15:9–10 NIV

Remaining in Christ's love is the only way to bear fruit that will last. John 15 gives us a beautiful picture of what bearing fruit means. What kind of fruit are we talking about here? The kind of fruit that makes a difference for Christ. The fruits of the Spirit are love, joy, peace, patience, kindness, goodness, faithfulness, gentleness, and self-control (Galatians 5:22–23). These are the fruits that honor God and come from a life that is growing in Him.

The Bible says that if we remain in God's love, we will bear much fruit. So how do we remain in His love? John 15:10 tells us the answer: "If you keep my commands, you will remain in my love." We can have complete joy and bear all kinds of spiritual fruit if we follow God's Word and live a life that pleases Him.

Just as a branch that has been cut off from the vine can do nothing, we can do nothing that matters if we aren't connected to the vine.

Father, help me stay connected to You so that I can bear the kind of fruit that matters. I know I can do nothing good without You. Amen.

Lift Mine Eyes

*"I lift up my eyes to the mountains—where does my help come from?
My help comes from the LORD, the Maker of heaven and earth."*
PSALM 121:1–2 NIV

Jenna looked at her checkbook and at the pile of bills, sighing. She
would once again have to be creative in deciding what would get paid
and what wouldn't. Her circumstances were discouraging. Jenna and
her husband were upside down on their house, owing more than it
was worth. Her husband had been looking unsuccessfully for work for
almost a year. Her earnings, the only income for their family, had not
kept up with inflation. It seemed they were always behind.

We all feel discouraged sometimes, especially when our
circumstances seem to press on us so heavily we can't see all the good
things that we have. The Lord reminds us that He is our sustaining
power, greater than anything, and that we should keep our eyes on
Him, not our circumstances. Our circumstances can change, and
usually do. The Lord is constant and never changing. What a blessing
that is!

*Dear Lord, I am reminded that You are a Friend greater than any of
my circumstances. I look to You as my Source of strength. You are
the One who is worthy, and forever will be. Praise to You and Your
faithfulness. I am eternally grateful. Amen!*

Hungry

*We also have the prophetic message as something completely
reliable, and you will do well to pay attention to it,
as to a light shining in a dark place, until the day dawns
and the morning star rises in your hearts.*
2 PETER 1:19 NIV

Sally hurried off to a morning meeting, neglecting breakfast.
Thankfully, soon into the ride to Toledo, she remembered that she had
thrown a bag of dried edamame seeds into the glove compartment.
Relieved to have some food, she carefully managed driving, opened
the bag, and grabbed a big handful of the healthy snack.

Gobbling them up and beginning to chew, her eyes grew
suddenly wide with panic. The seeds were hot. Very hot! So hot, she
shook her head in disbelief. She pulled a small plastic garbage bag up
to her face and began to spit wildly while trying to keep her eyes on
the road.

After gaining her composure, she picked up the bag of edamame
seeds from the passenger seat. Down at the bottom of the label it
read, "Wasabi."

That was information she wished she had paid attention to in the
store—or at least before she threw a handful in her mouth.

*Lord God, thank You for funny moments that remind us to pay
attention—to Your Word and the many details in life! Amen.*

Loving Ourselves Properly

"Honor your father and mother. Love your neighbor as yourself."
MATTHEW 19:19 NLT

There's a difference between humility and self-loathing. Too many women believe that in order to be properly humble, they need to beat themselves up. But Jesus said we should love our neighbor as ourselves. Of course He wasn't talking about mistreating our neighbor!

We need to see ourselves as God sees us, with His help. Then we can obey His command to look after others. In addition, we should practice godly self-care, especially in highly stressful seasons.

Leslie Vernick, LPC, encourages women in her book *How to Find Selfless Joy in a Me-First World* to do three things: "[1] realize God is the source of our joy and we seek Him with gusto; we're desperate without Him. [2] discipline ourselves (exercise, eating right, resting, not spending too much, etc.) so that we are at our best and not out of control. One of the fruits of the spirit is self-control, and we will grow in this as we grow closer to God. [3] accept our limitations—there are some things ONLY God can do."

Selfishness is not taking care of ourselves or asking for what we want. Selfishness is *demanding* to get what we want. Love yourself as God loves you, and then you can love your neighbor the way He wants you to.

God, give me a proper view of myself—not too high and not too low. Thank You for creating me the way You did. Amen.

Hannah's Prayer

The eyes of the LORD search the whole earth in order to strengthen those whose hearts are fully committed to him.
2 CHRONICLES 16:9 NLT

There are many great prayers in the Bible. There are prayers for wisdom and for unity, prayers of repentance and negotiation with God. Hannah's was an anguished prayer for a child.

Hannah was barren. She prayed before God with a broken heart and promised God that if He gave her a child, she would commit him to the Lord all the days of his life. God heard and answered her prayer. Does God always answer the prayer for a child in this way? No, He doesn't. There are women whom God loves deeply and unconditionally who will not bear a child in this life. But in this case, God granted Hannah a male child whom she named Samuel. She only had Samuel for a short time before she took him to Eli, the priest. Samuel was not an ordinary child. He heard the voice of God at a very young age. He grew up to become a judge and prophet that could not be matched in all of Israel's history.

God is looking for ordinary men and women whose prayers reflect hearts completely committed to Him. He found such commitment in Hannah, and He answered her prayer.

Father, may my prayers reflect a deep commitment to You, and may all that I ask for be for Your kingdom and not for my own glory. Amen.

Ready for Change

*"If my people, who are called by my name, will humble themselves
and pray and seek my face and turn from their wicked ways,
then I will hear from heaven, and I will forgive their sin
and will heal their land."*
2 CHRONICLES 7:14 NIV

How we yearn for the "good old days." Many of us remember our childhood years with nostalgia about a kinder, gentler time. We think that
things were much better then. King Solomon might have thought the
same thing when this verse was given to him at the dedication of the
temple. The verse is a call for revival.

Revival doesn't have to be a corporate event. Sometimes, it
needs to be personal. The statement is conditional: if we will meet the
requirements on our end, we can be sure that God will move on His end.

*Sovereign God, I come to You wanting revival in my life. I humble
myself before You, understanding that I cannot do anything without
You. Please rekindle my desire for You and hear my pledge to erase
anything from my life that does not please You. I know that You will
hear me; help me and heal me as You have promised. Amen!*

Ask Him

*"Call to me and I will answer you and tell you great and unsearchable
things you do not know."*
JEREMIAH 33:3 NIV

After a long day at work, Sue went home, where more frustration
awaited her. Bills needed payment without enough money to pay them
all. Another of the cars needed repair. One of the kids was having
issues that gave him a bad day, too. And on top of it all, she had a spat
with her husband.

Sue once again spent some time yelling out to God for answers.
"God," she said, "I'm tired of having to come to You for help! Why
can't You just be with me all the time to help me?"

There were tears and a pause, and she was taken aback. His still,
small voice reminded her that He never leaves her—not ever. Sue
realized that she was the one who veered away from Him. After more
calling out to God, in a calmer tone this time, she began to see His
direction and how she should respond to her challenges.

*Lord God, help us to continually seek Your strength and guidance.
Thank You that You are right there waiting, all the time. Amen.*

Stay Teachable

*When Apollos wanted to go to Achaia, the brothers and sisters
encouraged him and wrote to the disciples there to welcome him.*
ACTS 18:27 NIV

Apollos was a powerhouse for the Lord. The scriptures describe him
as "a learned man, with a thorough knowledge of the Scriptures. . .
he spoke with great fervor and taught about Jesus accurately" (Acts
18:24–26).

So it's interesting that even with those credentials, Priscilla and
Aquila, having heard him, invited him to their house for additional
teaching. Afterward, Apollos desired to preach in Achaia, and the
couple encouraged him to do so. They immediately contacted the
disciples there to welcome him. The result? Apollos refuted the Jews
in public debate, proving that Jesus was the Messiah while helping
the apostles at the same time (Acts 18:27–28).

We all have room for spiritual growth and godly knowledge no
matter how long we have known the Lord. The Bible urges us to
encourage one another. What would happen to advance the kingdom if
all believers, despite their position or spiritual seniority, exercised the
humility of Apollos? Though scholarly, he accepted more instruction
from other believers who, in turn, encouraged his ministry. Jealousy,
pride, or one-upmanship didn't exist.

We are to encourage one another, just as God encourages us.

*Lord, keep me teachable so that I can become more effective
for You to encourage others in their ministries. Amen.*

No Harm

Love does no harm to a neighbor.
Therefore love is the fulfillment of the law.
ROMANS 13:10 NIV

Love does no harm. Ever. That is a powerful statement.

If love does no wrong to a neighbor, that means love never utters cruel words. Love never gossips. Love is never violent, never impatient, never easily angered. And love certainly never plans out mean, vicious actions.

Love does only good to the people around us. Only good.

Unfortunately, none of us loves perfectly—yet. And we won't love perfectly until we're made perfect by our Creator, when we stand before Him. Until then, we will mess up. We will act in unloving ways sometimes.

The key is to make love a habit and admit when we've not acted in love. When we catch ourselves thinking unkind thoughts, we need to get our thoughts in line, for unkind thoughts lead to unkind actions. When we let our tongues slip and we say cruel things, we should apologize. And we need to continually examine our hearts and our motives, to see if we're being ruled by love.

Love always builds up, always points people to the Source of love—God. And since God's love for each and every one of His children is perfect and complete, we must work to deliver that kind of love as well.

Dear Father, forgive me for the times I have been cruel or
thoughtless and have not acted in love. Help me to make
love a way of everyday life. Amen.

The Lord Is Close

Everything the LORD does is right. He is loyal to all he has made.
The LORD is close to everyone who prays to him,
to all who truly pray to him.
PSALM 145:17–18 NCV

Do you ever feel like you go to God in prayer with the same things over and over again? Is your prayer life in need of a little lift? The Psalms are full of prayers and truth. To find a road map for prayers and promises, look to the Psalms.

The authors of the Psalms knew the truth of this scripture—that the Lord is close to those who pray to Him. They expressed their honest emotions to God—their joy, their fears, their praise. They understood that God loved them and wanted to have a personal relationship with them—just like He does with us.

If you're struggling with how to pray to God or what to pray about, use the Psalms as your guide. Pray through a psalm every day. Add your own personal thoughts and feelings as you pray. Pretty soon, you'll realize that you have begun a personal friendship with the Creator of the universe.

How amazing that You, Lord, Creator of heaven and earth, want to know me intimately! Thank You for loving me and showing Yourself to me through Your Word and Your creation. Thank You for being close to me so that I can know You and live for You. Amen.

Prayer or Brevity Mania?

God knows how often I pray for you. Day and night
I bring you and your needs in prayer to God. . .
ROMANS 1:9 NLT

Our language is laden with abbreviations, or as one called it—
brevity mania. Organizations are known for their acronyms—MADD,
CARE, WAVES—and abbreviations like the AMA, ADA, NRA, and
AFT abound. And how about texting—using symbols and letters to
translate whole phrases or emotions? Crying equals :'-(and FWIW
means "for what it's worth."

Although abbreviations—designed to lessen verbiage—are in
vogue, they puzzle the over-fifty crowd. Is it too much to ask for the
vocalization of a phrase for those of us who find stopping for a MAIB
(mental abbreviation interpretation break) distracting?

Likewise, our prayers are often lost in the obscurity of brevity.
We love fast food and instant success. All the while we struggle to
take the time to utter a few extra syllables to God. We shoot "arrow"
prayers while expecting God's response ASAP. We expect the Lord,
who knows all, to interpret our every need.

Although arrow prayers are sometimes needed, God asks us
to pray *specifically* and often for the person or problem just as
Paul did. God made us to fellowship with Him. That includes open
communication void of brevity mania!

Lord, forgive me for my abbreviated prayers, void of substance and
heart. Teach me to pray in specifics and less in generalities as I openly
pour out my innermost needs and desires to You. Amen.

Peace Like a River

*"I have told you these things, so that in me you may have peace.
In this world you will have trouble. But take heart!
I have overcome the world."*
JOHN 16:33 NIV

It was starting out to be a rotten day. Beth overslept and got a
speeding ticket on the way to work. Upon arriving, she found that
the receptionist had called in sick and the other assistant was on
bereavement leave. Beth was responsible to cover everything in
her small office. The sales team didn't seem to understand why she
couldn't keep up with their rapid-fire requests. On the brink of tears,
Beth felt overwhelmed and discouraged.

Life often feels like a stormy sea instead of a calm, peaceful river.
Circumstances have the capacity to upend us, making us feel unstable
and out of control. True, flowing peace comes from Jesus. It is in
Jesus that we can have confidence and a mind that is calm, tranquil,
and unmoved. The events of life can cause us to take our eyes off
Jesus. Our river of peace lies in our Savior.

*Gracious and loving Father, we thank You for Your peace, the peace
that surpasses all understanding. When circumstances cause me to
take my eyes off You, please remind me that You are my peace, my
confidence, and my joy. Circumstances can change. You never do!
Thank You for loving me so. Amen.*

Be Known for Love

*Dear friends, let us love one another, for love comes from God.
Everyone who loves has been born of God and knows God. Whoever
does not love does not know God, because God is love.*
1 JOHN 4:7–8 NIV

"God is love." It is a verse many remember learning in Sunday school
or Vacation Bible School. But what does it mean? God is, by His very
nature, love. All that He does is out of a heart overflowing with
unconditional love. God's unconditional love surpasses any other that
we have ever received or given.

Christians are to be known by our love. Lyrics of a song written
many years ago put it this way: "We are one in the Spirit. We are one
in the Lord. . . . And they'll know we are Christians by our love." But
do they? Do the people within your sphere of influence know that you
are a Christian by your love? Or do you blend in with the crowd? Be
a vessel of grace and peace. Let love be your trademark, a distinctive
sign that you are a believer. You may never know the impact this will
have for the kingdom.

What does love look like? It takes all shapes and forms. Some
examples might be helping others, going the extra mile, offering
words of encouragement, or putting your own ambitions aside in order
to put others first.

*Father, in my family and in my workplace,
please use me as a vessel of love. Amen.*

Keep Talking

The LORD is near to all who call on him,
to all who call on him in truth.
PSALM 145:18 NIV

God is everywhere, all the time. In a sense, He's near to everyone, since there's no place we can hide from His presence. But the word *near* in this verse refers to a sense of spiritual, emotional closeness. I might be in the same room with a hundred strangers, but I wouldn't consider myself *close* to any of them. But if you ask me about my best friend who lives across the country, I'd tell you we're very close.

When we call on God, no matter our circumstances, we become close to Him. He sees our hearts, He has compassion on us, and He longs to pull us into His arms and hold us there. When we call on Him, when we spend time talking to Him and telling Him what's on our minds, we strengthen our relationship with Him.

We get *close* to Him.

When we feel far from God, sometimes the last thing we want to do is talk to Him. But it is through honest, heartfelt conversation, however one-sided it may seem to us, that we draw God's presence. When we feel far from God, we need to keep talking. He's there.

Dear Father, thank You for Your promise to listen to me.
I love You, I need You, and I want to be close to You. Amen.

Raise the Roof

*Come, let's shout praises to GOD, raise the roof for the Rock
who saved us! Let's march into his presence singing praises,
lifting the rafters with our hymns!*
PSALM 95:1–2 MSG

In the 1600s, lyricist Johann SchÐtz penned these words in his song
"Sing Praise to God Who Reigns Above": "Thus all my toilsome way
along, I sing aloud Thy praises, That earth may hear the grateful song
my voice unwearied raises. Be joyful in the Lord, my heart, both soul
and body bear your part: To God all praise and glory."

What a wonderful exhortation for us today. Toilsome way?
Weary? Sing! Be joyful in your heart! Not many had it rougher than
King David, who curled up in caves to hide from his enemies, or
Paul in a dark dungeon cell, yet they still praised God despite the
circumstances. And our God extended His grace to them as they
acclaimed Him in their suffering.

The Lord wants to hear our shouts of joy and see us march into
the courtyard rejoicing. He hears our faltering songs and turns them
into a symphony for His ears. So lift up your voices and join in the
praise to our Creator and Lord. Let's lift the rafters and allow Him to
filter our offerings of joy with His love.

*Dear heavenly Father, I praise Your holy name. Bless You, Lord.
Thank You for Your grace and mercy toward me. Amen.*

Solitary Prayer

Come near to God and he will come near to you.
JAMES 4:8 NIV

Do you have a prayer closet? Jesus said, "And when thou prayest, thou shalt not be as the hypocrites are: for they love to pray standing in the synagogues and in the corners of the streets, that they may be seen of men. Verily I say unto you, they have their reward. But thou, when thou prayest, enter into thy closet, and when thou hast shut thy door, pray to thy Father which is in secret; and thy Father which seeth in secret shall reward thee openly" (Matthew 6:5–6 KJV). So, what did Christ mean by "closet"? The original word is from the Greek *tamion*. It means an inner chamber or secret room.

Jesus warned against people praying in public with the intent to show others how pious they are. Instead, He advocated solitude. Jesus often went off by Himself to draw near to His Father and pray, and that is what He suggested in the passage from Matthew.

A secret room isn't necessary, rather a quiet place where one can be alone with God. Maybe your tamion is your garden or the beach. It might be in the quiet of your own home when your husband and children are away. Wherever it is, enjoy some time alone with God. Draw near to Him in prayer, and He will draw near to you.

Dear God, when we meet in the quiet place,
allow me to breathe in Your presence. Amen.

Providing It All

*For God so greatly loved and dearly prized the world that He [even]
gave up His only begotten (unique) Son, so that whoever believes
in (trusts in, clings to, relies on) Him shall not perish (come to
destruction, be lost) but have eternal (everlasting) life.*
JOHN 3:16 AMP

Beginning with Adam, God provided for His loved ones: a ram for
Abraham to spare his son, manna for the wandering Jewish people. The
Bible resonates with the provisions of a mighty God. And the Word says
our God is the same today as He was then. So we know He will provide
for our needs. True love reflected by His care for us every day.

His provision is not just for our material needs, but more
importantly He extends us unmerited favor, grace, when we least
deserve it. He provides us with an all-encompassing love once we
accept it. And He seals His promises with the gift of the Holy Spirit
making us heirs to the throne. When we realize the depth of care
we've received from our heavenly Father, it is breathtaking.

Always a step ahead, He made provision before any need existed.
God gave us His all, His best, when He gave us His Son. He provided
it all. We serve a glorious and mighty God.

*Lord, Your encompassing love amazes me. Thank You for all
You have done and will continue to do in my life. Amen.*

Cleaning the Pantry of Your Soul

Brethren, I count not myself to have apprehended: but this one thing I do, forgetting those things which are behind, and reaching forth unto those things which are before, I press toward the mark for the prize of the high calling of God in Christ Jesus. Let us therefore, as many as be perfect, be thus minded: and if in any thing ye be otherwise minded, God shall reveal even this unto you.
PHILIPPIANS 3:13–15 KJV

Businessman and minister John G. Lake once said, "Beloved, if any unholiness exists in the nature, it is not there by the consent of the Spirit of God. If unholiness is in your life, it is because your soul is giving consent to it, and you are retaining it. Let it go. Cast it out and let God have His way in your life."

As you grow in Christ, you will find that old thinking has to go to make room for the new understanding of God's desires and plans for your life. It's cleaning the pantry of your soul. Old mind-sets and habits are like junk food or packages with expired dates. As you throw out the old, you find the new thoughts and habits bring renewed life and strength in Christ.

Heavenly Father, I want to think Your thoughts and know Your ways. Help me to let go of the old ways and live in the new today. Amen.

When You Can't Pray

*And the Holy Spirit helps us in our weakness. For example, we don't
know what God wants us to pray for. But the Holy Spirit prays for us
with groanings that cannot be expressed in words. And the Father
who knows all hearts knows what the Spirit is saying, for the Spirit
pleads for us believers in harmony with God's own will.*
ROMANS 8:26–27 NLT

Sometimes we literally cannot pray. The Holy Spirit takes over on
such occasions. Go before God; enter into His presence in a quiet
spot where there will not be interruptions. And just be still before
the Lord. When your heart is broken, the Holy Spirit will intercede for
you. When you have lost someone or something precious, the Holy
Spirit will go before the Father on your behalf. When you are weak,
the Comforter will ask the Father to strengthen you. When you are
confused and anxious about a decision that looms before you, the
Counselor will seek God's best for you. You are not alone. You are a
precious daughter of the Living God. And when Christ ascended back
into heaven, He did not leave you on this earth to forge through the
wilderness on your own. He sent a Comforter, a Counselor, the Holy
Ghost, the Spirit of Truth. When you don't know what to pray, the
Bible promises that the Spirit has you covered.

*Father, please hear the groaning of the Holy Spirit who intercedes on
my behalf before Your throne. Amen.*

Building Friendships

*A friend loves at all times, and a brother is born
for a time of adversity.*
PROVERBS 17:17 NIV

Today's world isn't designed for friendship. It's too fast paced, with too many demands and too much stress. Oh, we're connected to everyone, all the time, through text messaging and cell phones and Facebook. But as fun as Facebook may seem, it robs us of face-to-face time. We're so distracted with everything at once, we find it hard to focus on one thing, one person at a time.

But friendship demands one-on-one, face-to-face time. And although most of us don't feel we have a lot of time to give, we must! We simply must make friendship, and building real flesh-and-blood relationships, a priority.

God created us for relationships. And although a well-timed e-mail or text message may lift us up at times, there's simply no replacement for a real, live hug. There's no substitute for a friend sitting beside you in the hospital, holding your hand. And we won't have those things unless we're willing to put aside our high-tech gadgets and invest time in the people around us.

Today, let's make it a point to turn off our cell phones. Let's step away from our computers for a while and have a real conversation with someone. That person may just turn out to be a true friend.

*Dear Father, teach me to be a true friend. Help me to make friendship
a priority and invest in the people around me. Amen.*

The Way Out

*No temptation has overtaken you except what is common to mankind.
And God is faithful; he will not let you be tempted beyond what
you can bear. But when you are tempted, he will also provide
a way out so that you can endure it.*
1 CORINTHIANS 10:13 NIV

Everyone faces temptation. Scripture says that no one escapes it, and all become its victims (Romans 3:23). But don't be discouraged. God provides a way out.

Believers learn to endure and stand up to temptation by God's grace. When they rely on the power that comes from the Holy Spirit, then God provides them with strength to resist. Jesus said that this willpower comes by watchfulness and prayer. "Watch and pray so that you will not fall into temptation. The spirit is willing, but the flesh is weak" (Matthew 26:41 NIV).

As hard as people try, temptation sometimes wins. God has a plan for that, too. He sent His Son, Jesus, into the world to take the punishment for the sins of everyone who believes in Him. Not only did Jesus suffer the consequences of sin but also through His sacrifice He provided God with a way to forgive sinfulness and to promise believers eternal life.

Watch and pray today that you don't fall into temptation, but if you do, then remember this: sin might win in the moment, but God's grace and forgiveness are forever.

*Dear Lord, lead me not into temptation but
deliver me from evil today and always. Amen.*

Lord, Help!

*"LORD, help!" they cried in their trouble, and he saved them
from their distress. He calmed the storm to a whisper
and stilled the waves. What a blessing was that stillness
as he brought them safely into harbor!*
PSALM 107:28–30 NLT

Prayers do not have to be eloquent or majestic. There are no
requirements for them to be long and labored. The only thing
necessary is that you communicate with God. Your words can be
heart-wrenching—rising deep from the very bottom of your soul—
or calm and gentle as a whisper. However you speak to Him, you can
know that He hears you and will answer.

Samuel Morse, the father of modern communication, said, "The
only gleam of hope, and I cannot underrate it, is from confidence in
God. When I look upward it calms any apprehension for the future,
and I seem to hear a voice saying: 'If I clothe the lilies of the field,
shall I not also clothe you?' Here is my strong confidence, and I will
wait patiently for the direction of Providence."

The answer to your prayer does not depend on you. Your
expressions of your heart spoken to your Father bring Him onto the
scene for any reason you need Him.

*Father, thank You for hearing my prayers. I know that You are always
near to me and You answer my heart's cry. Help me to come to You
first instead of trying to do things on my own. Amen.*

Forever Love

*Love each other with genuine affection,
and take delight in honoring each other.*
ROMANS 12:10 NLT

Clara wanted a garden swing. Throughout their fifty years of marriage, she had asked Walter to build one, but other projects took priority. A swing wasn't that important. She wanted it mostly to watch the sun set over the lake and see the stars come out.

One day, Walter decided to surprise his wife. He had discovered something long forgotten, tucked away in the barn, something that would make the perfect swing seat.

When Clara left for a few days to visit her sister, Walter got busy. He built the swing's foundation and then a sturdy lattice roof to which he attached two strong chains. Then, from the barn, he hauled out the front seat from his 1946 Plymouth—the seat where he and Clara had shared their first kiss. He scrubbed it well and fastened it to the chains just minutes before she returned home.

"Oh, my!" Clara gasped when she saw it. "Oh. . .my."

It wasn't the swing that she'd had in mind, but still, it was the most beautiful swing she had ever seen. As the sun set, Clara and Walter sat there together. He wrapped his arm around her shoulder and gently kissed her cheek. "God blessed me with you, dear," he said. "I love you now and forever."

*Thank You, Lord, for blessing me with love,
and thank You for loving me forever. Amen.*

A Bigger Battle

*For though we live in the world, we do not wage war as the world
does. The weapons we fight with are not the weapons of the world.
On the contrary, they have divine power to demolish strongholds.*
2 CORINTHIANS 10:3–4 NIV

One of Janice's acquaintances was talking badly about her. It seemed
that the only motivation behind the unkind words was jealousy.
Nonetheless, Janice felt upset when she heard the things that were
being said. She searched herself for something offensive she might
have said or done and hadn't realized, but she could think of nothing.

After talking with a trusted friend who also knew the person
speaking badly of her, Janice's friend stated clearly, "It's not you."

Janice couldn't help think how the enemy had twisted something
to achieve this. Some bit of information was received wrongly, or a
thought was planted. Any number of things could have been contorted
by the enemy who loves to destroy.

Rather than make Janice bitter, this experience helped her
consider how often any of us may be unknowingly influenced by the
enemy. Most importantly, she renewed her commitment to being
more spiritually alert. What the enemy meant for evil, God once again
used for good!

*Loving God, thank You for being the One we can go to, to change
the influence, to break the strongholds of the enemy. Amen.*

Just in Time

*Let us then fearlessly and confidently and boldly draw near to the
throne of grace (the throne of God's unmerited favor to us sinners),
that we may receive mercy [for our failures] and find grace to help
in good time for every need [appropriate help and well-timed help,
coming just when we need it].*
HEBREWS 4:16 AMP

As believers, our lives become exciting when we wait on God to direct
our paths, because He knows what is best for us at any given moment.
His plans and agenda are never wrong. We just need to practice living
on His schedule and spending time in prayer. But that's easier said
than done! Often we are chomping at the bit, and it's hard to wait.

Once we fully realize He knows best and turn our lives over to the
Spirit for direction, we can allow God to be in charge of our calendar;
His timing is what is paramount

When chomping at the bit for a job offer or for a proposal, His
timing might seem slow. "Hurry up, God!" we groan. But when we
learn to patiently wait on His promises, we will see the plans He has
for us are more than we dared hope—or dream. God promises to
answer us; and it never fails to be just in time.

*Lord, I want Your perfect will in my life.
Help me learn to wait upon You. Amen.*

Rest in His Unfailing Love

*Many are the woes of the wicked, but the LORD's unfailing love
surrounds the one who trusts in him.*
PSALM 32:10 NIV

Over the course of several brutal months, Alecia and her husband
were shaken and stretched in ways they never imagined. Their
business collapsed; two of their aging parents had heart attacks; and
their relationship went through turmoil. However, a year before her
stressful season began, Alecia had memorized several psalms, as well
as New Testament passages about God's love and peace.

God knew that Alecia's heart would need to be strengthened by
biblical truth. Even as her family dealt with financial, emotional, and
relational problems, she experienced unexplainable joy.

In the book *Jesus Today*, Sarah Young writes, "When you are
suffering, your need for Me is greater than ever. The more you choose
to come near Me, affirming your trust in Me, the more you can find
hope in my unfailing love. You can even learn to be joyful in hope
while waiting in My presence—where joy abounds."

In God's paradoxical economy, the more we suffer, the more God
gives us His love, strength, and peace. He also imparts joy and hope,
which the world will never understand. But just ask Alecia—they're
very, very real.

*Father, thank You for the spiritual gifts of love, joy, peace, and hope.
Give me daily reminders to draw close to You in the midst of good
times and bad, because You are waiting for me. Amen.*

Praise Him When It Hurts

Trust in the LORD with all thine heart; and lean not unto thine own understanding. In all thy ways acknowledge him, and he shall direct thy paths.
PROVERBS 3:5–6 KJV

Bridgett and her youngest daughter were alike in many ways. As her daughter became a young adult, though, their relationship sometimes felt like it would break in two. Bridgett's heart ached for the times when her daughter adored her—the times when "Mommy" was the only one who could fix her hurts and dry her tears.

Bridgett had learned that any words she had to say about her daughter's life choices would only widen the gulf between them. So she took her own hurts to her heavenly Father daily and prayed for God's grace and direction for both their lives. "Lord, I trust You to bring about Your purpose and plan for us."

Each time she was tempted to worry about her daughter and the choices she was making, she intentionally praised God for working in her heart. A little more than a year passed and Bridgett began to see change. Her daughter's heart softened, and God-ordained opportunities opened up for her. The mother-daughter relationship improved, and Bridgett knew her prayers were being answered through her decision to praise God through prayer.

Father, I choose to trust You with my worries. Thank You for working in my life according to Your plans. I give it to You, and I praise You in advance! Amen.

A Loving Friend

A generous person will prosper;
whoever refreshes others will be refreshed.
PROVERBS 11:25 NIV

Are you convinced that you don't have enough friends—or perhaps your friends aren't meeting your needs? Consider what kind of friend you are. The timeworn axiom "To have a friend, be one" rings with truth.

Good friends listen deeply. We all need someone who can share our load and with whom we can be gut-level honest. This type of friend is invaluable when you feel you can't go one more step.

Good friends also mentor gently and lovingly. Single mom Leticia, thirty-five, has a best friend, Naomi, who's in her seventies. Naomi pushes Leticia to take care of herself and not forget her own needs in the midst of career, kids, and church activities. Maybe there is someone you could nudge into a healthier lifestyle or more active spiritual life.

Finally, good friends forgive freely. They don't judge too harshly or take things extremely personally. Instead, they give friends the benefit of the doubt, knowing that no woman is perfect and sometimes people make mistakes. They are thankful for grace-filled friends and try to forgive as God has forgiven them.

Heavenly Father, thank You for friends. Give us the ability to be forgiving, godly, listening friends—and provide us with relationships that will help us grow and mature. Most of all, thank You for the Friend we have in Jesus.

Heed the Burden to Pray

*And in their prayers for you their hearts will go out to you,
because of the surpassing grace God has given you.*
2 CORINTHIANS 9:14 NIV

Trisha couldn't get her adult son off her mind. One evening her
heart's burden overwhelmed her. Hours earlier John visited his mom
before going out for the evening. She knew all too well what "going
out" meant. Before he left, Trisha lovingly said, "John, God's grace
and mercy has kept you safe for many years. One day God will lift that
grace."

Puzzled, her son replied, "Oh don't worry, Mom."

Immediately Trisha began intercessory prayer. "Lord, do what
You must to bring John to salvation. I only ask that You spare His
life." Heavy-hearted, she continued to pray all evening.

Then the phone call came. On his way home from a nightclub,
John drove off the road. The entire car except the driver's seat was
smashed like a tin can. Miraculously, John crawled out the window
and arrived at his grandparents' home, bloodied and in shock. Later he
explained that he had no idea how he got there. Trisha also discovered
that the accident was one of two that evening. Another minor accident
had occurred on his way to the bar.

When we sense a burden to pray, it's for a reason. That burden
originates from God's mercy and grace for whom we pray. John
eventually came to Jesus. But suppose his mother had ignored God's
leading to pray that night? The outcome might have been quite
different.

Father, thank You for prayer and how it changes lives. Amen.

Biblical Encouragement for Women

Don't be concerned about the outward beauty of fancy hairstyles,
expensive jewelry, or beautiful clothes. You should clothe yourselves
instead with the beauty that comes from within, the unfading beauty
of a gentle and quiet spirit, which is so precious to God.
1 PETER 3:3–4 NLT

The world encourages women to dress provocatively, to invest in
expensive products and styles, all to make them "better." This is not
how God judges a woman's heart. God is concerned with what is
on the inside. He listens to how you respond to others and watches
the facial expressions you choose to exhibit. He sees your heart.
Certainly it is fun to buy a new outfit or spend some time and effort
accessorizing. There is nothing wrong with this in and of itself. Where
the trouble comes is when the world's messages drown out God's call
on your life. The Lord desires that you clothe yourself with a gentle
and quiet spirit. He declares this as unfading beauty, the inner beauty
of the heart. Focus on this and no one will even notice whether your
jewelry shines. Your face will be radiant with the joy of the Lord and
your heart will overflow with grace and peace.

Lord, grant me a quiet and gentle spirit. I ask this in Jesus' name.
Amen.

Who God Hears

The LORD is far from the wicked,
but he hears the prayers of the righteous.
PROVERBS 15:29 NLT

One of the countless, wonderful things about God is that He's a gentleman. As powerful as He is, He rarely pushes in where He's not wanted, except in cases where justice demands it.

God remains far from the wicked, for the wicked push Him away. They don't want Him around. They make choices against the Almighty and disregard His ways. Then, when they land themselves in trouble with no way out, help is nowhere to be found. They choose to exclude the One who could help them. In the end, they have no one.

But when the righteous call His name, He hears. Though none of us is righteous on our own, we can claim righteousness through Jesus Christ. He alone is righteous, and He covers us like a cloak. When we call on God, He sees the righteousness that covers us through Christ and recognizes us as His children. He leans over and listens carefully to our words, because we belong to Him. He loves us.

Next time it seems like God isn't listening, perhaps we should examine our hearts. Have we pushed God away? Have we accepted the price His Son, Jesus Christ, paid on our behalf? If not, we can't claim righteousness. If we have, we can trust that He's never far away. He hears us.

Dear Father, thank You for making me
righteous through Your Son, Jesus. Amen.

Your Heart's Desire

*Trust in the LORD and do good. Then you will live safely
in the land and prosper. Take delight in the LORD, and he will
give you your heart's desires. Commit everything you
do to the LORD. Trust him, and he will help you.*
PSALM 37:3–5 NLT

It's easy to look at this verse and think, "Hey, if I just delight in the
Lord, He'll give me everything I want!" But when we really start to
delight in the Lord, God changes our hearts so completely that all we
ever want is what *He* wants. When you commit everything you do to
the Lord, you will begin to see how your desires line up with God's
desires.

What does this look like in everyday life? Start your morning with
thankfulness. Ask God to bless your day and to provide opportunities
to be a blessing to those you encounter. Interact with God about each
issue and problem you face. Thank Him for big and little blessings
that come your way. Seek His will and guidance when you make
plans. Pray for loved ones who don't know Christ. Intercede for friends
and neighbors who need divine help. Be on the lookout for new ways
to delight yourself in the Lord.

*Lord, I commit my whole heart to You—and all of my plans and ideas.
I want Your will in my life. Thank You for Your blessings and Your
great love for me. Show me how to delight in You, Lord. I love You.
Amen.*

Praying for Unbelievers

*"Pray to the LORD. We have had enough of God's thunder and hail.
I will let you go; you do not have to stay here any longer."*
EXODUS 9:28 NCV

Hannah frowned as she boarded the plane. The flight looked full, and she was tired. She wanted to read, drink a Diet Coke, and not talk to anyone.

Then the Holy Spirit reminded her of her pastor's words the previous Sunday: "Ask God to give you opportunities to share His love with others, wherever you go."

Hannah took her seat toward the back of the plane. "I'm available, Lord," she whispered.

Her seatmates included two people who didn't speak English. During the three-hour flight, Hannah prayed silently for them, smiling occasionally, and when the seat belt sign went off, she walked to the back of the plane.

After using the restroom, Hannah heard sniffling. A flight attendant sat in the jump seat next to the galley kitchen, crying softly. Hannah paused. "Are you okay?" she asked the woman.

"Not really," the attendant said, shaking her head. "I just got bad news before the plane took off."

"Can I pray for you?"

"I don't really believe in God, but I guess it couldn't hurt. . . ."

Hannah smiled, bowed her head, and quietly prayed on behalf of her new acquaintance.

*Father, give us the courage and faith to let You lead us.
Give us opportunities to share the hope we have through
Jesus with a world that desperately needs it. Amen.*

Calm Yourself

Anxiety weighs down the heart, but a kind word cheers it up.
PROVERBS 12:25 NIV

How could there be a garbage truck and a school bus in front of her on the same morning? Sara finally got to the parking lot, zipping into a spot. She threw the car into PARK and quickly gathered her file bag, purse, and coffee. After pushing the door shut with her foot, she walked swiftly toward the office, going over in her head all the things that needed her attention that day.

She realized she was taking shallow breaths when she nearly gasped for air, and she felt her tenseness all of a sudden. "Lord," she prayed quickly, focusing her mind for a moment. Remembering His promise to provide peace, she slowed her steps, took a deep breath, and looked around at His creation for the bit of time she had before getting to work. She hadn't noticed until then the symphony of birds or the sound of the leaves rustling in the gentle breeze of summer.

It was just like God to help her get to a place of calm and clear thinking. Her mind turned to thanking Him for many things rather than getting anxious over the issues she was facing.

Lord, thank You for Your faithfulness to remind us of the peace that passes all understanding. You are the only One who can provide it for us. Amen.

No Greater Love

For God so loved the world that he gave his one and only Son,
that whoever believes in him shall not perish but have eternal life.
For God did not send his Son into the world to condemn the world,
but to save the world through him.
JOHN 3:16–17 NIV

Probably the most memorized passage of scripture, John 3:16 is
the Gospel in one sentence. We memorize it at an early age so our
ears become accustomed to hearing it. But have you allowed it to
completely change your life?

God didn't send Jesus to condemn us! He came to save us by
giving up His life for ours. John 15:13 (NLT) says "there is no greater
love than to lay down one's life for one's friends." That is the very
foundation of Christianity. As C. S. Lewis said, "Christianity, if false, is
of no importance, and if true, of infinite importance. The only thing it
cannot be is moderately important."

The next time you hear a child recite John 3:16 or listen as this
verse is being read aloud, allow the words to truly seep into your soul
once again. Thank God for His amazing gift of life and His unfailing
love for us.

Heavenly Father, thank You for the cross and its infinite
importance in my life. Thank You for making a way for me to
know You and live eternally with You. I give my life fully to You.
Teach me how to live for You. Amen.

Second Chances

*"I, even I, am he who blots out your transgressions,
for my own sake, and remembers your sins no more."*
ISAIAH 43:25 NIV

How many of us have hung our heads low, knowing we really messed up? Wishing we could redo that homework assignment, take back the unkind words that leaped from our mouths without thinking, or even pull back that e-mail message right after we clicked SEND. We've all done something we wished we could undo. Often, we think we have failed not only ourselves but also God.

In fact, the Bible is full of people that God used despite their errors. Moses had an anger problem. David was lustful. Jacob was deceptive. The wonderful thing about our faith is that we serve a God of second chances. Not only is He willing, but He also wants us to confess our sins so He can forgive us. Sing praises for the wonderful blessing of starting over!

*Gracious and heavenly Father, we are grateful that we serve a
God of second chances. In fact, You give us more than two chances,
and You don't keep score. We are all prodigals, and we need to feel
Your love and forgiveness. Thank You for loving me enough to not
give up on me. You are still with me! Amen.*

Loving in Spite Of

*Live in harmony with one another. Do not be proud, but be willing
to associate with people of low position. Do not be conceited.
Do not repay anyone evil for evil. Be careful to do what is right
in the eyes of everyone. If it is possible, as far as it depends
on you, live at peace with everyone.*
ROMANS 12:16–18 NIV

Jason didn't know what bothered him more about Matt, the grizzly
looking army veteran: the fact that Matt obviously hadn't bathed
recently or his vile, angry attitude. What Jason did know was that this
man needed help. His house was almost literally falling down around
him; he didn't have a car; and he wasn't eating well.

Jason kept trying to befriend Matt. Most people wouldn't have
bothered. But Jason saw Matt as someone who really needed to
experience God's love and continued to minister to him, although
often it was extremely difficult. Eventually, Jason's persistence paid
off. Matt dedicated his life to Christ.

*Abba Father, You are the author and finisher of our faith. We look to
You to help us love others with an agape love, a love from You. It is
difficult to love unconditionally, and it can only be done with Your
help. Thank You that You give us the strength, the conviction, and the
grace to love in Your name. Amen.*

Good Gifts

*"If you, then, though you are evil, know how to give good gifts
to your children, how much more will your Father in heaven
give good gifts to those who ask him!"*
MATTHEW 7:11 NIV

It's a natural, God-bred instinct to care for our children. Even parents who seem to have little parental aptitude usually try to provide the basics. Yet where parents sometimes fall short, God never will.

God loves us, and He delights in caring for us. When our own children are tired or hungry or hurt, we don't want them running to some stranger for comfort. We want them to run to us, snuggle into our arms, and trust us to care for them. God is no different.

Sometimes, though, our children ask us for things we know might hurt them. A two-year-old boy might seem fascinated by the sharp knife Mommy is using to fix dinner, but she won't give it to him, and he may throw a tantrum. He won't understand that it's out of love his mother withholds the knife.

We become distracted and enamored with shiny things, too. Often we see something that seems exciting and good, and we want it for ourselves. We get frustrated when God won't give it to us. But we can always trust God's heart. We can know that even when He withholds things we think will bring us happiness, He does it out of love.

*Dear Father, thank You for supplying all my needs
and many of my wants. Amen.*

Have You Thanked Someone Today?

They have been a wonderful encouragement to me, as they have been to you. You must show your appreciation to all who serve so well.
1 CORINTHIANS 16:18 NLT

Have you thanked your pastor, friends, or family who have encouraged or helped you just when you needed it?

Paul wrote to the Corinthian church, explaining how Stephanas and his family were the first converts in Achaia and how they devoted themselves to serve others. He reminded them that when Stephanas, Fortunatus, and Achaicus arrived in Corinth they supplied whatever needs the people had and they "refreshed my spirit and yours. . ."

When true believers serve, they serve from the heart not an inward desire for outward praise. This is what Stephanas did, yet Paul still prompted the church to show appreciation for God's servant and what he did for them.

Do you ever feel taken advantage of? Do you labor and receive little to no recognition? As God's servants, we work because we love Christ; yet an occasional display of appreciation is always. . . well, appreciated. That's what Paul communicated. "Hey guys, let's encourage our brothers through showing our appreciation to them for all they did for us!"

Paul's suggestion holds true today. Thank someone who has refreshed your spirit. It will encourage them and you to keep persevering on life's pathway.

Lord, encourage me to show my appreciation to those who have touched my life with Your love and grace. Amen.

Help My Unbelief!

"What do you mean, 'If I can'?" Jesus asked.
"Anything is possible if a person believes."
The father instantly cried out, "I do believe,
but help me overcome my unbelief!"
MARK 9:23–24 NLT

This story in the New Testament tells of a man who brought his demon-possessed son to Jesus for healing. First he asked the disciples to drive out the demon, but they could not. Then he said to Jesus, "But if you can do anything, take pity on us and help us."

The man had his focus on his problem instead of on Christ. He was thinking about how long his son had been possessed and the great damage that had been done. He wasn't convinced that Jesus could do anything about it. But Jesus corrected the man and showed him that anything is possible through Christ.

Are you facing hard times right now? Does your faith feel a little weak? When you are tempted to let your problems get the better of you and you feel that your faith isn't strong enough to overcome, pray for God to change your thinking from doubt to firm faith in Christ. And remember, when you are weak, He is strong!

Heavenly Father, my problems seem too big to handle right now.
I trust You, and I want to believe that You are bigger than
anything I'm facing. Help my unbelief! Amen.

Stand Firm!

Cast your cares on the LORD and he will sustain you;
he will never let the righteous be shaken.
PSALM 55:22 NIV

The storm tore through the neighborhood, upending patio furniture and blowing trash cans down the street. After the tempest passed, the residents ventured outside to inspect the damage. Roof shingles were found in some yards. Several large tree branches had narrowly missed damaging vehicles, while some trees were completely uprooted. It was a horrendous and frightening sight, one that was very unsettling to many.

We believers often have horrible storms in our own lives: unemployment, death of a loved one, serious illness, wayward children. He who stands with Christ stands firmly, as if anchored to the ground. Although it seems as if we will be destroyed in these life storms, God will not allow it. To quote the great preacher Charles Spurgeon, "Like pillars, the godly stand immoveable, to the glory of the Great Architect."

Dear Lord, I will trust in You, despite what life throws at me.
You have promised to never let the righteous be shaken,
and I am holding on to that promise by holding on to You.
Thank You that You can be trusted to keep Your promises
to protect and sustain me. In Jesus' name. Amen.

Breaking Barriers

*Now the gates of Jericho were securely barred because
of the Israelites. No one went out and no one came in.
Then the LORD said to Joshua, "See, I have delivered Jericho
into your hands, along with its king and its fighting men."*
JOSHUA 6:1–2 NIV

Anastasia started walking with Christ in her twenties. That's when
she began praying for her father to know God, too. She invited him
to church often, and once in a while he joined her at an Easter or
Christmas service. In her thirties she still called him Daddy, and she
was still praying, but now she had a husband praying with her, too;
and as the years went along, her children joined in.

This circle of prayer for Daddy and Granddaddy grew and
continued. Anastasia would not give up seeking God for her father.
When Anastasia was in her fifties, Daddy was a great-granddaddy,
and they kept praying. He would still come along to church with them
most holidays, though it was getting much more difficult with his cane
and hearing impairment.

One year Anastasia's daughter died tragically in a car accident.
Anastasia struggled deeply but kept her focus heavenward, where she
knew her daughter was. Her father was angry with God but couldn't
help but notice the depth of his daughter's faith.

When her daddy was in his eighties, the persistence of the
enlarged circle of prayer finally saw its answer, and he came to Christ.
Anastasia shared the news with everyone she had ever asked to pray
for him. It was a glorious day of rejoicing!

*Father God, thank You for Your instructions to be persistent
and for Your work in breaking down the barriers. Amen.*

Sound Advice

*The sweet smell of perfume and oils is pleasant,
and so is good advice from a friend.*
PROVERBS 27:9 NCV

Did you ever snub unsolicited advice such as: "You know, I think
if you'd only cut down on chocolate, you could lose that extra ten
pounds." Or the backhanded approach: "I don't care what others
think, you're a wonderful person."

When someone who knows or cares little about you offers
criticism, it is offensive. Yet the Bible emphasizes that constructive
criticism, offered in love, is a pleasant perfume. In fact, the scriptures
instruct us to beware of flattery and embrace godly correction.

Trish approached a friend for some sound advice. Afraid to
offend, the friend told Trish what she thought she wanted to hear.
Though flattered, her advice helped little. Days later, she talked with
her close friend Phyllis. After listening to Trish's problem, Phyllis was
straightforward, yet Trish wasn't offended because Phyllis swaddled
her comments in love and concern. She was direct yet tactful, honest
yet nonabrasive, poignant yet sensitive, communicative yet never
once abused their friendship by exceeding her boundaries. The result?
Phyllis's advice empowered her to see the situation clearly to take
steps to rectify it.

Receiving and giving criticism is risky business, but both are
necessary elements to our Christian growth. Although we may
grimace at first, loving criticism diminishes tunnel vision and serves
as a springboard to positive changes.

As for the unsolicited advice from self-ascribed counselors? Snub it!

*Father, thank You for friends who care enough to season their
suggestions with love. Amen.*

A Forever Password

*If we are [His] children, then we are [His] heirs also: heirs of God
and fellow heirs with Christ [sharing His inheritance with Him].*
ROMANS 8:17 AMP

In today's high-tech society, passwords are required for so many
things in our lives: bank ATMs, computer settings, bill paying. These
passwords identify the user and are intended to keep others out of our
business.

Rejoice. Because God loved us so much, He gave us an eternal
password: Jesus. Once we acquire this password through salvation
and set our hope in Him, we become heirs of Christ. Children of the
King. Precious saints. These are names given to us by the Father to
set us apart from the world because of His great love.

Unlike the security passwords for business, this password can
never be compromised. We are safe and secure in the Father's arms
and able to access His promised gifts. Open your Bible and discover all
that is available to you as a believer: eternal life, provision, blessing
upon blessing. Then praise Him for His wondrous love. His awesome
care. Jesus. That's the most important word you'll use. As children of
the King, you have rights to so much through your special relationship
and kinship. What a blessing it is to know Jesus is the password to the
Kingdom of God.

*Heavenly Father, thank You for Your everlasting love. I will store the
password You have given me in my heart, for all eternity. Amen.*

Pray through Trouble

"Is anyone among you in trouble? Let them pray."
JAMES 5:13 NIV

Mona and her sister argued about their mother. The elderly woman had been self-sufficient, but lately she had trouble caring for herself. Mona's sister decided that putting their mother into a nursing home was the best option. But Mona disagreed. She felt that she and her sister could take turns staying with their mother so she could remain in her house. Communication broke down between the two sisters, and Mona didn't know what to do next—until she remembered the words of Philippians 4:6: "Do not be anxious about anything, but in every situation, by prayer and petition, with thanksgiving, present your requests to God." Mona knelt down in her living room and prayed. "Dear God, help me to mend my relationship with my sister, and help us both to do what is best for Mom."

In everyday life, people get tangled in webs of anxiety, and they sometimes forget to consult God. In Philippians 4:6, Paul reminds Christians not to let that happen. He says in *every* situation, pray. And not only bring requests to God but bring them with thanksgiving.

The great evangelist and Christian teacher Oswald Chambers said, "We have to pray with our eyes on God, not on the difficulties." How do you handle the difficulties in your life? Do you pray with your eyes on God?

Dear Father, You are able to fix all of my problems.
I praise You for that! Amen.

Different Kinds of Love

*This is my commandment, that ye love one another,
as I have loved you.*
JOHN 15:12 KJV

Not all love is the same according to the Greek translation of God's
Word. For instance, *philia* is defined as a loyalty and friendship for
family members or friends. *Eros* is a passionate, sensual desire. *Storge*
is a natural affection shown between parent and child.

The one most familiar comes from the word *agape*, meaning not
only general affection but to hold someone in high regard. The New
Testament applies agape love in the relationship between Jesus and
His disciples. It is one of self-sacrifice and a giving spirit to all, both
friend and foe.

Jesus commands us to love our neighbor as we love ourselves
(Matthew 22:39). He doesn't say, "Love your neighbor as long as they
keep their dogs from barking or if they maintain their yard and stay on
their side of the fence." Rather, He commands us to love as He loves us.

That's God's agape love. It's unconditional and powerful. Agape
love builds not destroys; it accepts others' imperfections and is
tolerant of people who do things differently than we do.

What's your definition of love? Take some time today and
exercise God's love in the same manner He loves you, and see what
happens!

*Lord, thank You for loving me unconditionally with all of my
faults and flaws. Help me to love as I am loved. Amen.*

Worry vs. Prayer

Don't worry about anything; instead, pray about everything.
Tell God what you need, and thank him for all he has done.
PHILIPPIANS 4:6 NLT

Do not worry. This is a tall order for women. We are worriers by
nature, aren't we? We worry about our children and friends. We worry
about what people think of us and what we will do if such-and-such
happens. We are the queens of the what-if's! But the Bible tells us not
to worry about *anything*. In the book of Matthew, we are reminded
that if God cares for the birds of the air, providing them with food
as they need it, He is certain to take care of His children! But if we
give up worrying, what will we do with all the time we spent being
anxious? Exchange it for time in prayer. Go before God with your
concerns. Cast all your cares on Him, for He promises to care for you.
Tell God what you need, and thank Him in advance for what He will
do. God will always provide. He will always show up. He does not
want you to worry.

Lord, replace my worry time with prayer time. It is in Jesus' name
that I come before You now, presenting You with my requests.
Thank You for Your provision in my life. Amen.

Waiting for the Storm to Pass

You do not know what will happen tomorrow! Your life is like a mist.
You can see it for a short time, but then it goes away. So you should
say, "If the Lord wants, we will live and do this or that."
JAMES 4:14–15 NCV

Summer monsoon seasons in Tucson, Arizona, can bring a haboob—a
violent, desert dust storm. Dust forms a high wall with winds up to
thirty miles per hour. The storm can last up to three hours. People
respond differently to the storms. Some drivers try to press through
with extremely low visibility. Others wait it out.

One individual, Dex, shared with a friend, "When Ann and I got
caught in the haboob last night, instead of trying to press on through
it, we decided to enjoy it. We stopped, went to a movie, ate dinner
out, and made it home before 10 p.m."

The storms of life are always going to come. The next time you
see a storm on the horizon, follow Dex and Ann's example and choose
to have a little fun while you are waiting for the storm to pass!

Lord, sometimes I get lost in the storm. I'm looking at the damage
that storm can do instead of looking to You. Help me to rest in Your
peace and have a little fun while waiting for the storm to pass. Amen.

Blessable

*Love the LORD your God and. . .serve him with all your heart and with
all your soul—then I will send rain on your land in its season.*
DEUTERONOMY 11:13–14 NIV

We all want God's blessings. We want it to rain on our crops; we want
the sun to shine on our picnics; and we want a gentle breeze to relieve
us from summer's scorch. We want job security and bigger paychecks.

Though God allows some blessings to grace every person in the
human race, there are some keys to receiving more of God's goodness.
If we want God's blessings, we must be blessable.

So how do we become blessable? We must love God. And we
must serve Him with all our hearts.

Loving God is the easy part. But the evidence of that love comes
through our service to Him, and that's a little harder.

When we love God, we serve Him by loving others. We serve Him
by taking the time to mow the widow's lawn or prepare a meal for
someone who's ill or provide a coat for someone who's cold. We serve
Him by offering a hand of friendship to the friendless or by saying
something positive about the victim of gossip.

When we love God and our actions show evidence of that love, we
become blessable. That's when God will pour out His goodness on us
in ways we could never imagine.

*Dear Father, I love You. Show me ways I can serve You today.
Amen.*

Hanging On

He spreads out the northern skies over empty space;
he suspends the earth over nothing.
JOB 26:6–8 NIV

An old, dry petunia bloom had fallen from its hanging pot and was caught in a mere two-threaded spiderweb. Suspended in midair, it was seemingly held by nothing at all and flittered wildly in the softest of breezes. God and the curious cat are likely the only ones who knew how long it had been there.

Do you ever feel this way? Barely hanging on, struggling like crazy, and no one seems to notice. When the struggle *is* recognized by others, they can't see why it's so hard; and then, on top of your hardship, you may be judged, too. Sometimes the only person who notices knocks you around, like the cat leaping and batting at the hovering debris.

Does God notice? Is He going to help you?

Remember that God absolutely notices and cares immensely. He holds up the universe, and He holds you up even when you feel alone, mocked, and discouraged. He will not forget your plight.

Lord God, thank You for knowing exactly where we are all the time
and for holding us up even when we don't understand the hows
and the whys. Amen.

Thank You, Lord

I will praise the LORD at all times; I will constantly speak his praises.
PSALM 34:1 NLT

While imprisoned, the apostle Paul gave thanks to God, even singing
His praises, and it resulted in the salvation of the jailers. What a great
lesson for every Christian—when you feel least like giving thanks,
that's precisely when you should!

What is your response when you find yourself trapped in traffic,
late for a meeting, frustrated in your plans, sick in bed, hurting
emotionally, overwhelmed with work, lonely, tired, or confused? Our
human nature teaches us we should gripe and fret. Yet scripture says
we should give thanks. Only when we surrender our lives to Him and
His control is this possible.

Learn to thank Him. Thank Him for being your help in time of
trouble. Thank Him for His great wisdom and power. And thank Him
for causing every situation in your life to work together for your good.

Giving thanks may not change your circumstances significantly,
but it will change you. You'll feel yourself focusing on God—His
goodness, kindness, and grace—rather than your own anger, pride,
sickness, or inconvenience. Maybe that's why it's such fertile soil for
miracles. The biblical commentator Matthew Henry stated it well:
"Thanksgiving is good, but thanks-living is better."

*Lord, I choose to give You thanks today for whatever comes my way.
I love You, Lord, and I am grateful for Your goodness. Amen.*

A Heart of Peace

*Look at those who are honest and good,
for a wonderful future awaits those who love peace.*
PSALM 37:37 NLT

Before the sun came up each Friday morning, Shanna was in her car driving toward the hospital. She spent the thirty-minute drive talking to the Lord about her time there. She entered the hospital with great anticipation of what God would do in the hearts of the tiny patients in the neonatal intensive care unit. "Father, consume me with Your peace this morning, so that I am a comfort to the babies today."

As a "cuddler," she took her opportunity to comfort the tiny ones with the love and peace of God. She whispered words of encouragement, hummed songs of faith, and offered a calm and soothing peace as they rested in her arms. "It's my greatest hope that the Lord Himself will minister peace and healing to these little ones," Shanna said.

Our lives are stressful and full of day-to-day struggles. People in general are moving forward at a hurried pace, frenzied when others get in their way. God desires for His peace to strengthen you and for you, like Shanna, to share His peace with others.

*Lord, You are my peace. No matter what I'm facing in this life,
help me to accept Your peace and strength each day. Give me the
patience to drink it in and then share it with others. Amen.*

A Friend Who Sticks Closer than a Brother

When David had finished speaking to Saul, the soul of Jonathan was knit with the soul of David, and Jonathan loved him as his own life.
1 SAMUEL 18:1 AMP

The relationship between David and Jonathan was like that of brothers. Proverbs 18:24 (NIV) says it this way: "One who has unreliable friends soon comes to ruin, but there is a friend who sticks closer than a brother." Everyone hits a rough patch now and then. This world is not our home. As believers, we are aliens here. One day we will truly be at home in heaven with the Lord. Until then, it is important that we stand strong with one another through the ups and downs of life. Consider the depth of Jonathan's love for David:

Jonathan, the son of King Saul, protected David from death when Saul grew jealous of David. He created a secret way of getting the message to David that he indeed needed to flee the kingdom. The two hated to part, but it was their only option. In the end, the Bible tells us it was David who wept the hardest when he had to leave Jonathan. No doubt, David recognized the value of his true friend who stuck closer than a brother. Do you have a friend in need? Life gets busy. Don't ever be too busy to help your friends, to be there for them as Jonathan was for David.

Father in heaven, may I be a friend who truly sticks closer than a brother. Amen.

Share Your Hope

*We have this hope as an anchor for the soul, firm and secure. It enters
the inner sanctuary behind the curtain, where our forerunner, Jesus,
has entered on our behalf. He has become a high priest forever.*
HEBREWS 6:19–20 NIV

Anne Frank, a German Jewish teenager, and her family hid from those
who could very well take their lives. They spent just over two years in
annexed rooms above her father's office in Amsterdam during World
War II. Once they were discovered by the Nazis, she and her family
were sent to concentration camps, where Anne died of typhus at
fifteen years old.

Anne's desire to share hope through writing didn't die with her.
Her diary, first published in 1947, has been translated into sixty-
seven languages. Within the pages of her masterpiece—one of the
most widely read books in the world—she penned the words, "In spite
of everything, I still believe that people are really good at heart."

Though Anne's time on earth was cut short, her hope is shared
through the words she carefully recorded. She lives on each day as
people continue to turn the pages of her life and see God's hand in the
midst of the Holocaust.

*Lord, my hope is not in this life but in the life to come. Help me to
anchor my soul in the truth of Your love. Remind me each day to
share Your hope with others. Amen.*

When Trials Come

Dear brothers and sisters, when troubles come your way, consider it an opportunity for great joy. For you know that when your faith is tested, your endurance has a chance to grow.
JAMES 1:2–4 NLT

Kristina shuns difficult people because she finds them exhausting and annoying. Belle never asks her boss for extra work, even though she might advance within her company if she would complete those tasks well. And Hilda decides not to pursue a missions opportunity because she is afraid of the difficulties she might face overseas.

What about you? Do you often want to run away from trials, seeing them as inconveniences (at best) or terrorists (at worst)?

In the New Testament book of James, the brother of Jesus wrote to early believers, encouraging them to see trials as opportunities for growth. He said that the testing of our faith leads to perseverance, and perseverance leads to maturity.

Jesus never turned from difficulties; instead, He saw them as steps leading to His final glory. Can we do the same? In God's strength, we can.

Jobs, marriage, parenting, relationships, and ministry assignments are usually more difficult—and more rewarding—than we can imagine. However, instead of shunning trials, let's rest in the Lord and run toward Him, believing that the things that test us lead us to maturity—and deep, deep joy.

Lord, give us courage to run toward You in the midst of our difficulties, knowing that You grow our faith during times when we feel afraid and unsure. Amen.

God's Unfailing Love

*I have always been mindful of your unfailing love
and have lived in reliance on your faithfulness.*
PSALM 26:3 NIV

When her Sunday school teacher asked for examples of love, little Terri exclaimed, "Love is when you smile no matter how tired you are." Terri's answer reflected her home life. Her brother, Jason, was a special-needs child requiring around-the-clock care, and Terri's mother, Sue, cared for him selflessly and diligently without complaining. At church and wherever she went, Sue always brought a smile and a sunny disposition.

One day, Sue's pastor asked her how she managed to smile when surely she must be weary. She answered, "God's love gives me strength." She shared that she began each day with God's promise in Isaiah 54:10 (NIV): " 'Though the mountains be shaken and the hills be removed, yet my unfailing love for you will not be shaken nor my covenant of peace be removed,' says the LORD, who has compassion on you."

Every day, Sue went about caring for Jason's needs, relying on God's compassionate love and believing that He would give her strength. Each night, she thanked Him for loving her through the day.

Sue's sunny disposition reminded others that if she could face her trials with a smile, then so could they by trusting in God's abiding love.

*Dear Lord, I will be glad and rejoice in Your unfailing love, for You
have seen my troubles, and You care about the anguish of my soul.
Amen (Psalm 31:7 NLT).*

The Gift of Prayer

First of all, then, I admonish and urge that petitions, prayers,
intercessions, and thanksgivings be offered on behalf of all men. . . .
For such [praying] is good and right, and [it is] pleasing
and acceptable to God our Savior.
1 TIMOTHY 2:1, 3 AMP

There is such joy in giving gifts. Seeing the delight on someone's face
to receive something unexpected is exciting. Perhaps the absolute
greatest gift one person can give to another doesn't come in a box.
It can't be wrapped or presented formally, but instead it is the words
spoken to God for someone—the gift of prayer.

When we pray for others, we ask God to intervene and to make
Himself known to them. We can pray for God's plan and purpose
in their lives. We can ask God to bless them or protect them. You
can share with them that you are praying for them or do it privately
without their knowledge. Who would God have you give the gift of
prayer to today?

Lord, thank You for bringing people to my heart and mind who need
prayer. Help me to pray the things that they need from You in their
lives. Show me how to give the gift of prayer to those
You would have me pray for. Amen.

Exceedingly More

*Now to him who is able to do immeasurably more than all we ask
or imagine, according to his power that is at work within us.*
EPHESIANS 3:20 NIV

On a beautiful, sunny Saturday morning, Raeshel sat on her front
porch and reflected back to a year ago when it wouldn't stop raining
on her uneven, poorly landscaped lawn, where her son's wedding
would be the following spring.

It had been difficult to imagine how she and her family would
get it all done with so much work needed and so much relentless
rain. Yet there she sat a year later admiring the hard work that she,
her husband, and their sons had done. The grass where the wedding
tent sat in May was level, thick, and bright green. The landscaped
area that they had previously nicknamed "the weed patch" now had a
bench, a brick path, and a birdbath amid blooming daylilies.

Best of all, the feeling of accomplishment came with great
memories of a beautiful wedding celebration. God had blessed her
with much more than she had anticipated.

*God, thank You for the promise that You will do exceedingly,
immeasurably more, even when it doesn't appear that way to us
at first. Help us to trust You every step of the way. Amen.*

Staying on Track

I have fought a good fight, I have finished my course,
I have kept the faith.
2 TIMOTHY 4:7 KJV

In our hustle-bustle world, it's easy to get so busy we forget our priorities. Hopefully, as believers, we've established our priority list with God at the top. Staying in touch with Him and walking in His will should be our number one goal.

Paul knew this when he exhorted the churches to stick closely to the teachings of Jesus. He knew the fickle heart and how easy it would be for them to stray. In his letters to Timothy, he reminded the young man of the importance of drawing close to God, hearing His heartbeat. Despite the pain and afflictions Paul suffered in his life, he kept his eyes on Jesus, using praise to commune with God.

Likewise, we can keep in constant communion with the Father. We are so blessed to have been given the Holy Spirit within to keep us in tune with His will. Through His guidance, that still, small voice, we can rest assured our priorities will stay focused on Jesus. As the author A. W. Tozer wrote, "Lord, guide me carefully on this uncharted sea as I daily seek You in Your word. Then use me mightily as Your servant this year as I boldly proclaim Your word in leading others."

Lord, no better words have been spoken than to say I surrender to
Your will. Amen.

Encourage One Another

Therefore encourage one another and build each other up,
just as in fact you are doing.
1 THESSALONIANS 5:11 NIV

"Runners, get ready. Set. Go!"

Carol Ann fixed her eyes on the finish line and sprinted ahead in her first-ever Special Olympics race. As she ran, all along the way family members and friends shouted words of encouragement. "Go, Carol Ann! You're doing great! You're almost there!" Carol Ann beamed as she crossed the finish line and fell into the arms of her coach. "Good job!" said the coach as she embraced Carol Ann. "I knew you could do it."

Whether it is a race, a daunting project, or just getting through life, human beings need encouragement. Paul wrote in his letter to the Thessalonians, "Encourage one another. . .build each other up."

Encouragement is more than words. It is also valuing, being tolerant of, serving, and praying for one another. It is looking for what is good and strong in a person and celebrating it. Encouragement means sincerely forgiving and asking for forgiveness, recognizing someone's weaknesses and holding out a helping hand, giving humbly while building someone up, helping others to hope in the Lord, and praying that God will encourage them in ways that you cannot.

Whom will you encourage today? Get in the habit of encouraging others. It will bless them and you.

Heavenly Father, open my eyes to those who need encouragement.
Show me how I can help. Amen.

Good Friday

When he had received the drink, Jesus said, "It is finished."
With that, he bowed his head and gave up his spirit.
JOHN 19:30 NIV

"Good Friday," perhaps finding its origin in *Holy Friday*, *Sorrowful Friday*, or *God's Friday*, does not seem good at all. It is the day we commemorate our Savior's death on the cross.

Crucifixion was a terrible death—painful, tortuous, and reserved for the worst criminals. Jesus was forced to carry His own cross. He was mocked and ridiculed. They hung a sign above His head and placed a crown of thorns on His head. "*King of the Jews!*" they laughed as they raised a vinegar-soaked sponge to His lips. He had come humbly into the world, born in a stable, raised in the household of a carpenter. Little did they know that the nails that pierced His wrists and feet were driven there for them. Their jeers rang out in the darkness, but the Light of the World loved them with an everlasting love. That Friday *was* good. It was the fulfillment of the prophecies. Christ Jesus paid a price we could not pay that day. And as He cried out, "It is finished!" a gift of goodness was offered to the world that can never be matched. Good Friday. God's Friday. The day Jesus made a way for our eternal life in heaven.

Oh, Savior, how good is Your free gift of salvation.
May I never take it for granted. You have given me life. Amen.

Sending God's Favor

You help us by your prayers. Then many will give thanks on our behalf
for the gracious favor granted us in answer to the prayers of many.
2 CORINTHIANS 1:11 NIV

"I'll pray for you." Why is it those words seem weak, almost trite at times? It's what we say when we don't know what to say. When we don't know what to do, but we long to do something.

Yet, those four words are probably the most powerful words we can speak, as long as we follow through. When we pray, we call upon all the power of the King of heaven. When we pray, we see results. When we pray, miracles happen.

When we pray, people are blessed.

Friends, the power of prayer is better in a crisis than a casserole. It's better than being there, holding someone's hand, or doing their laundry. The power of prayer does more for a missionary on the other side of the world than a box of clothes or even a check.

Prayer brings peace. Prayer brings wisdom and clarity. Prayer is powerful.

Next time we offer to pray for someone, we can say it with the confidence that our prayers will be heard. They will be answered. And they will make a beautiful difference in the lives of those for whom we pray.

Dear Father, thank You for hearing my prayers. Thank You for
showing favor to others at my request. Amen.

Resurrection Sunday

The angel said to the women, "Do not be afraid, for I know that you are looking for Jesus, who was crucified. He is not here; he has risen, just as he said. Come and see the place where he lay."
MATTHEW 28:5–6 NIV

Amid the colored eggs and new spring dresses, remember the reason for Easter. It had nothing to do with candy or baskets or chocolate bunnies. It had everything to do with Christ's victory over the grave. There were no egg hunts that day, no jelly beans, no Easter ham with all the side dishes. There was a stone rolled away. There were grave clothes tossed aside. There was a risen Lord! Nail scars in His hands were borne as prophecy fulfilled, death defeated, and sin debt paid. Not His own, for He knew no sin. But ours. Easter is Resurrection Sunday. It is Christ's love stamp on this world forever, the Christian's victory cry! Easter is *Jesus*, and He reaches out to you today. Whatever state you find yourself in—healthy or ill, empty or overflowing with blessing—remember Him. Celebrate Him! He remembered you on the cross. And when He rose on the third day, imagine the angels' songs in heaven! Raise your hymns of praise to our Risen Lord today.

Lord Jesus, thank You for paying the ultimate price for my life. You died in order that I might have abundant and eternal life. Amen.

The Resurrection: Our Hope

Jesus said unto her, I am the resurrection, and the life:
he that believeth in me, though he were dead, yet shall he live.
JOHN 11:25 KJV

When Martha and Mary's brother, Lazarus, became deathly ill, the two women sent word to Jesus, a personal friend. Though He loved the trio, Jesus waited to visit them until after Lazarus had died. Understandably, Mary and Martha were confused, hurt, and grief-stricken.

"I am the resurrection and the life," Jesus told them as they stood near the tomb. Only minutes later, Jesus raised Lazarus from the dead.

When we lose a loved one, intense pain can overtake our faith. After two teenagers died in a wreck, a journalist asked pastor and author Dr. Howard Batson why God allows good people to suffer.

Batson said, "What we all want is a hard and fast moral equation. [However,] terrible things happen to wonderful families and good things happen to evil men."

He continued, "But if there were never any uncertainties in life. . . we'd have little need to depend on God. . . He helps us through the chaos, but He doesn't always take away the chaos."

Like Martha and Mary, we will one day see the glory of God, too— if we only believe.

Jesus, forgive our unbelief and show us Your glory. May we have eyes
to see, ears to hear, and hearts open to see Your wonders—
in this life, and the next. Amen.

We Are All Missionaries

And on the sabbath we went out of the city by a river side,
where prayer was wont to be made; and we sat down,
and spake unto the women which resorted thither.
ACTS 16:13 KJV

When Jesus ascended after His resurrection, He instructed all of his followers to "go and make disciples" (Matthew 28:19 NIV) out of the nations. Every Christian is a missionary, whether he/she realizes it or not.

Joy is a Christian school teacher. One day on the way to work, she thought, *My mom is a kindergarten teacher in a public school in West Virginia. How cool would it be if my class called her public school class and sang to them?* She said, "When I arrived at school, I told my eighteen students that a missionary is someone who tells people about Jesus. We also talked about where West Virginia is. I thought it was humorous when one student asked what language they spoke! Then we called and sang 'Jesus Loves Me' to students at Kanawha City Elementary. They sang us the peanut butter song."

Joy had longed to teach her students about witnessing, and was faithful to follow up on a creative idea. Let's pray for new places, times, and ways to share the Gospel—and encourage others to do the same.

Jesus, thank You for opportunities to share You with others.
May we always be bold to follow through in obedience. Amen.

He Knows Your Name

Listen to me, O isles and coastlands, and hearken, you peoples from afar. The Lord has called me from the womb; from the body of my mother He has named my name.
ISAIAH 49:1 AMP

Courtney and her husband, Curtis, had chosen their son's name the day the doctor confirmed by ultrasound that the baby was a boy. Now in her sixth month of pregnancy, neither she nor Curtis could bring themselves to call the baby by the name they had agreed on. She continued to scan the book of baby names each evening and refused to tell friends and family the baby's name.

As they sat in bed that evening, Curtis looked at his wife. "It's not his name, is it?" Courtney shook her head no.

Curtis continued, "I've been praying about this, and I don't want to name him after someone but give him the name God has named him."

Courtney smiled as she handed him a list of "new" names she'd been thinking about.

The Lord knows you. Sometimes you may feel like you are invisible to the whole world, but He knew you before you ever made your appearance into the world. He knew your name and has a dream and destiny for your life. He has named your name.

God, You have a great destiny for my life. Whenever I have a rough day or feel invisible or undervalued by those around me, help me to remember that You named my name. You know me, and I belong to You. Amen.

At All Times

Pray in the Spirit at all times with all kinds of prayers.
EPHESIANS 6:18 NCV

When giving instructions about important things, it's good to be specific. The more specific the instructions, the more likely the task will be done correctly. That's why when Paul spoke to the Ephesians about praying, he didn't leave any question about when to pray.

Prayer isn't a ritual to practice before bed or first thing in the morning or when the sun is at a certain place in the sky. Though it's great to have specific times of concentrated, focused prayer, our conversations with God shouldn't be limited to a certain time on our calendar. God wants us to pray *all the time.*

After all, God wants to be included in our days. He wants to walk and talk with us each moment. Imagine if we traveled through the day with our children or our spouse, but we only spoke to them between 6:15 and 6:45 a.m.! Of course we'd never do that to the people we care about. God doesn't want us to do that to Him, either.

God wants to travel the journey with us. He's a wonderful Companion, offering wisdom and comfort for every aspect of our lives. But He can only do that if we let Him into our schedules, every minute of every day.

Dear Father, thank You for always being there to listen.
Remind me to talk to You about everything, all the time. Amen.

Perfect Peace

You will keep in perfect peace all who trust in you,
all whose thoughts are fixed on you! Trust in the LORD always,
for the LORD GOD is the eternal Rock.
ISAIAH 26:3–4 NLT

What does perfect peace look like? Is it a life without problems? Is it a smooth ride into the future without any bumps in the road? Not for the Christian. We know life on earth won't ever be easy, but God promises to keep us in perfect peace if our thoughts are fixed on Him.

Perfect peace is only found by having a moment-by-moment relationship with Jesus Christ. It is ongoing faith and trust that God really has it all figured out. It's believing that each setback, heartbreak, problem, and crisis will be made right by God.

You can live in peace even during the messy stuff of life. You don't have to have everything figured out on your own. Doesn't that take some pressure off?

And the God of all grace, who called you to His eternal glory in Christ, after you have suffered a little while, will Himself restore you and make you strong, firm, and steadfast (1 Peter 5:10). That's perfect peace.

Heavenly Father, thank You for offering me peace in the midst of the stress of this life. Thank You that I'm not in charge and that You have everything already figured out. I trust You. Amen.

Love for One Another

All the believers were together and shared everything.
They would sell their land and the things they owned and then
divide the money and give it to anyone who needed it.
ACTS 2:44–45 NCV

Alex and Kay rushed out of their garage to feel the heat of the forty-foot flames hot against their backs. They jumped in their cars and barely escaped the fire that burned their beautiful home and much of Oklahoma in 2012. As they pulled away, all they had were the clothes on their backs. Over the next twenty-four hours, they discovered that hundreds from their small, rural community had lost everything. Immediately, blessings began to pour in, and the people came together to care for one another.

A local church became the hub for relief supplies and encouragement to the displaced. Alex was overwhelmed when friends and family from several church congregations filled his car with food, clothing, and toiletries. One man asked Alex, "What size shoe do you wear?" Alex replied, "A ten." The man bent down, unlaced his work boots, and handed them to Alex. Alex drove home with tears of gratitude and thanks flowing from his heart.

Dear heavenly Father, help me to be the Church. It's not about a building where we come together but the love and care I demonstrate to others that makes me one of Yours. Show me how to give Your best to everyone You bring across my path. Amen.

Women of Faith

*I remember your true faith. That faith first lived in your
grandmother Lois and in your mother Eunice,
and I know you now have that same faith.*
2 TIMOTHY 1:5 NCV

When the apostle Paul thought of young Timothy, one thing stood
out. Timothy had true faith. He had been raised by his mother and
grandmother to love and trust the Lord. Perhaps you come from a long
line of Christian women, or maybe you are a first-generation Christ-
follower. Either way, these verses have a message for you. We all
influence children. Perhaps you have your own children or nieces and
nephews. Maybe you spend time with friends' children. Some of you
may be grandmothers. Others may work with children either in your
career or in a church ministry role. Whatever the situation, you have a
great impact on children that look up to you.

It is important to note the trait that stood out was not perfection.
It was faith. We cannot be perfect examples for our children. But
we can teach them about faith! The way you respond to life's trials
speaks the loudest. Children learn about faith when they see it lived
out before them. Like Eunice and Lois were wonderful examples for
Timothy, may you influence the next generation to place their faith in
Christ Jesus.

*God, help me to be a woman of faith, for I know that little ones
are watching and learning about You through me. Amen.*

Surrendering to Love

*Jesus replied, "Anyone who loves me will obey my teaching.
My Father will love them, and we will come to them
and make our home with them."*
JOHN 14:23 NIV

Author and speaker Mary DeMuth had been abused, foreclosed,
abandoned, and betrayed—but it was just enough to bring her to a
place of surrender, piece by precious piece.

In that surrender, she found the freedom of giving everything to
God. In her book *Everything*, Mary writes, "There is always another
risk God asks us to take, always another adventure around the corner.
But if we stay in the 'good old days,' we won't take the risk or live the
adventure today."

What are you afraid of? Who are you afraid of? What is holding
you back from serving God with every fiber of your being? Risk
trusting Him. Risk believing Him.

The world is dying from lack of God's love; but we are too afraid
to reach out, afraid of what it will cost us. We wonder what sacrifices
we'll have to make, when He already made the biggest sacrifice.

God is love. And if we love Him, we will obey Him, no matter the
cost. Remember, whatever He requires of you, He is big enough to get
you through it. Dare to take Him at His word. . .to live fully. . .to obey
wholeheartedly.

*Precious Jesus, You are our everything. Forgive us for not risking
enough, for holding back and not surrendering to You. Amen.*

Casting Cares

Cast all your anxiety on him because he cares for you.
1 PETER 5:7 NIV

Do you have tiresome work that beckons, follows, and awaits you? No matter how demanding it is, the way you handle that work can reflect God.

Do you have relationship challenges with a spouse, parent, friend, or child? The way you handle those challenges can be a bright spot for everyone involved.

Are you fearful about the future, either for yourself or your children? The way you handle that fear can be a blessing into eternity.

Are there health issues that you or a loved one face? What you do with those can speak to the lives of many.

Do your friends, neighbors, or coworkers have things they are deeply struggling with that they have asked you to talk about with them or pray for? Listening and praying can make a world of difference for them in so many ways.

Does it seem that there are too many burdens, people, problems, and things to pray for? Give them all to God. He wants to take care of every one.

*Lord God, thank You for being the Sovereign Almighty
who can handle all of the cares we have. Amen.*

Love and Faithfulness

So the Word became human and made his home among us.
He was full of unfailing love and faithfulness. And we have
seen his glory, the glory of the Father's one and only Son.
JOHN 1:14 NLT

God came in human flesh—fully knowing what would be done to Him—to allow complete access to God. Jesus says that the only way to God is through Him (John 14:6). Before Jesus came, one could know about God. Through Jesus, we all can have an intimate relationship with God.

Christ came full of unfailing love and faithfulness. No other relationship can fill you with the love that comes through Jesus. No other relationship can meet all of your needs. No other relationship can be depended upon in the way that you can trust God's faithfulness.

Earthly relationships will leave you lacking if you come to count on them for your happiness. People will let you down. It's a guarantee. Even your most trusted loved ones cannot be faithful all the time. But Jesus' love is unfailing. He promises to never leave or forsake you (Hebrews 13:5). Put your faith and trust in the only One who is worthy.

Heavenly Father, I'm eternally grateful that Your love and faithfulness
will never leave me. Help me depend fully on Your faithfulness
alone, and give me a healthy perspective and balance
in my earthly relationships. Amen.

Walk a Mile in the Master's Shoes

*For this very reason, make every effort to add to your faith goodness;
and to goodness knowledge.*
2 PETER 1:5 NIV

Remember when you bought a new pair of shoes and had to break them in? They tended to pinch the toes a bit. But after a few weeks, they conformed to your foot and became more comfortable. So it is with the Christian life. When we start out on our walk of faith, it's not always a comfortable journey; we try to emulate Christ and His ways, to walk in His shoes, and we need to learn it takes time to get the correct fit.

God, in His infinite grace and mercy, knows we'll stumble. We can place our hope in Him with confidence He'll understand. He's not there with a "giant thumb" to squash us as we toddle along, new in our spiritual walk. He doesn't look for opportunities to say, "Aha, you messed up!" Quite the contrary: He encourages us with His Word.

For example, we read that the patriarchs in the Bible weren't perfect. Filled with flaws, David was still called "a man after God's own heart." In the same way, as we grow and learn with the aid of the Spirit, our lives will also reflect more of Him. And as we grow ever more sure-footed, we'll reach our destination—to be like our Father.

Gracious Lord, thank You for Your ever-present guidance. Amen.

Neighborly Love

"Do not seek revenge or bear a grudge against anyone among your people, but love your neighbor as yourself. I am the LORD."
LEVITICUS 19:18 NIV

Sophie kept to herself, tended her garden, and complained whenever she could. If a child's ball came over her fence, she kept it. If someone stopped to admire her flowers, she rapped on her front window and signaled for them to move on. She even called the police when the laughing at her next-door neighbor's baby shower annoyed her. Yes, Sophie was a difficult neighbor, and everyone stayed away.

One day, the flowers in Sophie's garden looked wilted. The grass had grown tall. Her neighbors felt that something was wrong, but should they get involved? They drew straws to decide who would check on Sophie.

Elaine Keller got the short straw. She knocked on Sophie's door, and the old woman answered, leaning on crutches, her right foot in a cast.

"We were worried," Elaine said. "We want to help you."

"No need," said Sophie.

"But we *want* to!" Elaine protested, and before long she was watering Sophie's flowers, and her husband was cutting the grass.

Sophie never did warm up to her neighbors, but they learned to accept her just as she was—the way that God accepts us. Some people are hard to love; yet that is exactly what God commands of us—in all circumstances to love our neighbors.

Dear Lord, help me to love my neighbors patiently and consistently.
Amen.

Praying Together

*For where two or three are gathered together in my name,
there am I in the midst of them.*
MATTHEW 18:20 KJV

The pastor stood before his congregation on a rainy Sunday morning.
"You have made a good choice today!" he stated, along with a joke
about all those that stayed at home and pulled the covers up over
their heads. "Yes, you have made a good choice," he repeated. "We
have an honored guest. God is here with us this morning!" He then
read Matthew 18:20: "For where two or three are gathered in my
name, there am I in the midst of them."

Of all the passages in the Bible that emphasize the importance of
gathering for worship and prayer, this one stands out. It is short and
sweet and to the point. Why should we gather together to pray with
other Christians? Because when we do, *God shows up!* The Lord is in
our midst.

As you gather with other Christians in your church or even in
your family, God is honored. He loves to listen to the hearts and
voices of His children unified in prayer. He will be faithful to answer
according to His perfect will.

*Father, thank You for the promise that where we gather in Your name,
there You will be also. Help me never to give up the practice
of praying with fellow believers. Amen.*

Blessed Redeemer

For God so loved the world that he gave his one and only Son, that whoever believes in him shall not perish but have eternal life.
JOHN 3:16 NIV

Compassion is "sympathetic consciousness of others' distress together with a desire to alleviate it" *(Merriam-Webster).* Oh, how our God loved us and showed His compassion. He knew we were a sinful people, and we were in peril. Our eternal lives were at stake. And He had a plan. He provided a way for redemption.

Despite the fact we did not deserve His unmerited favor and grace, He gave it to us anyway. He looked down on mankind and desired to bridge the separation between us. He sent His Son, Jesus, to die on the cross for our sins, so we might live the resurrected life. Once we've accepted this free gift, we can rejoice!

We were in distress, and God came to the rescue. What a mighty God we serve! And how He loves us. The rescuing Shepherd came for His flock. He bore what we deserved because He had such compassion. True love, which our Father gives, is eternal. He loved us before we loved Him. What an amazing concept He desires us to grasp! Know today that your heavenly Father loves you.

Dear Lord, how gracious and loving You are to me.
Thank You, Father, for Your arms about me this day. Amen.

Love the Unlovable?

Bless those who curse you. Pray for those who hurt you.
LUKE 6:28 NLT

Do you know of anyone like this? Lydia was demanding, incorrigible, and cynical. She manipulated every situation, and if she couldn't, she whined and complained. Gossip was the norm for her, and she'd often spread unsubstantiated rumors. Some family members and coworkers accommodated her shifting moods and bursts of unrestrained anger in an effort to keep peace. Others simply distanced themselves.

So how do we bless those who curse us, as Jesus commands? Ralph Waldo Emerson once said, "If you would lift me up you must be on higher ground." Christians stand on higher ground. We stand in our faith in Jesus Christ and His Holy Word. We stand on Christ's shoulders to lift up others to receive the same saving grace and forgiveness that we embrace.

That's how and why we can bless those who curse or hurt us. Because Jesus based everything He did, and does, on His love for us, how can we do anything less? That doesn't mean we need to befriend every unconscionable person or accept unacceptable behavior. But it does mean that we are to pray for and attempt to understand and love the unlovable, because God loves them.

The Lord never calls us to a task without equipping us to fulfill it. As we pray, He helps us to see that person through His eyes.

Father, help me look past the person and see the need. Amen.

Before You Ask

*"Seek the Kingdom of God above all else, and live righteously,
and he will give you everything you need."*
MATTHEW 6:33 NLT

"Dear God, please. . ."

Do your prayers begin that way? "Dear God, please help me to be patient with my kids." "Dear God, please heal my friend's illness." "Dear God, please provide enough money to pay this month's bills." God wants believers to ask for whatever they need. But Jesus reminds them that there is a right way to pray, and prayer is more than asking.

In the Lord's Prayer, Jesus teaches His followers how to pray. He begins, "Our Father in heaven, may your name be kept holy. May your kingdom come soon. May your will be done on earth as it is in heaven" (Matthew 6:9–10 NLT). First, Jesus honors God's holiness. Next, He shows faith in God's promise of reigning over the earth and redeeming His people. Then He accepts God's perfect will. Praise, faith, and acceptance come before asking. Jesus reminds believers to honor God first, put God's will second, and pray for their own needs third. His prayer begins with God and ends with Him: "For thine is the kingdom, and the power, and the glory, for ever. Amen" (Matthew 6:13 KJV).

Bring your requests to God. Ask specifically and confidently, but remember Jesus' model—put God first in your prayers.

*Dear God, I praise You. My faith rests in You,
and I accept whatever Your will is for my life. Amen.*

Always There

*When I said, "My foot is slipping," your unfailing love, LORD,
supported me. When anxiety was great within me,
your consolation brought me joy.*
PSALM 94:18–19 NIV

Dayna exited the conference room all smiles and hurried back to her desk. She had just landed a big account, and she wanted to share her news. Imagining just how proud her father would be, she reached for her phone and dialed his number. She stopped, realizing he wouldn't be there. In her excitement she had forgotten, for just a moment, that he was gone. Just six weeks ago she'd stood next to her sister at his memorial service.

Dayna put the receiver down and took a deep breath. She bowed her head and prayed, *Heavenly Father, I miss my dad. Comfort me in his absence. Thank You for blessing me with favor with my new client and giving me inspiration and wisdom to do my job well. Thank You for always being there for me.*

One of the things people grieve most in losing loved ones is trying to overcome that strong desire to reach out, only to find them no longer there. The good news is that God is always there. Through your relationship with Him, you can celebrate the goodness of each new day.

*Thank You, God, for always being there. Help me to remember
that I don't have to do this alone. Amen.*

Ask in Faith

But when you ask God, you must believe and not doubt. Anyone who
doubts is like a wave in the sea, blown up and down by the wind.
JAMES 1:6 NCV

What does it mean to ask God for something *in faith?* Does it mean
we believe that He *can* grant our requests? That He *will* grant our
requests? Exactly what is required to prove our faith?

These are difficult questions. Many who have prayed for healed
bodies and healed relationships have received exactly that, this side of
heaven. Others who have prayed for the same things, believing only
God could bring healing, haven't received the answers they wanted.

There is no secret ingredient that makes all our longings come
to fruition. The secret ingredient, if there is one, is faith that God
is who He says He is. It's faith that God is good and will use our
circumstances to bring about His purpose and high calling in our lives
and in the world.

When we don't get the answers we want from God, it's okay
to feel disappointed. He understands. But we must never doubt His
goodness or His motives. We must stand firm in our belief that God's
love for us will never change.

Dear Father, I know that You are good and that You love me.
I know Your love for me will never change, even when my
circumstances are hard. Help me cling to Your love,
even when You don't give the answers I want. Amen.

Joyous Light

*Whom having not seen, ye love; in whom, though now ye see him not,
yet believing, ye rejoice with joy unspeakable and full of glory.*
1 PETER 1:8 KJV

Artist Thomas Kinkade was called the "painter of light." His work
reflects light shining from the canvas, brightening his pictures.
Wouldn't it be wonderful to be known as someone who lightens the
places he or she goes? Most often those who light up a room do so
because they contain such a measure of love and joy, often contagious
joy. Light-filled people who love the Lord are infectious with a
dazzling light illuminating the darkness.

Jesus is the Light of the World. When we accept Him, the light
is poured into us. The Holy Spirit comes to reside within, bringing
His light. A glorious gift graciously given to us. When we realize the
importance of the gift and the blessings that result from a life led by
the Father, we can't contain our happiness. The joy and hope that fill
our hearts wells up. Joy uncontained comes when Jesus becomes our
Lord. Through Him, through faith, we have hope for the future. What
joy! So let it spill forth in love. Be a contagious, light-filled Christian
spreading your hope, joy, and love to a hurting world.

*Lord, help me to be a light unto the world,
shining forth Your goodness. Amen.*

Encourage Yourself

David encouraged himself in the LORD his God.
1 SAMUEL 30:6 KJV

David and his army went off to fight, leaving their families behind in Ziklag. While they were gone, their enemy the Amalekites raided the city, burned it, and captured the women and children. When the men returned, they found just a smoking pile of rubble. Enraged and weeping uncontrollably, some blamed David and wanted him killed. What did David do when no one was around to encourage him? He encouraged himself in the Lord (1 Samuel 30:1–6).

David had a personal relationship with God. He knew the scriptures, and He relied on God's promises. Instead of giving in to discouragement, he applied those promises to his own situation and found strength. David relied on God to build him up. Many believe that he wrote these words in Psalm 119:15–16: "I will study your commandments and reflect on your ways. I will delight in your decrees and not forget your word" (NLT). *I will delight myself in Your decrees.* In the middle of his grief and loneliness, David delighted himself in the Lord.

Christians never have to face discouragement alone. As they trust God, they can also recall past times when He brought them success. They can communicate with Him through prayer and find support in His Word.

Remember, God is always on your side, always there, and always ready to lift you up.

*Dear God, thank You for encouraging me with
Your promises and Your love. Amen.*

Mother's Day

When Jesus therefore saw his mother, and the disciple standing by,
whom he loved, he saith unto his mother, Woman, behold thy son!
Then saith he to the disciple, Behold thy mother! And from that hour
that disciple took her unto his own home.
JOHN 19:26–27 KJV

Jesus knew the value of a mother. Mary held a special place in His
heart. She brought Him into this world. Straight from heaven's glory,
He was wrapped in swaddling clothes by Mary's loving hands and laid
in a manger bed. Years later, from the cross, in agony, breathing His
dying breaths, Jesus made preparations for His mother's care. He told
the disciple dearest to His heart, believed to be John, to take Mary as
his own mother.

There is a lesson here for all of us. When we are children, our
mothers care for us. Inevitably, at some point, the tables turn. Our
mothers need our care. Follow the example laid out for you by your
Savior. Honor your mother all the days of your life. Honor her by
living well, spending time with her, and by meeting any needs she
may have. No mother and child relationship is perfect, but God's Word
is clear in its command to honor our mothers. Love and serve your
mother. . .for this pleases God.

God, help me to honor my mother. May my words and actions
bring glory to You as I love my mother well. Amen.

Scoring an Inheritance

An inheritance that can never perish, spoil or fade.
This inheritance is kept in heaven for you, who through faith
are shielded by God's power until the coming of the salvation
that is ready to be revealed in the last time.
1 PETER 1:4–5 NIV

Sarah's best friend was helped out of a financial hole just in the nick of time by an unexpected family inheritance.

While Sarah was happy for her friend, she began feeling sorry for herself at the same time. After all, what was wrong with her that she had no inheritance and probably never would? On the contrary, if there were an inheritance coming from her family it would be their debt, but thankfully that couldn't really happen. A piece of furniture or two, that was all there appeared to be.

Sarah made sacrifices to pay down her mortgage faster and save some money. Meanwhile, her best friend paid off her entire house and credit card debt while making plans to pay cash for a barn they were going to have built.

It was a monumental task for Sarah not to be incredibly jealous. She struggled with it all until God showed her in the Word the inheritance she did have coming, and this one would last forever!

Lord, thank You for the promise of an eternal inheritance that
will never fade like the things in this life do. Amen.

Already Loved

*"Behold, what manner of love the Father hath bestowed upon us,
that we should be called the sons of God. . ."*
I JOHN 3:1 KJV

Sheila struggled with feelings of resentment when she heard about
fellow authors' successes. Years of late-night toil had led to one
book and a weekly newspaper column. But low sales figures on her
book and repeated rejections left her discouraged. She prayed for
contentment, realizing that her problems were small compared to the
rest of the world.

One day, Sheila was playing a computer game with her toddler.
On the desk was a copy of her first book. Jenny looked at the
illustration of a frazzled mom on the cover and said, "Is that you?"

"No, sweetie," Sheila said, "but Mommy's name is on the cover.
See here—it says, 'by Sheila Masters.'"

"Oh!" Jenny said, grinning, "I *love* Sheila Masters!"

Sheila blinked back tears. As she hugged her child, she thanked
God for such a simple reminder that whether or not she ever reached
the best-selling list, she was already loved—by her family, but more
important, by the Father who had given her a gift with words.

*Father, thank You that You give us friends and family members to
remind us of Your care for us. Help us to be content with where
we are and what You've called us to do, knowing that Your love is
unconditional, bountiful, and always available. Amen.*

He Carries Us

In his love and mercy he redeemed them.
He lifted them up and carried them through all the years.
ISAIAH 63:9–10 NLT

Are you feeling broken today? Depressed? Defeated? Run to Jesus and not away from Him.

When we suffer, He cries. Isaiah 63:8–10 (NLT) says, "In all their suffering he also suffered, and he personally rescued them. In his love and mercy he redeemed them. He lifted them up and carried them through all the years."

He will carry us—no matter what pain we have to endure. No matter what happens to us. God sent Jesus to be our Redeemer. He knew the world would hate, malign, and kill Jesus. Yet He allowed His very flesh to writhe in agony on the cross—so that we could also become His sons and daughters. He loved me, and you, that much.

One day, we will be with Him. "Beloved," He will say, "no more tears. No more pain." He will lift us up and hold us in His mighty arms, and then He will show us His kingdom, and we will, finally, be whole.

Lord Jesus, thank You for coming to us—for not abandoning us when we are broken. Thank You for Your work on the cross; for Your grace, mercy, and love. Help me to seek You even when I can't feel You; to love You even when I don't know all the answers. Amen.

Everyday Ways

*The heavens declare the glory of God,
and the skies announce what his hands have made.*
PSALM 19:1 NCV

Another day had come and gone. It wasn't a special day—that Janet knew of anyway. She sat in her backyard and watched the sun set. Glorious shades of orange melded with yellow and bright red, all artfully meshed at the edges with a now navy-blue sky. It was unlike any sunset she had ever seen. *God showing off again*, she mused.

As she thought about it, no two sunsets were ever the same. The sun went down in a slightly different location along the horizon each day at a slightly different time depending on the season. The color variations were never exactly the same, as if an artist had painted it.

But then, a great artist did paint it. Every day. Something new.

Janet thought about how deeply God must love her and each of His children to give us a fresh work of art in the skies every day of our lives. Many duties and burdens may fill our days, and He loves us in the midst of all of it, enough to provide beauty and wonder all along the way.

*Father, thank You for Your everyday ways. Let the wonder of
Your creation continue to deepen our understanding
of Your great love for us. Amen.*

Linking Hearts with God

*"You will receive power when the Holy Spirit comes on you;
and you will be my witnesses. . .to the ends of the earth."*
ACTS 1:8 NIV

God knows our hearts. He knows what we need to make it through
a day. So in His kindness, He gave us a gift in the form of the Holy
Spirit. As a Counselor, a Comforter, and a Friend, the Holy Spirit acts
as our inner compass. He upholds us when times are hard and helps
us hear God's directions. When the path of obedience grows dark,
the Spirit floods it with light. What revelation! He lives within us.
Therefore, our prayers are lifted to the Father, to the very throne of
God. Whatever petitions we have, we may rest assured they are heard.

We can rejoice in the fact that God cared enough to bless our
lives with the Spirit to direct our paths. God loves the praises of His
people, and these praises revive the Spirit within you. If you are weary
or burdened, allow the Holy Spirit to minister to you. Seek the Holy
Spirit and His wisdom, and ask Him to revive and refresh your inner
man. Place your hope in God and trust the Spirit's guidance, and He
will never let you down.

*Father God, how blessed I am to come into Your presence.
Help me, Father, when I am weak. Guide me this day. Amen.*

Girlfriends

Two people are better than one, because they get more done by
working together. If one falls down, the other can help him up.
But it is bad for the person who is alone and falls,
because no one is there to help.
ECCLESIASTES 4:9–10 NCV

Magda had been hurt by girls in middle school and high school. Her
experiences included name calling and backstabbing at the expense
of her heart. She chose to hang out with the guys as much as she
could and threw herself into work to put herself through college. She
promised herself she'd never trust another female.

Years went by, and she found herself in a counseling session
with a woman who came to be both a mentor and a friend. She led
Magda to the Lord, and He began to connect her to other women who
genuinely cared about her. Through the love of these other women,
she began to see herself in a new way. She opened her heart to those
the Lord directed her to connect with. She needed women to speak
truth into her life, and those women also needed to hear what Magda
had to share.

If you've been hurt by girls who pretended to be your friends,
know that God wants you to have friends—ones who will love you like
He does and pray for you.

Lord, show me the friends that You want to put into my life.
Help me to be the friend to others You desire me to be. Amen.

A Decision

*Eat honey, my son, for it is good; honey from the comb is sweet to
your taste. Know also that wisdom is like honey for you: If you find it,
there is a future hope for you, and your hope will not be cut off.*
PROVERBS 24:13–14 NIV

Becky had a big decision to make. As a young woman with student
loan debt, broken dreams, and a dead-end job, she had an invitation to
live with friends out West and work a summer job.

Should she take the chance of making a new start, even if it
involved quitting a job that paid the bills? What if she didn't find
employment after the summer job ended? What would she do then?
Would she be stuck imposing on her friends?

After much thought, she decided to go. God blessed Becky with
a summer filled with growth, adventure, and new connections and
friends. And although at the end of the summer it was best to move
back home where another job opened up, she could see that she had
needed this time away to refresh and start a new chapter.

*God, thank You for the wisdom You give us to make good decisions.
Guide and bless us in each decision we make today. Amen.*

The Power of God's Love

*Above all things have intense and unfailing love for one another,
for love covers a multitude of sins [forgives and disregards
the offenses of others].*
1 PETER 4:8 AMP

Let's face it—we're human. As Christians, we endeavor to follow
the teachings of Christ but fall short. Periodically our actions take
the course of a runaway train. Maybe a brother tested your patience
and your intolerance of his behavior ignited you to lash out in anger.
Perhaps a sister in Christ took the credit publicly for some good work
you did in private and you seethe. Or maybe someone falsely accused
you and you retaliated.

Every believer is flawed, and too often we fail miserably. Peter—
endowed with a few flaws of his own—admonished the Church to
love one another intensely. He, above all, had learned the power of
repentance and forgiveness, having denied Christ three times after
the Roman soldiers apprehended Jesus. Yet Peter was one of the first
to see Jesus after His resurrection, and it was Peter who first reached
Jesus on the Sea of Galilee. There, the Lord commissioned Peter to
feed His sheep. After Jesus' ascension, Peter—the spokesman of the
apostles—preached the sermon that resulted in the conversion of
approximately three thousand souls (Acts 2:14–41).

Christ's love forgives and disregards the offenses of others. His
love covers a multitude of sins. That's the power of God's love at
work. Love resurrects, forgives, restores, and commissions us to reach
others for the kingdom.

Jesus, teach me to love rather than to judge. Amen.

Love and Mercy

*"Therefore, I tell you, her many sins have been forgiven—as her great
love has shown. But whoever has been forgiven little loves little."*
LUKE 7:47 NIV

The woman in this verse recognized who Jesus was and washed
His feet with her perfume. The Bible says that she lived a sinful life
but that her faith in Christ saved her. She, who was guilty of much,
was forgiven much. She experienced amazing grace and undeserved
mercy. She loved Jesus and did what she could to worship Him.

Have you ever received a speeding ticket? Then you most likely
deserved it. But have you ever deserved a speeding ticket and the
officer let you off the hook? What a huge relief! That's mercy. The
Bible tells us that the punishment for sin is death, but the gift of God
is eternal life (Romans 6:23). The sinful woman didn't deserve mercy,
and neither do we. But through Christ, we have been forgiven much.

God's Word says that if you've been given much, much is
expected (Luke 12:48). This applies to many situations. Have you been
given love and mercy? Yes, indeed! Then you're expected to show
love and mercy in return.

*Dear Jesus, I don't deserve what You have done for me.
Help me to remember how much I've been forgiven so that
I can extend that love and mercy to others. Amen.*

The Crown of Life

*Blessed (happy, to be envied) is the man who is patient under trial
and stands up under temptation, for when he has stood the test
and been approved, he will receive [the victor's] crown of life
which God has promised to those who love Him.*
JAMES 1:12 AMP

Stephen is known as the first Christian martyr. Stoned to death for
preaching Christ unashamedly, as he entered heaven, he saw Jesus
standing at the right hand of God. Stephen stood up for Jesus, and
Jesus stood up to welcome him home to heaven! Stephen endured a
great trial. He paid a high price—his life. Stephen received the crown
of life that day as he entered into the glory of heaven. In fact, did you
know that his name means "crown"?

As you face temptations and trials in your life, be encouraged.
Realize that Christ-followers through the ages have endured
persecution. The temptations you face have been struggles for
believers for centuries. The good news is that the Bible tells us God
will always provide a way out when we are tempted. Look for that
way! Cling to that Christian support system when you are tempted
to stray from God. Make necessary changes that will help you to
defeat Satan's desire that you succumb to his traps. One day you, like
Stephen, will receive the crown of life!

*Father God, in the name of Jesus, I will stand against Satan's
schemes. I will not give in to temptation. I love You, God. Amen.*

Powerful Praying

Therefore confess your sins to each other and pray for
each other so that you may be healed. The prayer of
a righteous man is powerful and effective.
JAMES 5:16 NIV

When someone we know well, someone we admire and respect, talks to us about something, we usually listen. But if a different person— someone we don't know well or who hasn't earned our respect—talks to us about the same thing, we may not listen with the same intensity. We tend to listen more to people we respect. And when the people we admire ask us for something, we'll often bend over backward to give them what they want.

God is the same way. When we have God's approval, when we live with integrity and faith, He listens to us. But when we consistently make poor choices and disregard God's guidance, He may not take our prayers as seriously.

Oh, He will never take His love from us, no matter what. And He will always listen when we ask for help out of our sin. But if we want our prayers to hold extra power, we need to live righteously. When we have God's approval on our lives, we can also know we have God's ear about all sorts of things. When we walk in God's will, we have access to God's power.

Dear Father, I want my prayers to be powerful and effective.
Help me to live in a way that pleases You. Amen.

The Hand of God

*For I am the LORD your God, who takes hold of your right
hand and says to you, Do not fear; I will help you.*
ISAIAH 41:13 NIV

If there is a scripture you need to have handy in times of trouble, this
is it! Post it on your fridge; write it on a sticky note to tack up in your
car; commit it to memory so that the Spirit of God can bring it to mind
when you need to hear it most.

Psalm 139 tells us that God created us and knows everything about
us. He knows when we sit and when we get up, and He knows every
word that's on our tongue before we speak it. Psalm 139:7–10 tells us
that no matter where we go, His hand will guide us and hold us.

Heading to the emergency room? Repeat Isaiah 41:13 and
remember that God is holding your hand. Afraid of the future? Stop
worrying and trust the God who loves you and has great plans for you.
Facing a problem that you cannot possibly bear? Take hold of God's
mighty hand and believe that He will help you.

*Father God, help me not to fear. Take hold of my hand
and guide me. I put my faith and trust in You alone. Amen.*

Grace Accepted

But because of his great love for us, God, who is rich in mercy,
made us alive with Christ even when we were dead in
transgressions—it is by grace you have been saved.
EPHESIANS 2:4–5 NIV

Have you ever been wrongly accused of something or completely misunderstood? Have the words of your accusers struck your heart, making you feel like you have to make it right somehow, but no amount of reasoning with them seems to help?

If anyone understands this situation it's Christ Himself. Wrongly accused. Misunderstood. Yet He offered unfathomable grace at all times and still offers it today.

This reminds us that we are to aim to offer this same grace to our accusers and those who misunderstand us. We will be misunderstood when we try to obey and follow God in a culture that runs quite contrary in many ways. Our job is to first accept God's grace and then offer it up to others as lovingly as we can. Like Christ.

God, help us to continually accept Your grace through Christ and
reflect You by offering that same grace to others. Amen.

You Are a Woman of Worth

*A wife of noble character who can find? She is worth far more than
rubies. Her husband has full confidence in her and lacks nothing of
value. She brings him good, not harm, all the days of her life.*
PROVERBS 31:10–12 NIV

Are you the woman of worth that Jesus intends you to be? We often
don't think we are. Between running a household, rushing to work,
taking care of the children, volunteering for worthwhile activities,
and still being a role model for our families, we think we've failed
miserably. There just isn't any way we can be that perfect Proverbs 31
woman!

Sometimes we don't fully realize that learning to be a noble
woman of character takes time. We learn many valuable lessons
through our family experiences, from time management to fiscal
responsibility to diplomacy. Our experiences can be offered to another
generation seeking wisdom from others who have "been there." You
are a woman of worth. God said so!

*Father God, thank You for equipping me to be a woman of noble
character. You tell me that I am more precious than jewels,
and I claim and believe that wholeheartedly. I love You, Lord,
and I will continue to put You first in my life. Help me to
be the woman You intend me to be! Amen.*

Asking and Imagining

For though we live in the world, we do not wage war as the world
does. The weapons we fight with are not the weapons of the world.
On the contrary, they have divine power to demolish strongholds.
2 CORINTHIANS 10:3–4 NIV

Most of us do not see ourselves as soldiers. In fact, we see ourselves
as anything but soldiers. However, we are called to be the militant
church. Satan is our enemy in a war for minds and souls.

As Paul says in today's verse, we do not wage war as the world
does. We do not use tanks, guns, or even fighter bombers. We must
fight in the Spirit and use these weapons: the Blood of Jesus, the
Name of Jesus, and the Word of God. Spiritual battles cannot be won
in the flesh but only by the power of prayer. When we come to God
in prayer and give Him full control of the situation, we acknowledge
His sovereignty in that area. However, He will not act unless we ask.
Never underestimate the power of your prayer to a loving, caring God
who can do all things, even more than we ask or imagine.

Loving Father, thank You for the power of prayer! Remind me that
no prayer goes unheard and that You wish us to partner with You in
this, to change people and situations. What an awesome privilege and
opportunity to be a part of this life-changing work! Amen!

Like Little Children

Some people brought their little children to Jesus so he could touch them, but his followers told them to stop. When Jesus saw this, he was upset and said to them, "Let the little children come to me. Don't stop them, because the kingdom of God belongs to people who are like these children. I tell you the truth, you must accept the kingdom of God as if you were a little child, or you will never enter it."
MARK 10:13–15 NCV

Have you ever heard a child pray from his heart? Not just a memorized prayer that he repeats before lunch but a real, honest prayer? A four-year-old boy prayed this: "Dear God, I really don't like all the bad dreams I've been having. Will you please make them stop?"

His prayer was so pure and honest. He prayed, believing that God would listen to his prayer and do something about it. He wasn't afraid to say how he really felt.

This passage in Mark tells us that no matter how old we are, God wants us to come to Him with the faith of a child. He wants us to be open and honest about our feelings. He wants us to trust Him wholeheartedly, just like little kids do.

As adults we sometimes play games with God. We tell God what we think He wants to hear, forgetting that He already knows our hearts! God is big enough to handle your honesty. Tell Him how you really feel.

Father, help me come to You as a little child and be more open and honest with You in prayer. Amen.

God's Promises

*"God is not human, that he should lie, not a human being,
that he should change his mind. Does he speak and then not act?
Does he promise and not fulfill?"*
NUMBERS 23:19 NIV

Our opinions of God are often shaped by our experiences with people. When we've been hurt, we see God as hurtful. When people lie to us, we subconsciously think of God as a liar. After all, if humans are created in His image, it only stands to reason that God would be like the people in our lives. Right?

Well, no. Yes, we were created in God's image. But we humans are a fallen, broken race. We're sinful. God is without sin.

Humans lie. God doesn't.

Humans go back on their word. God doesn't.

Humans can be mean and hurtful. God is love, and He only acts in love.

God promised good things to those who love Him, those who live and act according to His will. That doesn't mean others won't hurt us or that we won't experience the effects of living in a sin-infested world. But where there's pain, we have a Healer. Where there's brokenness, we have a Comforter. And where we feel alone, we know we have a Friend.

And one day we'll experience the perfect fulfillment of all His promises without the burdens of this world to weigh us down.

Now that's something to look forward to.

*Dear Father, thank You for Your promises. When I feel discouraged,
help me to remember those promises. Amen.*

Without Love

*If I speak in the tongues of men or of angels, but do not have love,
I am only a resounding gong or a clanging cymbal.*
1 CORINTHIANS 13:1 NIV

Without love, all the good deeds in the world are just a bunch of noise!
Like resounding gongs or clanging cymbals, the Pharisees of Jesus'
day went about their good works. Over and over, they repeated them.
They were duties, not desires of the heart. They based everything on
ritual rather than relationship. Are there Pharisees among us today?
Certainly! Our job as Christ-followers is to show the world the love
of God. We do this with open hearts and open arms. We do it in the
workplace, in the marketplace, and in our homes. We do it as we
come and go; with our children and with other people's children;
with our spouses, neighbors, and coworkers. The world desperately
needs to see extravagant love in us, love that cannot be explained
by any means other than the fact that we walk with the Author and
Creator of love. Don't go about your good deeds out of guilt or so that
someone will notice how nice you are. Do good deeds so that others
will notice Jesus in you and glorify your Father who is in heaven. Do
good deeds out of love. It will always come back to you tenfold.

*Lord Jesus, give me opportunities to love this world
so that others might see You in me. Amen.*

Darkest before Dawn

*Though the fig tree does not bud and there are no grapes on the vines,
though the olive crop fails and the fields produce no food, though
there are no sheep in the pen and no cattle in the stalls, yet I will
rejoice in the LORD, I will be joyful in God my Savior.*
HABAKKUK 3:17–18 NIV

Rick gave his order to the server at the restaurant. He overheard a
man at a nearby table tell his companions that a tornado had touched
down on the other side of town. Immediately, customers began to look
for a place of safety, "just in case." Within minutes, the lights began
to flicker and then went dark. Customers and staff began to quickly
move to the safety of the kitchen. Soon a deep roar and sounds of
breaking glass assaulted their ears.

Rick was not the only one praying for a miracle that day. During
this calamity, many in that restaurant were hoping in Him, asking for
Him to save them. And He did. Thankfully no one at that restaurant
was seriously hurt during the catastrophic EF5 tornado that hit Joplin,
Missouri, in May 2011.

*Gracious Father, thank You for Your faithfulness, even in difficult,
trying, and sometimes frightening times. You are in them. We can be
confident and thankful that You have heard our prayers. I will rejoice
in who You are—that You are in control—and be joyful
that I am Your child. Amen!*

Loving Sisters

*But Ruth replied, "Don't urge me to leave you or to turn back
from you. Where you go I will go, and where you stay I will stay.
Your people will be my people and your God my God."*
RUTH 1:16 NIV

The story of Ruth and Naomi is inspiring on many levels. It talks of
two women from different backgrounds, generations, ethnicity, and
even religion. But rather than being obstacles to loving friendship,
these differences became invisible. Both women realized that their
commitment, friendship, and love for each other surpassed any of
their differences. They were a blessing to each other.

Do you have girlfriends who would do almost anything for you? A
true friendship is a gift from God. Those relationships provide us with
love, companionship, encouragement, loyalty, honesty, understanding,
and more! Lasting friendships are essential to living a balanced life.

*Father God, thank You for giving us the gift of friendship.
May I be the blessing to my girlfriends that they are to me.
Please help me to always encourage and love them and to be
a loving support for them in both their trials and their happiness.
I praise You for my loving sisters! Amen.*

Prayer Time

*Rejoice always, pray continually, give thanks in all circumstances;
for this is God's will for you in Christ Jesus.*
1 THESSALONIANS 5:16–18 NIV

In her thirties Jenna began attending a Bible study that her neighbor invited her to. As a newer Christian, Jenna grew like crazy, just soaking up everything she could as she relied on God to help her understand things.

Prayer was something she wasn't sure she was getting, though. One of the ladies referred to her daily morning prayer time during the group discussion. The woman wasn't bragging or anything, but Jenna wondered how in the world she would ever carve out that time with her family's early-morning demands.

Jenna began to think of when she did pray. There were the many times while driving the kids all over the place. While she was alone in the kitchen she often prayed. When she took walks, she found herself talking to God and thanking Him for the beauty of His creation.

She began to have a peace about her prayer time. Her walk with God did not have to look like her friends' or the saints' down the street. It was just a steady thing with her and God. Anytime. Anywhere.

*Lord God, thank You for communing with us anytime
and for being available to us all the time. Amen.*

Breath of Life

He heals the brokenhearted and binds up their wounds
[curing their pains and their sorrows].
PSALM 147:3 AMP

As a result of sin, every person on the earth is born into a fallen world. The sinful condition brings hurt and heartache to all men—those who serve the Lord and those who don't. The good news is, as a child of God, you have a hope and eternal future in Christ. Jesus said, "I have told you all this so that you may have peace in me. Here on earth you will have many trials and sorrows. But take heart, because I have overcome the world" (John 16:33 NLT).

When your life brings disappointment, hurt, and pain that are almost unbearable, remember that you serve the One who heals hearts. He knows you best and loves you most. When the wind is knocked out of you and you feel like there is no oxygen left in the room, let God provide you with the air you need to breathe. Breathe out a prayer to Him and breathe in His peace and comfort today.

Lord, be my breath of life, today and always. Amen.

Staying Close

"Be strong and courageous. Do not be afraid; do not be discouraged, for the LORD your God will be with you wherever you go."
JOSHUA 1:9 NIV

It's easy to tell others not to worry. It's easy to remind our friends that God is with them and He's got everything under control. And it's easy to remind ourselves of that, when everything's going smoothly.

But when life sails us into rough waters, our natural instinct is to be afraid. We worry and fret. We cry out, not knowing how we will pay the bills or how we will face the cancer or how we will deal with whatever stormy waves crash around us. When life is scary, we get scared.

And believe it or not, that's a good thing. Because when we are afraid, when we are overwhelmed, when we realize that our circumstances are bigger than we are, that's when we're in the perfect place for God to pour out His comfort and assurance on us.

He never leaves us, but sometimes when life is good, we get distracted by other things and don't enjoy His presence as we should. When we feel afraid, we are drawn back to our heavenly Father's arms. And right in His arms is exactly where He wants us to be.

Dear Father, thank You for staying with me and giving me courage. Help me to stay close to You, in good times and bad. Amen.

High Expectations

*"They found grace out in the desert. . . . Israel, out looking for a place
to rest, met God out looking for them!" GOD told them, "I've never quit
loving you and never will. Expect love, love, and more love!"*
JEREMIAH 31:2–3 MSG

Grace out in the desert. What a refreshing thought. Have you been in
a desert place, lost, lonely, disappointed, feeling the pain of rejection?
Often our immediate response is to berate ourselves, look within to
see how we have been the one lacking, plummeting our self-esteem.
Dejected we crawl to that desert place to lick our wounds.

Behold! God is in our desert place. He longs to fill our dry hearts
with His healing love and mercy. Yet it's so hard for us—with our
finite minds—to grasp that the Creator of the universe cares for us
and loves us with an everlasting love, no matter what.

Despite their transgressions, God told the Israelites He never
quit loving them. That is true for you today. Look beyond any
circumstances and you will discover God looking at you, His eyes filled
with love. Scripture promises an overwhelming, unexpected river of
love that will pour out when we trust the Lord our God. Rest today
in His Word. Expect God's love, love, and more love to fill that empty
place in your life.

*Father, we read these words and choose this day
to believe in Your unfailing love. Amen.*

Pray Expectantly

*"But when you ask, you must believe and not doubt,
because the one who doubts is like a wave of the sea,
blown and tossed by the wind."*
JAMES 1:6 NIV

Do you pray expecting God to answer? George Müller did. Müller was a nineteenth-century evangelist known for his faith in prayer. He studied the Bible and trusted in God's promises. Müller documented fifty thousand answers to prayer, giving credit to his meditation on the scriptures and unbending faith in God. The answers to some of his prayers came in less than twenty-four hours, and others took much persistence and waiting. By faith, Müller trusted God to provide an answer without him asking for anyone's help. He wanted to prove that God is faithful and that He hears when people pray.

George Müller's prayers were rooted in faith. His example suggests that the one who prays must be willing for God to answer in His own time, in His own way, and by His own power. The latter was at the center of Müller's prayers. Instead of trying to find the answer himself, Müller relied on God alone. He opened his heart to God's answer, whatever it was, and he trusted God to answer according to His plan.

Prayer takes faith, persistence, and a willingness to let God have His own way. Try praying daily with that in mind, and expect God to answer.

*Father, I trust that You will answer my prayers in a way
that is best for me and most useful to You. Amen.*

Desert Discipline

No discipline is enjoyable while it is happening—it's painful!
But afterward there will be a peaceful harvest of right living
for those who are trained in this way.
HEBREWS 12:11 NLT

Malory had to leave her job; clearly it was time. Knowing it was the right thing to do, she stepped out in faith to pursue her writing career full-time.

What she found very quickly was that the bills were impossible to pay as a fairly new independent writer. So when she heard about a job as a writer for a newspaper in a nearby city, she jumped at it.

There she spent the better part of a year working long hours with a commute, leaving for work every morning before she could see her children off to school, and eking by financially. All of this to work in a very challenging and unaffirming environment.

It was a desert season, to be sure. She began spending all of her free time at home hunting for another full-time job. Anything, she thought, would be better than this.

When God brought her to that next job, He clearly showed it to her. It was a position that He had truly equipped her for.

Looking back, Malory could see that the dry, exhausting season she had gone through had all been a part of that preparation. It had been painful but, in the end, worth it.

God, give us peace in the hard times, knowing that
You have purpose in the unpleasantries of life. Amen.

Setting the Lonely in Families

God sets the lonely in families.
PSALM 68:6 NIV

Helen grew up as an only child in a small town. Her mother and father had adopted her after many years of infertility. Their church family consisted of mostly older adults. Helen had few friends outside of school, where most of the students seemed intent only on drinking and dating, and she often felt lonely. Her best companions were books, her journal—and Jesus.

Four years at a Christian college changed Helen's life. She became involved in a missions-minded church, where she met several kindred spirits. That led to adventurous experiences—and the man who would ultimately become her husband.

One year at Thanksgiving, Helen glanced around the table, which was filled with lovely food and several family members. Her three children argued over who would say the blessing, while her elderly parents brought in the last of the scrumptious-smelling dishes. She looked at her husband, who was checking his smartphone for the Cowboys' football score.

It's loud, and chaotic—and just what I always wanted, Helen thought. She smiled, sending God a premeal prayer of thanks that her greatest need these days was for alone time.

*Lord, thank You for providing us with family—whether by birth,
adoption, marriage, or through our church homes.
Give us the courage to seek out friends who will enrich our lives,
and thank You for being our best Friend.*

A Continual Feast

The cheerful heart has a continual feast.
PROVERBS 15:15 NIV

Ellen left lunch with a friend in a foul mood, which lasted through afternoon errands, dinner preparation, and kitchen cleanup. Finally, the truth dawned on her: she felt terrible because her friend, who never seemed happy, had complained through their entire lunch.

Ellen vowed to back off on weekly lunches with her friend, instead keeping their communication to short phone calls or texts. *I can pray for her*, she thought. *But I don't have to spend a lot of time with her.*

Our choice of companions has much to do with our outlook. Negativity and positivity are both contagious. The writer of Proverbs says that a cheerful heart has a continual feast. So it's safe to assume that a grumpy heart will feel hungry and lacking, instead of full.

While God calls us to minister to those who are hurting, we can do so with discernment. Next time someone complains, ask them to pray with you about their concerns. Tell them a story of how you overcame negativity or repaired a relationship. You could help turn their day around, and you won't feel like you've been beaten up afterward.

God, help me be a positive influence on my friends and family. Give me wisdom and the unwavering hope that comes from Christ, that I may share Your joy with others. Amen.

Opportunities to Love

"If you love those who love you, what credit is that to you?
Even sinners love those who love them."
LUKE 6:32 NIV

On a Jamaican vacation, an American couple admired the beautiful sun-kissed shores and blue skies as they walked to the local marketplace. On the way, a young woman begged, "Lady, I braid your hair; I braid your hair." The American woman said no, but the young woman's advances continued.

Then a towering man with dreadlocked hair approached: "Hey mon, you want some stuff?" The couple knew what that meant and politely told him they were Christians. "Ahhh, you *Krischans*," he said as he backed away.

Unfamiliar surroundings unnerved the couple. Yet God had another plan. Approaching the marketplace, the American woman prayed for God's love for the very people who made her uncomfortable.

Soon others approached the couple: a boy selling handmade yo-yos, a man asking questions, a young single mother. Unlike before, the couple stopped to talk with them. They bought a yo-yo from the boy and handed him a child's Bible tract that was tucked in the bottom of their bag. They shared Christ with him as others gathered to listen. They exchanged addresses with the single mother, and she later came to Christ. As the couple returned to the hotel, the drug pusher sat curbside with his friends. Suddenly he bellowed, "Hey Krischans! Pray for me."

God waited to pour out His love, and the couple nearly missed the opportunity because of their unfounded discomfort. Now that's uncomfortable.

Lord, keep me in constant contact with the lost
so that You can express Your love. Amen.

A Good Morsel

Taste and see that the LORD is good;
blessed is the one who takes refuge in him.
PSALM 34:8 NIV

Parents sometimes have to encourage children to eat foods they may not even want to try. This may be because of the way it looks, smells, or because they've gotten the notion it's just not going to be tasty. Having more life experience, adults know that not only is it good but also good for them.

The world gives the idea to nonbelievers that God isn't worth a taste. The world emphasizes a self-focus, while the Lord says put others before self and God before all. In reality, walking and talking with God is the best thing you can do for yourself. As you walk with God, learning to pray and lean on Him and operate in His will, you are storing up treasures for yourself in heaven. In the world you are demonstrating the love of Christ and being an influence to get others to taste of the Lord.

Like so many foods that are good for us, all it requires is that first taste, a tiny morsel, which whets the appetite for more of Him. Then you can be open to all the goodness, all the fullness of the Lord.

Lord, fill my cup to overflowing with Your love, so that it pours out of me in a way that makes others want what I have. Amen.

Love Made Perfect

*There is no fear in love. But perfect love drives out fear,
because fear has to do with punishment. The one who fears is
not made perfect in love. We love because he first loved us.*
1 JOHN 4:18–19 NIV

It's good to fear God, isn't it? God is awesome and fierce in His power. Yet, while we need to have a healthy respect for God, we don't need to be terrified of Him. At least, not if we really love Him.

Those who truly love God with all their hearts and souls have nothing to fear, for we know He loves us even more. We know that although He may allow us to walk through some difficult things, His plans for us are always good. When we love God, His love is made perfect in us. Our love for God causes His love for us to reign.

It's only when we choose not to love God that we need to fear Him, for though God's patience is long, He is a just God. He will not let the guilty go unpunished. When we love God with our lives, there's no need for punishment. When we love God with our lives, we love others and put their needs ahead of our own. And that, dear friends, is how His love is made perfect in us.

*Dear Father, thank You for loving me. I want to love You
with my life and honor You with my actions. Amen.*

Look Who Is Cheering You On!

*Therefore, since we are surrounded by such a huge crowd of
witnesses to the life of faith, let us strip off every weight that
slows us down, especially the sin that so easily trips us up.
And let us run with endurance the race God has set before us.*
HEBREWS 12:1 NLT

Meagan's boss let her know he needed her to make phone calls to
inform customers of a delay in shipping of items they had ordered.
The company needed her to fill the gap since a wave of the flu had
left them extremely short-handed. He knew this would be difficult for
Meagan but encouraged her to step outside her comfort zone.

Numbers? She got. People—not so much! Meagan felt a wave
of nausea pass into the pit of her stomach. She took a deep breath
and tried to press through it. She bowed her head and asked God for
strength.

Perhaps there are things that you have to do that are outside your
comfort zone. Remember that you have a crowd of faithful witnesses
cheering you on. His strength is perfect to get you through.

*Lord, there are things that I have to do that make me a nervous
wreck. When I am called upon to do those things, please fill me with
Your strength and give me confidence to trust that You will
help me do what I need to do. Amen.*

A Humble Prayer

Then King David went in and sat before the Lord, and said,
Who am I, O Lord God, and what is my house,
that You have brought me this far?
2 SAMUEL 7:18 AMP

A rather obnoxious man stood in line at an airport, getting angry at the slow-moving queue. Finally, he shoved his way to the front counter, demanding to be waited on.

"I'm sorry, sir," the attendant said, "but you'll have to wait your turn."

Incensed, the man demanded, "Young lady, do you know who I am?"

The woman calmly picked up the microphone and announced, "Ladies and gentlemen, there is a man at the front counter who doesn't know who he is. If anyone can identify him, will you please step to the front of the line and help us out?"

Contrast this man's boastful self-image with David's humility. He asked God: "Who am I, that you would bless my family like this?"

David's prayer exemplifies the respect we should have in approaching God. A proper relationship with God changes a person's attitude from *Do you know who I am?* to *Lord, thank You for knowing who I am.* The first question focuses on us; the second focuses on God's perfection, omnipotence, and graciousness at allowing us to be in His holy presence.

Father in heaven, forgive me when I have let my ego overtake my
gratitude for Your presence. Give me a humble, contrite spirit, and
thank You for granting me daily mercy. Amen.

Be Happy!

Blessed are those who act justly, who always do what is right.
PSALM 106:3 NIV

Did you know that the Greek word for *happy* is the same one for *blessed*? It sounds strange to us because we think *happy* refers to an emotional state. The truth is that neither of these words means anything emotional but instead talks about the recognition that everything good or fortunate that happens to us is a gift from God.

In the world that we live in today, some might think that a bank error or a mistake on a bill in their favor would be justification for keeping the money without a word. But a true Christ-follower would not look at these kinds of situations as good or fortunate events. We would find happiness and blessedness in bringing such an error to the attention of the appropriate parties. Our happiness is being honest, doing what is right, because that happiness is the promised spiritual reward.

Because we want to be blessed by God, to be a happy follower of Him, we will seek to always do what is right.

Gracious and heavenly Father, thank You for Your blessings each and every day. I am thankful to be Your follower. When I am tempted to do something that would displease You, remind me that You will bless me if I act justly. My happiness will be a much better reward.
In Your name, amen.

Your Heavenly Father

The LORD's love never ends; his mercies never stop.
They are new every morning; LORD, your loyalty is great.
LAMENTATIONS 3:22–23 NCV

Today is a day set aside to honor fathers. It is a complicated day for many. Because we live in a fallen world, relationships are far from perfect. Perhaps your relationship with your earthly father is wonderful, but it may be messy or fragmented. Take time today to celebrate your earthly father. Call your dad or, if you live close, spend some time with him. If it is within your power, seek to restore any brokenness in your relationship with your earthly father.

Regardless of your relationship with your earthly father, your heavenly Father loves you with an *unfailing love.* He is faithful to walk with you through the ups and downs of life. Remember that every day is a day to honor your heavenly Father. Begin and end today praising Him for who He is. Express thanksgiving. Present your requests to Him. Tell Him how much you love Him. God longs to be your Abba Father, a loving Daddy to you, His daughter!

Father, for some, today is a happy occasion. For others, it stings a bit.
Thank You that You are a loving God, my Abba Father, my Redeemer.
Amen.

Building Trust

*Trust in the Lord with all your heart and lean not on your own
understanding; in all your ways submit to him,
and he will make your paths straight.*
PROVERBS 3:5–6 NIV

Many corporations take their executives to leadership training courses
to develop better working relationships. Divided into teams, these
people have to learn to trust one another. One favorite exercise is
on the ropes course. A person is trussed up in a harness, steps off
a tall tower, and is flung into a wide-open space, trusting his team
members will guide him safely back to the ground. It takes a measure
of courage to make yourself participate, but the results are usually
exhilarating.

Placing our trust in a loving heavenly Father can sometimes feel
like stepping off a precipice. Why? Perhaps it is because we can't see
God. Trust is not easily attained. It comes once you have built a record
with another over a period of time. It involves letting go and knowing
you will be caught.

In order to trust God, we must step out in faith. Challenge
yourself to trust God with one detail in your life each day. Build that
trust pattern and watch Him work. He will not let you down. He holds
you securely in His hand. He is your hope for the future.

Father, I release my hold on my life and trust in You. Amen.

Love Gone Cold

*Sin will be rampant everywhere,
and the love of many will grow cold.*
MATTHEW 24:12 NLT

In a messed-up world that continually gives us advice contrary to
what the Bible says, love and relationships get messed up, too. When
people become inconvenienced by their marriages and relationships,
the common response today is to run. They stop showing love for each
other and allow a cold heart to settle in.

God wants us to honor our commitments, and in doing so, we
honor Him. Relationships take a lot of work. Marriage is a constant
process of serving your spouse, trusting and forgiving each other
daily. Friendships take patience and understanding. Families need lots
of love and grace.

When you allow love to grow cold in your relationships, you turn
from God's will in your life. Our primary purpose on earth is to love
the Lord and love others (Matthew 22:37–39). Even when it's tough or
uncomfortable. Remember that love is a choice.

So when you feel love growing cold, pray for God's love to shine
in your heart and warm up your relationships.

*Heavenly Father, keep my love from growing cold.
Please give me the strength to keep loving when relationships
get difficult. Help me not to run the other way but to keep
my commitments and honor You. Amen.*

A Regular Offering

*The angel answered, "Your prayers and gifts to the poor
have come up as a memorial offering before God."*
ACTS 10:4 NIV

Jenna dropped off another load of clothes at the Goodwill then swung
by the school to help the first-grade class with reading group. She
loved this volunteer job! On her way to Mrs. Windom's class, she
dropped off her coin collection bank in the office. Her husband and the
kids had been helping her save extra change to give to the school's
building campaign.

At church on Sunday morning, Jenna asked her children to help
her carry in a few bags of canned goods they had packed for the
community food pantry drive. It was a simple thing she could do, and
the kids seemed to like helping with it.

That evening before bed, their family prayed for the needs they
knew of in the lives of their neighbors, friends, and loved ones.
Jenna's daughter asked her, "Mommy, why do we do all these nice
things? My friends' mommies don't do these things with them."

Jenna didn't think much about any of the acts of kindness; it just
felt right to do them. "Well, I don't know exactly, but when I feel a
nudge to do a nice thing, I think I just ought to do it, and I believe
God will do something with it someday."

*Lord, thank You for seeing and hearing every offering we give,
no matter how small. Amen.*

New Believers

*Then he said to his disciples, "The harvest is plentiful
but the workers are few. Ask the Lord of the harvest,
therefore, to send out workers into his harvest field."*
MATTHEW 9:37–38 NIV

The Bible tells about a woman named Lydia who, unlike many women
of her time, was a merchant. She sold expensive purple cloth. Lydia
worshipped the true God of Israel, but she had not yet become a
believer in Christ.

One day, Lydia and others gathered near a river just outside
the city of Philippi. It was the Sabbath, and Paul and several of his
companions were in town teaching the people about Jesus. They went
down by the river and talked with the women there. While Lydia
listened to them, God opened her heart to receive the message of
Christ. Lydia believed and was baptized. Then she persuaded Paul
and his companions to stay at her home for a while. This was the
beginning of Lydia's service for the Lord. The Bible suggests that her
home became a meeting place for believers.

Encouragement is important to new believers. When Lydia
accepted Christ, she was eager to learn more about Him. Paul and his
companions agreed to go to her home, where they encouraged her
in her faith. Perhaps you know a new believer who could use your
encouragement. Think of ways you can help them today.

*Dear Lord, whom can I encourage today? Show me a new
believer who could use my help. Amen.*

Start Your Day with God

*In the morning, LORD, you hear my voice; in the morning
I lay my requests before you and wait expectantly.*
PSALM 5:3 NIV

Mornings are hard for a lot of people—especially night owls who get more done in the evening. And verses like this one can tend to make night owls feel like they aren't as spiritual as those who get up early to be with God.

The reality is that God wants to be the very center of your life. He doesn't want to be at the top of your priority list—just another box to check off each day. He wants your heart and attention morning, noon, and night. You won't get more points with God if you read ten Bible verses before your morning cup of coffee.

So how can you start your day with God even if you haven't gotten up hours earlier for devotions? As you wake up in the morning, thank the Lord for a new day. Ask Him to control your thoughts and attitude as you make the bed. Thank Him for providing for you as you toast your bagel. Ask that your self-image be based on your relationship with Christ as you get dressed and brush your teeth. Continue to pray as you drive to work or school. Spend time in His Word throughout the day. End your day by thanking Him for His love and faithfulness.

God wants a constant relationship with you, and He is available and waiting to do life with you twenty-four hours a day.

*Dear Lord, thank You for the gift of a new day. Help me be
aware of Your constant presence in my life. Amen.*

Loving through Our Actions

He has shown you, O mortal, what is good.
And what does the Lord require of you? To act justly and
to love mercy and to walk humbly with your God.
Micah 6:8 niv

The lavishly adorned gift box was thrust in the direction of John's date. He hoped that the gift of an extravagant necklace would make the proper impression on her. Although they had been seeing each other for a while, John kept heaping gifts on her, hoping that she would fall in love with him.

How many of us have thought a similar thing about our relationship with God? If we're good enough, God will bless us richly. If we pray the right way or make sure we go to church every Sunday, He will make things go our way. Is this the right way to impress our Father? The prophet Micah names three great acts of love for God and fellow man that will glorify God—to be righteous and fair to everyone, to show kindness freely and willingly to all, and to live humbly in a conscious fellowship with a sovereign King. Our motives should be to please Him through the legitimate gift of selfless service to Him and our fellow man.

Gracious Father, thank You that You love me just as I am and there is nothing I can do that can make You love me more! May I continue to serve You by selfless service to others. Amen!

Our Prayer Calling

Then she lived as a widow to the age of eighty-four.
She never left the Temple but stayed there day and night,
worshiping God with fasting and prayer.
LUKE 2:37 NLT

Have you ever felt useless to the kingdom of God? Do you think you have little to offer, so you offer little? Consider the eighty-four-year-old widow woman, Anna. She stayed at the temple worshiping God through prayer and fasting. That was her calling, and she was committed to prayer until the Lord ushered her home.

Undoubtedly, this woman's primary focus in life was God. But admittedly, life consumes us with work, home, church, family, errands, and to-do lists. Women are extraordinary at multitasking, and all of these responsibilities tug at us like a five-year-old begging for the latest toy.

Often, as we age or as illness prohibits us from doing the things we once did, we feel useless. Yet the truth remains that as long as we have breath, God has a plan for our lives. He desires to use us for His glory.

We need not pray and fast like this dedicated woman did. (In fact, for health reasons, fasting is not always an option.) Yet we are all called to pray. We can pray right where we are, regardless of our age, circumstances, or surroundings. Like Anna, it's our calling.

Lord, please remind me of the calling of prayer on my life,
despite my circumstances. Amen.

Rest for Your Soul

"Come to me, all you who are weary and burdened, and I will give you rest. Take my yoke upon you and learn from me, for I am gentle and humble in heart, and you will find rest for your souls. For my yoke is easy and my burden is light."
MATTHEW 11:28–30 NIV

Jesus says, "Come to me." Just as He invited the little children to come to Him, Jesus calls us to come to Him and bring all of our burdens and lay them at His feet. He wants to help. He wants to relieve the load we're carrying.

A yoke is a harness placed over an animal or set of animals for the purpose of dragging something or carrying heavy equipment. Jesus liked to use visual imagery to get His meaning across. Can't you just picture all of the burdens you are carrying right now strapped to your back like an ox plowing a field? Now imagine yourself unloading each one onto Jesus' shoulders instead. Take a deep breath.

Jesus tells us many times throughout the Gospels not to worry. Worrying about something will never help you. Worry makes things worse and burdens seem larger. Worry clutters up your soul. Jesus wants us to find rest in Him. Hear His gentle words rush over you— "Come to me." Find rest for your soul.

Jesus, thank You for taking my burdens. I give them fully to You. Help me not to take them back! I want the rest and peace that You are offering. Amen.

Hand Holders

As long as Moses held up his hands, the Israelites were winning,
but whenever he lowered his hands, the Amalekites were winning.
When Moses' hands grew tired, they took a stone and put it under him
and he sat on it. Aaron and Hur held his hands up—one on one side,
one on the other—so that his hands remained steady till sunset.
So Joshua overcame the Amalekite army with the sword.
EXODUS 17:11–13 NIV

How do you view your pastor? Do you see him as the cheerleader of your congregation, trying to motivate them to be better Christ-followers? Perhaps the teacher? Maybe even the ultimate decision maker? The truth is, some pastors feel that they are expected to be all things to all people and to do it with perfection.

Our verse today shows that Moses was an ordinary (but called) person trying to do a huge job by himself. No one could be expected to hold his hands up for the duration of a battle. He needed help. One way we can help our pastors in the work they have been given is by the power of consistent prayer for them personally, for their families, and for their ministry.

Father, our pastors are precious to us. Yet, we know they have been
given big assignments with sometimes unrealistic expectations.
Remind us to keep our pastors, their families, and their ministry in
prayer. It is one way we can hold their hands high to You. Amen.

Comfort and Be Comforted

*Blessed be God. . .the Father of mercies, and the God of all comfort;
Who comforteth us in all our tribulations, that we may be able to
comfort them which are in any trouble, by the comfort wherewith
we ourselves are comforted of God.*
2 CORINTHIANS 1:3–4 KJV

Have you ever noticed that sharing your problems with someone
unfamiliar with your adversity is vastly different from sharing your
experiences with someone who has endured the same trial? Support
groups for those of similar situations are designed to encourage and
comfort people who are going through comparable hardships.

God, the Father of all comfort and compassion, comforts us in
our trials. Why? Because He loves us deeply, and He desires for us
to become channels of hope and comfort to those who face similar
situations. Moreover, He understands.

In some churches, Wednesday night services allow believers to
stand up and testify. Their testimonies of answered prayer or of how
God worked on their behalf in a particular situation initiate comfort
and hope among others in the congregation who might be undergoing
the same problem.

God comforts us so that we, in turn, can comfort others with the
same comfort we received from the Father. That's God's promise to
you today. Receive the comfort you need from the Lord. He, in turn,
will equip you to help, comfort, and encourage others.

*Lord, help me comfort someone today. Help me listen and encourage,
just as You have done and continue to do for me. Amen.*

Praying for God's Will

*For this reason, since the day we heard about you,
we have not stopped praying for you. We continually ask
God to fill you with the knowledge of his will through all
the wisdom and understanding that the Spirit gives.*
COLOSSIANS 1:9 NIV

The apostle Paul reminded the Colossians that he was continuously praying for them to be filled with the knowledge of God's will. Read the verse above closely. How did Paul ask God to fill them with the knowledge of His will? The only way that we can know His will—*through all the wisdom and understanding that the Spirit gives.* Paul was speaking to believers here. Christians have received the Holy Spirit as their Counselor and Guide. Those who do not have a personal relationship with Christ are lacking the Spirit, and thus, they are not able to discern God's will for their lives. Always take advantage of the wonderful gift that you have been given. If you have accepted Christ as your Savior, you also have the Spirit. One of the greatest things about the Holy Spirit is that it helps us to distinguish God's call on our life from the other voices of the world. Pray that God will reveal His good and perfect will for your life. His Holy Spirit at work in you will never lead you down a wrong path.

*God, help me to draw upon the wonderful resource that I have
as a Christian. Help me, through the power of the Holy Spirit,
to know Your will. Amen.*

How to Love

*My children, we should love people not only with words and talk,
but by our actions and true caring.*
1 JOHN 3:18 NCV

We've often heard the phrase, "Talk is cheap."

Of course, that phrase doesn't refer to money, does it? It's a reminder that while anyone can *say* they care about starving children, few will shell out the cash to actually feed them. While anyone can *say* they care about our current political climate, few will actually take the time to try to change things for the better. And when we're in a crisis, many people may *say* they care about us. But how many people will sit with us in the middle of the night because we're still not over the loved one we lost six months ago?

Not many.

It's easy to tell people we care about them. But God wants more from us than our words. Sometimes compassionate words and a prayer are all we can offer, but when that's the case, we need to make sure we do pray. And when it is in our ability to do more, we need to put action to our words. Do we really care about that teenage girl with low self-esteem? Don't just tell her she's beautiful and leave her with her dated, faded clothes. Buy her a new outfit.

Let's look for ways today that we can love those around us with our actions.

Dear Father, teach me to love like You love. Amen.

A Recipe of Love

*"Give, and you will receive. . . . The amount you give
will determine the amount you get back."*
LUKE 6:38 NLT

A delicious assortment of pies lined the glass showcase in a
rudimentary diner nestled in the Ponderosa pines of Mt. Lemmon,
Arizona. As a husband and wife entered the door, strangers greeted
them with warm hospitality. Soothing classical music played as the
couple squeezed into a corner table. Although the type of music
seemed out of character for the diner, its significance became clear as
the wife chatted with the diner's owner, Pam.

Pam's character matched her music. She appreciated life and
the gifts of others. "I can't paint, and I can't compose music,"
Pam admitted, "but I can bake. It's my way of giving back to the
mountain."

Pam discovered her "gift" in 1972 when she first started baking
her mother's Pennsylvania Dutch pie recipes for her customers. She
explained how her mother demonstrated her love through everything
she cooked or baked. "Now my mother touches people through my
hands," she explained. "I just want to reach people with God's love,
and it begins with giving, sharing the gifts I have."

"I am blessed," Pam shared.

The couple was, too. For a moment, their lives became as simple
as Pam's unpretentious surroundings and basic philosophy: "Whatever
you do, do it with love."

*Lord, whatever gifts I have, cause me to use them,
seasoned with Your love. Amen.*

I.C.E.

I will praise the LORD, who counsels me;
even at night my heart instructs me.
I keep my eyes always on the LORD.
With him at my right hand, I will not be shaken.
PSALM 16:7–8 NIV

Think about the people in your life whom you have on speed dial. Who do you call first when crisis hits? Many of our phones actually have an I.C.E. programmed at the top of our contact list so that EMTs can have a phone number to call "in case of emergency."

And while having an emergency contact is important and necessary, sometimes we can come to depend on these people more so than God. Especially if our first response to any kind of crisis is to call a best friend, a mentor, or a professional counselor instead of going straight to the Lord. We think that just because our friends have skin on, they'll be able to help us in more tangible ways.

The truth is that God is able to do way more than we could ever ask or imagine (Ephesians 3:20), and He wants us to come to Him with everything first. He will counsel us and set our feet in the right direction.

There is nothing wrong with calling a friend or spiritual mentor and getting godly advice! Oftentimes God uses those very people to help you. The problem arises when we put those people before God.

Heavenly Father, forgive me for the times that I haven't trusted You enough with my problems. Help me to come to You first. Amen.

Prayer Touches God

*He was a devout, God-fearing man. . .He gave generously
to the poor and prayed regularly to God.*
ACTS 10:2 NLT

In the book of Acts, a centurion named Cornelius received a vision
from God. Though a Gentile, this man loved God, praying and fasting
regularly. While he prayed, an angel of the Lord told Cornelius that
God heard and honored his prayers. Accordingly, God instructed the
centurion to go talk to Peter, God's servant.

Peter, having received a vision that God would cleanse and
accept anyone whom the Jews deemed "unclean," agreed to meet this
Gentile despite Jewish law. Cornelius invited his Gentile neighbors,
friends, and family members when he met Peter in Caesarea.
Realizing God orchestrated the meeting, Peter preached the Gospel
to Cornelius and all who joined him, and the entire group of Gentiles
received the Holy Spirit (Acts 10:44–48).

Jesus takes note of a praying, giving heart like Cornelius had.
Denominations mean little, while a contrite, teachable spirit touches
God. Cornelius was a good, God-fearing man who needed to hear
about salvation through Christ. So God honored his prayers and led
him to the preacher—while teaching the preacher a thing or two at
the same time.

Have you hesitated to share your faith with someone you think
unseemly or beyond your realm of comfort? Begin now. Look what
happened when Peter did.

*Father, forgive me for my self-righteousness. Open the way for me to
witness to whomever You have prepared to hear the Gospel. Amen.*

Listening Closely

I will listen to what God the LORD says.
PSALM 85:8 NIV

There is an old hymn called "Speak to My Heart" that should resonate
in a believer's life. "Speak to my heart, Lord Jesus. Speak that my soul
may hear." Doesn't that define our prayer life? In faith, we talk with
the Lord, and He wants to answer and wants us to listen.

In today's hurried world, with all of the surrounding noise, it's
easy to ignore the still, small voice nudging us in the right direction.
We fire off requests, expect microwave-instant answers, and get
aggravated when nothing happens. Our human nature demands a
response. How will we know what to do/think/say if we do not listen?
When we are "yielded and still," then He can "speak to my heart."

Listening is a learned art, too often forgotten in the busyness
of a day. The alarm clock buzzes, we hit the floor running, toss out a
prayer, maybe sing a song of praise, grab our car keys, and are out the
door. If only we'd slow down and let the heavenly Father's words sink
into our spirits, what a difference we might see in our prayer life. This
day, stop. Listen. See what God has in store for you.

Lord, how I want to surrender and seek Your will.
Please still my spirit and speak to me. Amen.

Time to Love God

*But do not forget this one thing, dear friends: With the Lord a day
is like a thousand years, and a thousand years are like a day.*
2 PETER 3:8 NIV

"The time is just flying by."

"I don't have time."

"There aren't enough hours in a day."

Surely you've heard those words. You've probably said them
yourself. In today's busy world, there just doesn't seem to be enough
time. People communicate instantaneously. They work quickly, play
fast, and live by tight schedules. Even when they pray, they expect
God to answer quickly. But God doesn't work that way. The Bible says
that to Him a thousand years are like a day.

God's patience toward us is a reflection of His love. There are
many examples of His loving patience in the Bible, but the best is His
patience with the Israelites. Psalm 78:41 says, "Again and again they
tested God's patience" (NLT). Still, God continued to love them, and His
patience with Israel exists to this day.

Patience requires time, and although it is not infinite, God's
patience is immense. He allows people time to know Him, to trust
Him, and to believe in His Son and the gift of salvation. He gives them
a lifetime in which to do it and after that, the promise of eternal life
with Him in heaven. Now, that's true love!

*Dear God, help me to love others patiently,
the same way that You love me. Amen.*

Peace for an Uncertain Future

*O LORD, revive thy work in the midst of the years, in the midst
of the years make known; in wrath remember mercy.*
HABAKKUK 3:2 KJV

Helen tossed and turned. Though her body was tired, her mind
wasn't. Too many questions flooded her brain, because she and her
family were moving in a week to a new town, where her spouse would
start a different career.

Helen felt like a little girl. She wondered if she would make
friends, find a good church, or be able to fit into the small community.
Her heart hurt at the thought of her sons having to walk into school
the first day as a "new" kid. She had hoped they would live in one
place for several more years—at least until her youngest graduated
from high school.

Realizing she needed to talk to God more than she needed sleep,
Helen quietly slipped out of her warm bed and padded into the living
room.

Helen closed her eyes and prayed, whispering quietly to avoid
waking her brood: "Lord, You've given me so much! But I'm scared.
Would You please give me peace and an excitement about where
we're going? Help me to be confident that You will give us friends we
can lean on, and a godly church home. Remind me of Your faithfulness
when I waver."

*Heavenly Father, thank You for Your awesome deeds in the past,
and help us to trust You for the future. Amen.*

Pioneering Freedom Even Today

It is for freedom that Christ has set us free. Stand firm, then,
and do not let yourselves be burdened again by a yoke of slavery.
GALATIANS 5:1 NIV

The Fourth of July can have as many different meanings as there are individuals on the earth. To some, it is a time to cook out with friends and family. To others, it is a time to honor those who followed their passion given to them by God to come to a new land, establish a country, and pioneer a new way of life.

Much like the pioneers who fought for and established our great country, as believers there is a pioneering spirit that continues as we take the truth of God's Word and build His Kingdom on the earth. As you live each day of your life, you have the opportunity to share spiritual dependence on God and the choice you've made to serve Him. You can share the gift of the Gospel in every area of influence He provides to you.

Let Independence Day speak a reminder to you today that God desires the freedom found only in Christ to be shared with each and every person on the earth.

Heavenly Father, I want to make a difference. I want to become
the pioneer that is bringing freedom to others as You use my
life to build Your Kingdom on the earth. Amen.

A Declaration of Dependence

*"Sacrifice thank offerings to God, fulfill your vows
to the Most High, and call on me in the day of trouble;
I will deliver you, and you will honor me."*
PSALM 50:14–15 NIV

Most of us value our relationships, whether they are with family, friends, or coworkers. We like being in relationships with those who offer love, commitment, and trust because we feel valued. Perhaps not so ironically, today's verse reveals that God wants the same things from us. He wants thankful, trusting, and faithful children, people whom He can delight in and who can delight in Him.

As our heavenly Father, He wants to help us, especially in times of trouble. That dependency on Him recognizes that everything we have comes from Him. The practical way to depend on Him comes through an honest, consistent lifestyle of prayer, where we offer ourselves and our needs. Through prayer, we draw near to Him and get to know Him better. In doing that, we'll become the thankful, trusting, and faithful children He desires.

Gracious and generous Father, thank You for loving me so much that You are interested in every facet of my life. I commit to bring everything to You in prayer and acknowledge that I am dependent on You for my provision and safety. I pray for the continued outpouring of Your Spirit in me, so I can ask for continued blessings for myself as well as others. I love You, Lord. Amen.

Pray about Everything

*"The LORD directs the steps of the godly.
He delights in every detail of their lives."*
PSALM 37:23 NLT

When Jennifer passed her six-year-old daughter's bedroom one morning, she saw the little girl kneeling by her bed praying. Jennifer decided not to interrupt her, but she was curious. Bedtime prayers were routine in their household, and she had never seen her daughter kneel and pray in the morning. Later, Jennifer asked Marissa why she had prayed.

"Did I do something wrong?" Marissa wondered.

"No, honey!" Jennifer said. "I just wondered what you were praying about."

"My tooth," said Marissa. "I told God that my tooth is getting loose, and I'd rather have it come out at home than at school."

The Bible says that the Lord delights in every detail of His children's lives. And no matter how old a believer is, they are and always will be God's child.

Adult prayers don't have to be well ordered and formal. God loves hearing His children's voices, and no detail is too little or dull to pray about. Tell God that you hope the coffeehouse will have your favorite pumpkin-spice latte on their menu. Ask Him to give you patience as you wait in line. Thank Him for how wonderful that coffee tastes! Get into the habit of talking with Him all day long, because He loves you and delights in all facets of your life.

*Dear God, teach me to pray about everything
with childlike innocence and faith. Amen.*

Relax

*"You will not have to fight this battle. Take up your positions;
stand firm and see the deliverance the LORD will give you."*
2 CHRONICLES 20:17 NIV

Why do we always feel we need to fight our own battles?

Oh, God wants us to use common sense and stand up for others and ourselves when it's appropriate. But sometimes, it's best not to defend ourselves at all. Sometimes, when we know we've done no wrong, when we know we stand innocent before God in whatever situation we find ourselves, it's good just to remain still and calm and let God be our defender.

Truly, the more we defend ourselves, the guiltier we sound sometimes. But when we can stand before God with clean hands and a pure heart, God will deliver us. Oh, it may not be in the way we want. It may not happen as quickly as we'd like. But when we decide to stand firm, to continue living godly lives, to continue seeking His approval in our words, thoughts, and actions, we can trust Him.

Let's remember today to rest in His goodness, despite the battles that rage around us. We don't have to live our lives fighting. We can relax. Our Father is the judge, and He will deliver us.

*Dear Father, thank You for being my defender.
Thank You for delivering me from all sorts of trouble.
Help me to relax and let You take care of me. Amen.*

The Alabaster Box

*As she stood behind him at his feet weeping, she began to wet
his feet with her tears. Then she wiped them with her hair,
kissed them and poured perfume on them.*
LUKE 7:38 NIV

The story of Mary and her alabaster box of high-priced perfume is a
familiar one. Historically, this kind of perfume was given to a woman
by her parents as a dowry. It was to be used on her wedding night,
to be poured out on her husband's feet in an act of submission. So
when Mary poured out this costly substance onto Jesus' feet, it was a
statement of her complete love, devotion, submission, and obedience.
She offered Him all of herself.

Many who witnessed the outpouring of this expensive perfume
were angered because it could have been sold for a lot of money and
used to fund ministry. They missed the point of her extravagant love.
She did not take cheap perfume but some of the most expensive ever
made. And she didn't use just a few drops but emptied the container!
Mary is a wonderful example for us—to love completely, being
humbled at the feet of her Savior, and to offer her complete self. How
beautiful and generous! May we be as well!

*Lord, I love You! May my love for You and Your people be like a
beautiful fragrance that leaves its essence everywhere I go. I give
myself wholly to You as You did for me. Amen.*

He Cares for You

*You yourselves have seen what I did to Egypt, and how I
carried you on eagles' wings and brought you to myself.*
EXODUS 19:4 NIV

Often we feel deserted. As though God doesn't hear our prayers. And
we wait. When Moses led the children of Israel out of Egypt toward
the Promised Land, he did not take them on the shortest route. God
directed him to go the distant way, lest the people turn back quickly
when things became difficult. God led them by day with a pillar of
clouds and by night with a pillar of fire. How clearly He showed
Himself to His children! The people placed their hope in an almighty
God and followed His lead. When they thirsted, God gave water. When
they hungered, He sent manna. No need was unmet.

The amount of food and water needed for the group was
unimaginable. But each day, Moses depended upon God. He believed
God would care for them.

If God can do this for so many, you can rest assured that He will
care for you. He knows your needs before you even ask. Place your
hope and trust in Him. He is able. He's proven Himself, over and over.
Read the scriptures and pray to the One who loves you. His care is
infinite. . .and He will never disappoint you.

*Heavenly Father, I know You love me and hear me.
I bless Your holy name. Amen.*

Earnest Prayer

*If My people, who are called by My name, shall humble themselves,
pray, seek, crave, and require of necessity My face and turn
from their wicked ways, then will I hear from heaven,
forgive their sin, and heal their land.*
2 CHRONICLES 7:14 AMP

The Amplified Bible specifies how believers are to humble themselves and pray. We are to "seek, crave, and require of necessity" God's face.

Have you ever watched children playing hide-and-seek? They look everywhere for the one they are after in the game! They put their whole hearts into it. We should *seek* God relentlessly.

Crave. The word brings about the thought of "fair food." Just inside the state fair entrance gate, tantalizing smells entice us. Cravings for pronto pups, funnel cakes, sweet cotton candy, or caramel apples are almost unavoidable. Our desire for God's presence in our lives ought to be strong and irresistible.

Necessity. What is it that you just can't live without? The cell phone with all its cool apps? That specially blended coffee each morning? Our hearts need God for survival. He is our one and only true necessity.

When you pray, call out to God with your whole heart. Prayer must be more than an afterthought to close each day, as eyelids grow heavy and sleep wins the battle. Seek God. Crave and require His face. Turn toward Him. He stands ready to hear, to forgive, and to heal.

Lord, be my greatest desire, my craving, my all. Amen.

A Joyful Heart

*Sarah said, "God has brought me laughter, and everyone
who hears about this will laugh with me."*
GENESIS 21:6 NIV

Kayla and her husband attended the funeral for the elderly mother
of one of his business associates. Afterward, Kayla complained to
her husband about how some of the grieving family members had
behaved.

"Did you see the two daughters standing at their mother's casket,
laughing? I couldn't believe my eyes."

Kayla's husband quickly came to their defense. "Yes, I heard
them talking," he said. "They were remembering their mother's good
sense of humor and some of the funny things she did when they were
children."

In the Bible, King Solomon says, "There is a time for everything,
and a season for every activity under the heavens" (Ecclesiastes 3:1
NIV). He adds this piece of wisdom: "Every day is hard for those who
suffer, but a happy heart is like a continual feast." (Proverbs 15:15
NCV) While the daughters' laughter might have seemed inappropriate,
it was exactly what they needed to start healing their broken hearts.

Are you or someone you know unhappy? A little laughter might
help. Begin with a smile. When you hear laughter, move toward it and
try to join in. Seek the company of happy friends, and invite humor
into your conversations. Most of all, praise God. Praise is the best way
to heal a hurting soul. Praise God joyfully for His many blessings.

*Lord, whenever my heart is heavy, encourage me to heal it with joy.
Amen.*

Unexplainable Love

*No power in the sky above or in the earth below—indeed,
nothing in all creation will ever be able to separate us from
the love of God that is revealed in Christ Jesus our Lord.*
ROMANS 8:39 NLT

Aaron was a hard kid. After fourteen foster homes in seven years,
he immediately began his normal routine of "impossible to love"
antics, but his newest foster parents didn't react the way all the
others had. It seemed no matter what he did, they weren't surprised
or shocked. Their words were always soft. And although he had seen
hurt sometimes in their eyes, not once had they mentioned calling his
caseworker.

After disciplinarian actions and hours of detention at another
new school, Aaron was suspended. Expecting to finally see a reaction,
Aaron began to pack his things. Mr. Kensington walked into his room
and asked, "What are you doing?"

Aaron mumbled, "Packing. I figure now you'll be sending me
back."

Mr. Kensington sat down on the bed. "Aaron, we're going to do
everything we can to help you succeed."

"Why would you do that?" Aaron snapped.

"Because we love you, and we'll never stop loving you."

Aaron's eyes filled with tears. He knew it was true. Aaron was
finally home.

*Father, help me to see that there is nothing that would cause You to
stop loving me. Even when I struggle to forgive myself, I know You
always forgive me. Thank You for Your unexplainable love. Amen.*

Be Happy Despite It All

*A twinkle in the eye means joy in the heart,
and good news makes you feel fit as a fiddle.*
PROVERBS 15:30 MSG

The apostle Paul had much he could've grumbled about. He was beaten, jailed, shipwrecked, and nearly drowned; yet through it all, he discovered God was the source of his contentment. Paul understood God was in control of his life, even when he was in those overwhelming, tragic situations. Remember his songs of praise from the jail cell (Acts 16)?

Sometimes we find ourselves in hard places, and life isn't going the way we planned. This is the time we have to look for the positive. We have to make the choice to "bloom where we're planted," and God will meet us there. In our songs of praise amid the difficulties, God will come. The Holy Spirit, the Comforter, will minister to our needs. The Lord has promised to never leave or forsake us, so if He is present, we should have no fear or worry. Without fear or worry, we can learn to be content. No fretting, no regretting, just trusting the Word is truth.

When we place our hope in Christ and He's our guide, He will give us the ability to walk satisfied, no matter our circumstances. He is our all in all.

*Lord, I give You thanks for all Your good gifts
but most of all for Your presence. Amen.*

Fix Your Thoughts on Truth

*And now, dear brothers and sisters, one final thing. Fix your thoughts
on what is true, and honorable, and right, and pure, and lovely, and
admirable. Think about things that are excellent and worthy of praise.*
PHILIPPIANS 4:8 NLT

In a world loaded with mixed messages and immorality of every kind,
it becomes increasingly difficult to have pure thoughts and clear
minds. What can a believer do to keep her mind set on Christ? Replace
the negative message with a positive message from God's Word.

Think about the negative messages that you struggle with the
most. Maybe you struggle with some of these: You're not thin enough.
You're not spiritual enough. You've made a lot of mistakes, etc.

Dig through the scriptures and find truth from God's Word to
combat the false message that you're struggling with. Write the
passages down and memorize them. Here are a few to get you started:

- God looks at my heart, not my outward appearance.
  (1 Samuel 16:7)
- I am free in Christ. (1 Corinthians 1:30)
- I am a new creation. My old self is gone! (2 Corinthians 5:17)

The next time you feel negativity and false messages slip into
your thinking, fix your thoughts on what you know to be true. Pray for
the Lord to replace the doubts and negativity with His words of truth.

*Lord God, please control my thoughts and help me
set my mind and heart on You alone. Amen.*

Love Your Neighbor as Yourself

*"'And you must love the LORD your God with all your heart,
all your soul, all your mind, and all your strength.' The second
is equally important: 'Love your neighbor as yourself.'
No other commandment is greater than these."*
MARK 12:30–31 NLT

Look out for number one. It is the message this world sends every day in a million ways. We are bombarded with it. If it feels good, do it. Do what is right for you. But is this the message of God's Word? Nothing could be further from the truth!

We are told to love our neighbors as ourselves. As you would treat your own body, your own heart, treat your neighbor the same. But who is your neighbor? Your neighbor is anyone within your sphere of influence. Those who live near you, certainly. But your neighbors also include your coworkers, friends, relatives, and even strangers on the street. When you make a purchase at a convenience store, treat the clerk as you would like to be treated. When you order dinner at a restaurant, imagine how hard the waitress is working. Treat her with kindness.

Consider others even as Christ considered you on the cross. The greatest commandment of all is to love God, and this goes hand in hand with the second commandment. Love one another. Love your neighbor as yourself.

*Lord, remind me that my neighbors are all around me.
Teach me to love others as I love myself. Amen.*

Create a "Smile File"

*The best that people can do is eat, drink, and enjoy their work.
I saw that even this comes from God.*
ECCLESIASTES 2:24 NCV

A woman's job—whether she's a mom, physician, schoolteacher,
CFO, or artist—can be tiring and discouraging. Workplaces can be
competitive, and children and husbands aren't always appreciative.

Be honest: Don't you, at times, feel trapped beneath the weight of
expectations, to-do lists, and fatigue? To avoid burnout, it's important
to regularly take note of your successes—especially when others don't
notice your tireless efforts.

Emmy, an aspiring songwriter, decided that for every rejection
she received, she'd note in her journal three productive things she
had done that same week to hone her craft. Administrative assistant
Bianca created an e-mail folder specifically for affirming notes she
received from her boss, kids, and husband. And Shelley, an executive
director of a nonprofit, keeps a hanging file of silly cartoons, jokes, and
pictures. When she is stressed or overwhelmed, she takes a moment
to read something fun. It never fails to lift her spirits.

Why not keep a "Smile File" of your own? Take a simple shoe box
or organizing bin and place encouraging cards, e-mails, and photos
inside. You never know when it might come in handy.

*Dear Lord, help me to not feel the full weight of difficulties in my
work. Give me ideas on how to avoid burning out; and thank You
for the encouragement others give. Amen.*

Side by Side

*Have no fear of sudden disaster or of the ruin that
overtakes the wicked, for the L*ORD *will be at your side
and will keep your foot from being snared.*
PROVERBS 3:25–26 NIV

Our world today is crammed with grim news. Television and Internet reports blast us with every detail of a disaster, often filling our hearts with dread. From the pulpit we hear "perfect love casts out fear." However, we frequently remain apprehensive. There are things of which we must be aware, but we do not need to become overtaken with fear and worry. For the Lord our God has given us a promise in His Word. He is at our side.

The Lord sees the concerns and dreads of His children and has surrounded us with His love. When we gaze into His face and seek His presence, the light of His love will flood any dark corners, dispelling the anxious thoughts and scary shadows. His hand is there to hold us close, allowing us to feel His heartbeat.

As a boat casts off its tether from the dock, we need to cast off the ties to fear and worry and drift upon the sea of peace offered by our heavenly Father. He is at our side and will keep us safe, for He is true love.

*Father, this day I surrender my cares to You,
for I know You love me. Amen.*

God Has Not Forgotten

Then said he unto me, Fear not, Daniel: for from the first day that thou didst set thine heart to understand, and to chasten thyself before thy God, thy words were heard, and I am come for thy words.
DANIEL 10:12 KJV

Sometimes it seems God is silent. When you pray and ask God to intervene in a situation or help you with a difficulty and you don't hear back right away, there is a temptation to interpret that as God is inactive. The truth is, He is never too busy to hear you.

Daniel had great concern for his people. He spent weeks fasting and praying, and he desperately wanted direction—an answer for his people. Imagine being fervently on your knees for three weeks, fasting and praying and *nothing*! Some would have given up and maybe even assumed that God had forgotten. Three weeks pass and an angel comes to let Daniel know that God heard his prayer and went to work the very hour he spoke it.

What are you on your knees before God about? What have you asked Him to do on your behalf? Know that God has not forgotten you. He is working behind the scenes to bring about good in your life. He has the answer you need. Hold on to Him, and believe He will come through for you.

Lord, help me hold on to You, believing that my answer is on the way.
Amen.

Making Allowances

*Always be humble and gentle. Be patient with each other,
making allowance for each other's faults because of your love.*
EPHESIANS 4:2 NLT

This verse contains such a simple, forgotten truth, doesn't it? God
wants us to be holy. He wants us to be righteous and good and godly.
But He knows we'll never get it exactly right until we're made perfect
in His presence.

Until then, we all have our faults. Numerous faults, if we're
honest with ourselves. And God doesn't want us standing around,
whispering and pointing self-righteous fingers of condemnation. God
is the only One who is allowed to wear the judge's robe. The only One.

And He doesn't condemn us. Instead, He pours His love and
acceptance into our lives, with a gentle admonition to "go and sin no
more" (John 8:11 NLT). In other words, "It's okay. You messed up, but
it's been taken care of. The price has been paid. I still love you. Just
try not to do it again."

Why do we find it so hard to extend grace to others, when so
much grace has been shown to us? As we go through each day, let's
make it a point to live out this verse. Let's be humble, gentle, and
patient, making allowances for the faults of others because of God's
love.

*Dear Father, help me to be gentle and loving with others.
Remind me of the grace You've shown me, and help me
show the same love to those around me. Amen.*

Deep Roots

*"They will be like a tree planted by the water that sends out
its roots by the stream. It does not fear when heat comes;
its leaves are always green. It has no worries in a year
of drought and never fails to bear fruit."*
JEREMIAH 17:8 NIV

Watering your garden doesn't seem difficult, but did you know you can train a plant to grow incorrectly, just in the way you water it? By pouring water from the hose for only a few moments at each plant, the root systems become very shallow. They start to seek water from the top of the soil, and the roots can easily be burned in the summer sun. By using a soaker hose, the water slowly percolates into the ground, and the plants learn to push their roots deeper into the soil to get water.

Jeremiah talked about a larger plant, a tree. A tree needs deep roots to keep it anchored in the ground, providing stability. The roots synthesize water and minerals for nourishment and then help to store those elements for a later time. Our deep spiritual roots come from reading God's Word, which provides stability, nourishment, and refreshment.

Father, I do not want to wither in the sun. Help me to immerse myself in Your Word. When I do, I strike my spiritual roots deeper into life-giving soil and drink from Living Water. Help me to be the fruitful follower of You that I am meant to be. Amen.

The Simple Things

In him our hearts rejoice, for we trust in his holy name.
PSALM 33:21 NIV

Think about the simple pleasures in everyday life—that first sip of coffee in the morning, waking up to realize you still have a few more minutes to sleep, or putting on fresh, warm clothes right out of the dryer on a cold winter morning. Perhaps it's a walk along the beach or a hike up the mountains into the blue skies that give you a simple peace.

God knows all the simple pleasures you enjoy—and He created them for your delight. When the simple things that can come only by His hand fill you with contentment, He is pleased. He takes pleasure in you. You are His delight. Giving you peace, comfort, and a sense of knowing that you belong to Him is a simple thing for Him.

Take a moment today and step away from the busyness of life. Take notice and fully experience some of those things you enjoy most. Then share that special joy with Him.

Lord, thank You for the simple things that bring pleasure to my day.
I enjoy each gift You've given me. I invite You to share
those moments with me today. Amen.

Praying for All People

*I urge, then, first of all, that petitions, prayers, intercession and
thanksgiving be made for all people—for kings and all those in
authority, that we may live peaceful and quiet lives in all godliness
and holiness. This is good, and pleases God our Savior, who wants all
people to be saved and to come to a knowledge of the truth.*
1 TIMOTHY 2:1–4 NIV

John and Charlie were friends. . .most of the time. It was when they
got into a political discussion that observers wondered where their
spirited conversation would lead. It seemed that both men thought
their point of view was the correct one.

Whether we like the person who is in office or not, God
commands us to pray for those He placed in authority over us. In
ancient times, this could have meant praying for those who hated
Christians and were possibly plotting harm to them. Even today, as
issues concerning Christ-followers emerge, we are called to pray
for all people, including those with whom we don't see eye to eye
politically. Today's verse reminds us that to do so is good and pleasing
to the Lord.

*Gracious Lord, thank You for the admonition to pray for all people,
including those whom we disagree with. All people are precious to
You, Lord. Please help me put my own feelings aside and be obedient
in praying for all those in authority. Amen.*

Communication Guard

Let your conversation be always full of grace, seasoned with salt,
so that you may know how to answer everyone.
COLOSSIANS 4:6 NIV

Lonnie thought she was careful about how she spoke of others. Then an acquaintance, Zella, blasted her with angry accusations that she had been running her mouth about Zella's family.

Lonnie searched herself and asked God to search her heart. There was plenty to sort out in the long list of allegations. It was sent to her via social media, but she wanted to give it all an honest look.

What she deduced was that Zella was angry about a disapproving look Lonnie had given her over poor behavior toward a mutual friend. Zella then concluded several things that were not accurate about Lonnie, all while weaving guilt and shame into her message.

Lonnie carefully responded with grace and humility, acknowledging her shortcomings but also the truth that she had not been speaking ill of Zella's family. Although Zella ignored Lonnie's response, Lonnie realized how important it is to guard not only her words but her facial expressions as well.

God, help us to reflect You in even the seemingly
silly dramas of daily life. Amen.

God's Mountain Sanctuary

And when he had sent them away,
he departed into a mountain to pray.
MARK 6:46 KJV

Do you need to get away from it all? Are the pressures of life smothering you?

Katy's responsibilities at work and home had zapped her energy. She couldn't even pray without interruption, so she made a decision few women make. She visited a mountain cabin for a one-night stay.

The serenity and silence were a welcome escape from life's mayhem. Eagerly she embarked on a solo expedition of a wooded path. Using a hollow log as a bench, she sat near a stream's edge, watching the crystal water splash over boulders protruding from its rocky floor.

Void of computers or cell phones, she talked to God—just as Jesus often did in seclusion. "Is there something You want to teach me, Lord?" she asked as she watched creation keep perfect cadence with its Creator. No one told the squirrels where to find food; no one commanded the trees to reach upward; no one forced the water to flow downstream. No one but God, and creation complied.

As she strolled back to her cabin, the Lord seemed to say, "Take the lessons of creation with you. Don't fret; don't fight; simply flow in the path I clear." In that moment, the words of author Robert Fulghum immerged: "There are Sabbath moments I need that don't happen sitting in a pew."

This was surely one of those, found in God's mountain sanctuary.

Father, help me find my mountain sanctuary right where I am. Amen.

Encourage Others

Worry weighs a person down;
an encouraging word cheers a person up.
PROVERBS 12:25 NLT

When was the last time you offered an encouraging word to someone?
This can be done in many ways. It can take the form of a card or an
e-mail. It can be spoken privately or publicly. Get creative in how you
encourage those around you! Write a note of encouragement and put
it in your child's lunch box. Stick a note on your husband's steering
wheel or briefcase. Place a piece of gum or a miniature chocolate bar
on a coworker's desk along with a note of specific encouragement. It
only takes a moment, but as Proverbs says, it cheers up the recipient's
heart. There is so much sorrow in this world. At any given time, there
are many people within your sphere of influence who are hurting.
Worry weighs them down as they face disappointment, loss, and
other trials. Think about how much it means to you when someone
takes the time to encourage you. Do the same for others. Be the voice
of encouragement. There is blessing to be found in lifting up those
around you.

Father, as I go through this week, make me an encourager.
Provide opportunities for me to encourage those around me.
I truly desire to cheer up the hearts of those who are worried.
Amen.

Forgiving Those Who've Wronged Us

*He who covers and forgives an offense seeks love, but he who
repeats or harps on a matter separates even close friends.*
PROVERBS 17:9 AMP

Shannon tossed and turned, unable to sleep. Finally she got up,
padded into the living room, and sat down on the couch.

"Okay, God," she said, "I know I need to deal with this. I just
don't know how."

Several months prior, Shannon's best friend, Amy, had stopped
talking to her. Shannon tried asking Amy what was wrong, to no
avail. It was as if a switch had been flipped. Amy wouldn't even look
at her when they were both in the same room. The worst part? Amy
had begun spreading vicious lies about her former BFF. Shannon felt
baffled, angry, and hurt.

"How can I forgive her, Lord? I don't know what I did or why she's
being so ugly to me—and I won't be getting an apology, since she won't
even talk to me!" Tears ran down Shannon's face and her shoulders
shook. She covered her face in her hands.

Then a voice whispered to her heart, "Give it to Me. Let Me deal
with Amy. I died so you could be free of sin."

Shannon sighed. *Yes,* she thought. *I want to be free. I will lay this
at Your feet, Jesus. I will forgive.*

*Lord, give us the strength to release our hurt, anger, and bitterness—
and thank You for forgiving our sins through Your work on the cross.*
Amen.

Whispers in the Wind

*Then Jesus told him, "Because you have seen me, you have believed;
blessed are those who have not seen and yet have believed."*
JOHN 20:29 NIV

The wind blew hard, as a good, old-fashioned Midwestern rainstorm
descended on the town. Trees bent over, their limbs thrashing about.
Leaves scattered across yards, and the wind chime clanged a raucous
song instead of the gentle, soothing one normally heard.

The wind is invisible. We can feel it as it crosses our skin. We can
sometimes smell it as it transports a scent. We can't see *it*, but we can
see the effect it has with the blowing leaves. It is powerful. The wind
is very much like our faith in God.

We can't see Him. We can't take Him by the hand or even
converse with Him face-to-face like we do a friend. But we still know
He is present in our lives because we can experience the effects.

God moves among His people, and we can see it. God speaks to
His people, and we can hear the still, small voice. And, just like we
can feel the wind across our cheeks, we can feel God's presence. We
don't need to physically see God to know that He exists and that He's
working.

*You are like the wind, Lord. Powerful and fast moving, soft and gentle.
We may not see You, but we can sense You. Help us to believe,
even when we can't see. Amen.*

Foreign

*You are to love those who are foreigners,
for you yourselves were foreigners in Egypt.*
DEUTERONOMY 10:19 NIV

Bob and Sue had an opportunity to travel to Rome one summer, but neither of them knew Italian or much about the culture.

When they arrived in the city, they had no local currency. The currency exchange kiosk at the airport was overpriced, so they decided to wait until they got to their hotel. The hotel bellman pointed down the street in answer to their request, but they were unclear as to where he was directing them. They enjoyed wandering around the city trying to figure it out. Until they got hungry, anyway. They found a restaurant that accepted their credit card, and they shopped the same way. The language barrier kept them from making progress. Exhausted but with full stomachs, they decided to work on it the next day.

Refreshed after a hotel breakfast they didn't have to hunt for, they asked again where to go. Still, they were unable to find the street and landmarks described in a beautiful language that made no sense.

In high frustration hours later, a local citizen overheard what they were looking for and gave them clear directions to get to the currency exchange. Later, Sue thought how much more she should be looking out for foreigners when she returned home.

*Lord, help us to extend grace to those around us no matter
where they're from, the same way You do for us. Amen.*

The Gift of Encouragement

*We have different gifts. . . . If it is to encourage,
then give encouragement.*
ROMANS 12:6–8 NIV

As a Christian, what is the inward desire of your heart? To witness? To serve? To teach? In the book of Romans, Paul lists the different gifts God gives His children according to His grace. These gifts of grace are inward desires and abilities used to further the kingdom of God. Encouragement is one of those gifts.

Have you ever met someone who seems to have the right thing to say at just the right time? Intuitively, she notices when someone is troubled and proceeds to listen and speak words to uplift and encourage.

Paul spoke of encouraging as a God-given desire to proclaim God's Word in such a way that it touches hearts to move them to receive the Gospel. Encouragement is a vital part to witnessing because encouragement is doused with God's love. For the believer, it stimulates our faith to produce a deeper commitment to Christ. It brings hope to the disheartened or defeated soul. It restores hope.

Perhaps you are wondering what "gift" you possess. The Bible promises us that every true believer is endowed with at least one or more spiritual gifts (1 Corinthians 12). How will you know your gift? Ask God, and then follow the desires He places on your heart.

*Father, help me tune in to the needs of those around me
so that I might encourage them for the Gospel's sake
for Your glory and their good. Amen.*

Loving the Unlovable

"You have heard the law that says, 'Love your neighbor'
and hate your enemy. But I say, love your enemies!
Pray for those who persecute you! In that way, you will
be acting as true children of your Father in heaven."
MATTHEW 5:43–45 NLT

Most of us have family members or people in our lives who are difficult to love. Those people that we would rather not run into in the store so we dart down another aisle hoping they'll check out before we do. You may have one person in your life like that, or many. Difficult people may surround us at every turn. But it's important not to go out of your way to avoid those people. Sometimes running into a difficult person can actually be a "divine appointment"! Maybe you're the only person they'll see all week who wears a smile on her face.

When you happen upon a difficult person whom you'd rather not talk to, take the time to pray for your attitude and then pray for that person. Greet her with a smile and look her in the eye. There is no reason to fear difficult people if you trust in God. He will show you what to do and say as you listen to His promptings (Luke 12:12).

Heavenly Father, I pray that You would help me not to shy away from
the people You have allowed to cross my path. Help me speak Your
truth and share Your love boldly. Amen.

Not Withholding

For the LORD GOD is a sun and shield;
the Lord bestows favor and honor;
no good thing does he withhold from
those whose walk is blameless.
PSALM 84:11 NIV

Gina's cat wanted to go out again as he did every evening. He pawed at the glass as if Gina didn't know the routine.

"It's raining out, kitty. Trust me, you don't want to go out tonight," she said, picking up her eighteen-pound, brown-and-black-striped feline that looked more like a bobcat. She held him calmly and looked in his beautiful green eyes. He promptly hissed at her.

Gina laughed and put him down, where he proceeded to paw more aggressively at the glass, as if to say, "Have you heard nothing that I've asked of you?"

I'm like that with God, Gina thought. *I ask Him to do something for me. I see He is completely able to do it. I also see His love for me. He clearly adores me. Yet He does not give me what I ask for. I forget that He sees beyond the door I am asking Him to open, and He knows when the time is right to either open it or redirect me.*

Father God, thank You for not withholding Your care and for knowing exactly when doors should open and close for me. Amen.

Sew in Love

*Do not be interested only in your own life,
but be interested in the lives of others.*
PHILIPPIANS 2:4 NCV

"Who sews anymore?" Karen said while sipping coffee with her Bible study group. "It makes me sad. My mother used to sew everything for us kids, and I sewed for my kids until it wasn't 'cool' anymore."

"I miss sewing, too," said another woman.

"So do I," said a third.

As the women continued to talk, they decided to organize a one-day sewing event at their church. Participants made shorts and shirts for a missionary to distribute to children in Africa. A shared interest in sewing turned into a selfless act of love.

Each day, God provides opportunities for His people to love one another in random ways. A woman in Oklahoma whose mother had been in a nursing home continued to volunteer there after her mother died. A former teacher in Texas offered free after-school tutoring. A lady who loved gardening helped seniors with theirs.

Acts of love don't need to be complex. Jesus said, "If you give even a cup of cold water to one of the least of My followers, you will surely be rewarded." Often, the simplest acts have the most lasting effects. Sometimes, the greatest reward is seeing a simple act of love bring about extraordinary results.

How can you share God's love today?

*Dear Father, as I go about my day, help me to see
opportunities to share Your love with others. Amen.*

The Difference Barnabas Made

But Barnabas accepted Saul and took him to the apostles.
Barnabas explained to them that Saul had seen the Lord on the road
and the Lord had spoken to Saul. Then he told them how boldly
Saul had preached in the name of Jesus in Damascus. And so Saul
stayed with the followers, going everywhere in Jerusalem,
preaching boldly in the name of the Lord.
ACTS 9:27–28 NCV

Did you know that the man we know as Barnabas was not given that name at birth? His name was Joseph. The apostles later gave him the name Barnabas, which means "one who encourages." Isn't it apparent why he was given this name? Barnabas was an encourager.

When Saul literally "saw the light" on the road to Damascus and instantaneously was converted, there were many who did not believe it. Saul had been a Jew among Jews, a Pharisee, a murderer of Christ-followers. The apostles did not want to accept him. They were skeptical. But Barnabas stood up for Saul. He testified to the change of heart he had witnessed in the man. Barnabas not only encouraged Saul, but he encouraged the apostles to accept him as a brother in the Lord. Did this encouragement make a difference? Indeed it did. It caused the apostles to accept Saul into the fold. He went throughout Jerusalem with them, preaching Christ as Savior. You never know when a bold word of encouragement may make all the difference in the world.

God, use me as an encourager in this world. Allow my bold words of
encouragement to make a difference in the lives of others. Amen.

Wait Expectantly

*Listen to my voice in the morning, LORD. Each morning
I bring my requests to you and wait expectantly.*
PSALM 5:3 NLT

Why would the psalmist say he waits *expectantly* upon praying to the
Lord each morning? Perhaps it is because he had seen God answer
prayers time and time again! When we develop a habit of prayer, of
seeking God and presenting Him with our deepest needs, we also
learn to expect Him to answer. When we pray, God listens. He shows
up. He never fails to hear His children.

Think about a baby who cries out in the night. The baby learns to
expect a parent to come and lift him out of the crib to provide comfort,
food, or a dry diaper. Babies in orphanages often stop crying. No one
comes when they cry. There is no use. The expectation for rescue and
provision wanes. Your heavenly Father is eager and ready to meet
with you when you come before Him in prayer. The Bible tells us that
His eyes are always roaming across the earth, searching for those who
are after His own heart. When you lift your requests to the Sovereign
God, rest assured that He is ready to answer. Wait expectantly!

*Lord, thank You that You are a God who hears my prayers and
answers. Thank You in advance for all that You are doing in my life.
Amen.*

Sincere Love

Love must be sincere. Hate what is evil;
cling to what is good.
ROMANS 12:9 NIV

The words *I love you* come easily for some people; for others, those words are withheld and only shared sparingly. As important as those three little words are, they're not nearly as important as the actions behind the words.

Sincere love clings to what is good. Sincere love always protects. It is always patient and kind. It always seeks to bring honor to others. Sincere love always builds up and never tears down.

Some families tell each other they love each other frequently. Yet they gossip and slander and backbite. They seek to dishonor one another at every opportunity. They harm each other's spirits and break each other's hearts. Their words of love aren't sincere.

Others speak the words less frequently, but their actions show kindness and love. The words they do speak bring honor; they build one another up and find ways of showing their love through action.

The words *I love you* are important; we need to hear them. But they ring shallow when they're not backed up with sincere, loving motives and actions. Let's work to show sincere love—backed by actions—to the people God has placed in our lives.

Dear Father, help me to love sincerely. Help me to recognize evil,
hurtful motives in my heart. I want to cling to what is good and love
others with my words and my actions. Amen.

Recycling

All praise to the God and Father of our Master, Jesus the Messiah. . . .
He comes alongside us when we go through hard times,
and before you know it, he brings us alongside someone else
who is going through hard times so that we can be there
for that person just as God was there for us.
2 CORINTHIANS 1:3–4 MSG

Have you ever considered how much use the Lord can make out of the garbage of our lives? As Christians, we can take the good and bad events we've experienced and use them to witness to others of the goodness of God. When we've walked a path and struggled with a problem, and God has seen us through to the other side, we need to reach out to a brother or sister. Ambassador Clare Boothe Luce once stated, "There are no hopeless situations; there are only people who have grown hopeless about them." That's when we might offer encouragement.

God weaves a life tapestry for each of us; when we focus on the knotted thread, we don't see any beauty. However, a fellow believer can show us his tapestry made from similar knots, and we see the picture. How precious of the Lord to allow us to share with one another. Never underestimate the power of your testimony.

Father, show me this day how You would have me
share what You have done in my life. Amen.

Public Prayer

*So I bow in prayer before the Father from whom every
family in heaven and on earth gets its true name.*
EPHESIANS 3:14–15 NCV

What an amazing sight! Groups of teenagers encircling the flagpoles in front of their schools, hands joined, heads bowed, praying. At schools around the world, nearly one million teens participated in the "See You at the Pole" global day of student prayer. Professing their faith in God, they interceded for their friends, families, teachers, schools, and nations. The sight of them praying together ministered to their peers and led some of them to Christ.

A heartfelt prayer offered in public glorifies God and allows others to feel His presence; however, the scriptures include a warning about public prayer. Matthew 6:5 advises people not to act like the hypocrites who want to be seen and heard praying just to show how pious and religious they are. Public prayer must be sincere and directed toward God and not toward others.

Every day, Christians gather together, bow their heads, and pray publicly in churches; at prayer groups, funerals, and memorial services; in restaurants before meals; and even around school flagpoles. They pray sincerely, sometimes silently and sometimes aloud, setting aside the world and entering into God's presence.

Are you shy about praying in public? Don't be. Step out in faith, bow your head, and pray like God is the only One watching.

*Heavenly Father, I am not ashamed to bow my head
and be in Your presence wherever I go. Amen.*

All about Me

*You know me inside and out, you know every bone in my body;
you know exactly how I was made, bit by bit, how I was sculpted
from nothing into something. . .all the stages of my life were
spread out before you, the days of my life all prepared
before I'd even lived one day.*
PSALM 139:15–16 MSG

Have you ever considered how matchless you are in this world?
No one is created in exactly the same way. We each have our own
personalities, gifts, ideas, and dreams. C. S. Lewis wrote, "Why else
were individuals created, but that God, loving all infinitely, should
love each differently?"

Accepting our individuality is a lifetime lesson since there will be
many times we will want to compare ourselves to others. But God has
shown His love through the unique manner in which He creates and
guides our lives. We are distinct, one from another. His presence in
our lives keeps us on a path He created just for us. It's hard to fathom
that kind of love.

With that knowledge, we can learn to love ourselves and others
with Christlike love and enrich our relationship with Him. Ever-
growing, ever-learning, we can trust the heavenly Father to mature us
into what He created us to be: "Just ME."

*Thank You, Father, for loving me each day.
Keep me on the path You created. Amen.*

God's Gift of Wisdom

*"Now give me wisdom and knowledge so I can lead these people in
the right way, because no one can rule them without your help."*
2 CHRONICLES 1:10 NCV

Dani suffered a miscarriage and a deep depression. Then she and her
husband were blessed with demanding jobs, children—and bills. Life
happened, and because of stress and busyness, Dani let her passion
for Christ dwindle. She found herself consumed with diapers, dishes,
and deadlines.

During a sermon that convicted her, she prayed for the desire to
spend time with Jesus. Slowly it came, along with confusion about
how to best fit Him into her demanding days.

But as Dani confessed her weakness, frailty, and disobedience
to God and asked Him for fresh ideas, she felt peace as her loving
heavenly Father whispered to her, "I'm so glad that you want to spend
time with Me. I love it when you do."And He gave her a few creative
ideas about how to seek Him in the midst of motherhood.

Now, Dani seeks the Lord daily—whether praying while she's
in the car-pool line, studying the Word during naptimes or music
lessons, or staying up a few minutes after her children go to sleep.
Dani prays that God will continue to give her a passion for Him, so
that she can impart that love to her children.

*Lord, give me creativity, discipline, and wisdom as
I seek You in the midst of life's demands. Amen.*

Hanging on to Hope

*Hope deferred makes the heart sick,
but a longing fulfilled is a tree of life.*
PROVERBS 13:12 NIV

Hannah's dreams seemed to elude her. All she hoped for was a simple family life. After a broken childhood, she was grateful for the husband God had given her. He was good to her, and they were growing in Christ together. But they both wanted children so very much and were medically unable.

A family. It was the life millions had and one that even the most unkind and unappreciative of people were granted. Yet for her, God held back.

Why? Hannah wrestled with God for years.

After Hannah and her husband became foster parents, they thought God had sent them a set of siblings to adopt. They were so excited, only to have the abusive parents regain custody of the children. Again, "Why, God?" Hannah continued to care for foster children and make a difference in their lives for however long they stayed. Then one day God sent two sisters who would never leave their loving home.

*Lord God, thank You for the hope You extend to us, deferred as it may
be at times. You truly love to fulfill our deepest longings. Amen.*

Unwavering Devotion

Give thanks to the LORD, for he is good; his love endures forever.
1 CHRONICLES 16:34 NIV

In the movie *Hatchi*, Richard Gere plays a college music professor who discovers a stray puppy at the train station where he daily returns home from the city. The puppy and professor form a unique bond. Soon, the dog begins seeing his master off to work each morning at the station and returning—at the sound of the evening train's whistle—to greet him each night.

Remarkably, after the professor dies suddenly, the canine returns to the station every morning and evening for ten years, until his own demise. The film is based on the true story of a dog in Japan named Hatchiko.

Hatchi's unwavering devotion is a picture of the love of God for His children. He desires to be with us at all times and waits for us when we leave His side. His loyalty to us far outweighs that of any friend, lover, or companion.

Have you strayed from His side? Are you weary and worried about how He'll react if you come back to Him? Don't be—He waits in joyful anticipation for you to come home.

Lord, thank You for Your faithfulness to me, even when I'm unfaithful to You. Give me the courage to move back toward You, where You wait with open arms for my return. Amen.

Drive-Time Prayer

Lift your eyes and look to the heavens: Who created all these?
He who brings out the starry host one by one, and calls forth
each of them by name. Because of his great power and
mighty strength, not one of them is missing.
ISAIAH 40:26 NIV

Unlike most people, Rachel loved her twenty-minute drive to work
each morning. After years of sliding behind the wheel and settling in
for the commute, lifting her voice to God in prayer as she drove felt
natural. She prayed for her own safety, for her husband, her family,
and her coworkers. She thanked God for His hand of protection on
their lives.

One Friday morning, halfway into her drive time, she was
conversing with God when a terrible accident unfolded just four car
lengths in front of her. She watched in what felt like slow motion.
She stayed in peace in God's presence as she pulled her foot off the
accelerator.

The speeding car that had caused the wreck—hitting several cars
in front of her but miraculously never touching her car—had stopped
sideways on the opposite side of the freeway. When she was clear
of the wreck, she pulled over to the shoulder and thanked God for
answering her prayers for protection and safety. Then she called her
husband to tell him how God had kept her from a serious accident.

Dear Lord, never allow me to discount Your promises. Thank You for
always answering my prayers according to Your will. Amen.

Standing in the Light

Though I have fallen, I will rise.
Though I sit in darkness, the LORD will be my light.
MICAH 7:8 NIV

Ever fall so low, you think you'll never get up again? We've all been there. Whether it's a job that's fallen through, a bad medical report, or a failed relationship, life has a way of knocking us down. When that happens, we often feel like we'll never stand again.

But with God, we know the low times aren't the end of our story. We may fall down, but He will lift us up. We may feel surrounded by darkness on every side, but He will be our light, guiding the way, showing us which step to take next. No matter where we are, what we've done, or what we're facing, God is our Rescuer, our Savior, and our Friend.

Satan wants to convince us that we have no hope, no future. But God's children always have a future and a hope. And someday, when death calls our name, even then we will be victorious. For on that day, we will be ready to experience total love and acceptance. We will know once and for all that we are special, we are cherished, and we belong to Him.

Dear Father, thank You for giving me confidence in a future filled with good things. When I'm down, remind me to trust in Your love. Thank You for lifting me out of darkness to stand in Your light. Amen.

The Love of Strangers

*If anyone has material possessions and sees a brother
or sister in need but has no pity on them, how can the love
of God be in that person? Dear children, let us not love
with words or speech but with actions and in truth.*
1 JOHN 3:17–18 NIV

When we think of hospitality in the modern sense, we often think
about being a good hostess, opening our home to friends and family,
perhaps bringing a housewarming gift to a new neighbor or a covered
dish to a family during an illness. Though all of that is hospitable,
the literal meaning of *hospitality* in the Greek means "the love of
strangers."

As Christ-followers, we are called to give generously and
sacrificially to all kinds of people, not just our friends or others that
we know. The work of the Holy Spirit transforms our hearts so that we
consider others before ourselves, sacrificing our time and resources to
give others provision and rest. Exercising true hospitality allows us to
use all our gifts for God's Kingdom.

*Loving Father, thank You for the many gifts You have given me—
time, talent, and financial resources. Show me how You wish me to
use each gift in a generous and hospitable way for Your kingdom.
I pray that You use me to be a rich blessing to others. Amen.*

The Moment You Prayed

As soon as you began to pray, a word went out,
which I have come to tell you, for you are highly esteemed.
Therefore, consider the word and understand the vision.
DANIEL 9:23 NIV

Megan had been challenged by a sermon on financial stewardship one Sunday. She and her husband had been setting aside some tithe money for a return mission trip to Poland, but it didn't look like they would be able to go. She began praying right away about what to do with the money and quickly felt nudged to give a large portion of it to the church building project where they had hoped to return for the short-term mission.

That afternoon she told her husband what she was praying over. Right away he felt good about the idea and suggested the same amount she had thought to give. That evening she e-mailed the pastor and his wife in Poland to let them know what they were going to send.

The pastor's wife shared that their church body in Poland had been praying specifically for God to move hearts to give to their building project. Megan asked what time the Poland church service was and discovered that it was the exact time that she and her husband were talking about what to give.

Lord God, thank You that You hear our prayers and move powerfully
to advance Your kingdom through our lives. You are amazing! Amen.

Praying for Peace

Pray for the peace of Jerusalem:
"May those who love you be secure."
PSALM 122:6 NIV

With the news of yet another outbreak of unrest in the Middle East, this phrase comes to mind: "Pray for the peace of Jerusalem." One might think that King David had prophetically understood how war torn this area of the world would be over the centuries. And, while it is good for us to pray for peace from war in Jerusalem and other places in the world, we should also be praying for peace with God.

As the Prince of Peace, Jesus overcame the world—its wars, pain, and evil. Jesus is the way to peace, both our inner peace and the peace of the world. But it all begins with us as we seek God's will for our lives; get closer to Him; quiet our minds; and listen to that still, small voice. There can be no lasting peace anywhere without being renewed day by day, praying for inner peace, growth of grace, and the love of ourselves and others.

Dear Father, thank You for sending the Prince of Peace to be our peace. Let me be a peacemaker by praying for peace for Jerusalem and elsewhere. I pray that I can be an instrument of Your peace and show love so that others will seek to love You with all their hearts. You are the God of peace; bless me with Your peace forever. Amen.

Shyness

*For the Spirit God gave us does not make us timid,
but gives us power, love and self-discipline.*
2 TIMOTHY 1:7 NIV

Carol got a late start as an author. She wrote to fill her time after
her son left for college. Christian novels became her niche, and to
Carol's surprise, her first three books made it onto a best-seller's
list. Her agent wanted her to do book signings and speak at writers'
conferences, but there was just one problem. Carol was painfully shy.
The thought of book signings and speeches gave her panic attacks.

At a coffee date with her friend, a pastor's wife, Carol complained
about the business part of writing. "Why can't I just stay home and
write books?" she said. "What's so important about speeches and book
signings?"

Her friend's answer was simple: "God."

"God?" said Carol.

"God," her friend repeated. "When you write, you write for
Him. When you sign books and speak, you do it for Him. Why do you
think your books sell so well? It's because they have an encouraging
message. Now God is giving you the opportunity to step out in faith
and share His message with even more women. All you have to do is
trust Him."

"Trust." That one word led Carol to become a proficient speaker.
Today, she confidently speaks all over the country and encourages
women to shed their shyness.

*Dear God, please give me strength in my weakness
and the courage to step out in faith. Amen.*

Call unto Me

Look to the LORD and his strength; seek his face always.
PSALM 105:4 NIV

A young woman received distressing news from her boss. In a panic, she phoned her mother to ask for guidance; she called her best friend for an opinion; she discussed the matter at lunch with coworkers. But not once did she seek the Lord's face.

Scripture encourages us to pray about everything—to send our cares and petitions heavenward. Why do we persist in running to others instead of Him? David, the psalmist, had no choice but to rely on the Lord as he fled his enemies. The lyrics of the Psalms remind us he was no stranger to loss and fear. Yet he cried unto the Lord. His words in Psalm 105 encourage us to remember what He has done before. Paul sat in the pits, literally, and sang songs of praise. While we might not be in dire straits like those men, we certainly have problems and can read scripture to see how the Lord has worked and have confidence He is near.

Let us work to seek His face always. Know the Lord cares about each detail of your life, and nothing is a secret or a surprise to Him. Reach for the best and expect results. It might require a time of waiting, but His answers are always unsurpassed.

Almighty Father, thank You for loving me so well.
In times when I fear, help me fall into Your embrace. Amen.

The Whole Truth

Let our lives lovingly express truth [in all things, speaking truly, dealing truly, living truly]. Enfolded in love, let us grow up in every way and in all things into Him Who is the Head, [even] Christ (the Messiah, the Anointed One).
EPHESIANS 4:15 AMP

When someone gives testimony in a court case, they are sworn in with the question, "Do you swear to tell the truth, the whole truth, and nothing but the truth, so help you God?" Sadly, it can take a court case to cause someone to tell the whole truth.

Physicians at the University of Michigan were counseled by risk-management executive Richard Boothman and his colleagues to own up to mistakes early. When they chose a more honest approach, the number of malpractice claims fell; they were esteemed by patients for their transparency; legal expenses went down; and patient satisfaction increased. Interestingly, patients seemed to recover faster.

Everyone makes mistakes. When we admit them and take responsibility—even asking for forgiveness—we build integrity in our relationships. It also opens doors when we offer grace to others when they make mistakes. Make a choice today to tell the whole truth and build strong relationships in your life today.

Lord, forgive me for the times I have been short on grace or even refused to give it to others. Thank You for Your mercy on my life. Help me to take responsibility when I make a mistake. Please grant me favor with others when I need grace from them. Amen.

Love God, Love Others

*Jesus answered, "'Love the Lord your God with all your heart,
all your soul, and all your mind.' This is the first and most important
command. And the second command is like the first:
'Love your neighbor as you love yourself.'"*
MATTHEW 22:37–39 NCV

It was Saint Augustine who said, "Love God and do what you will,"
meaning that if we're truly loving God, everything else will come
together as it should (Romans 8:28). We'll make the choices He wants
us to make as He guides us. We'll delight in Him and do His will. The
entire Word of God is summed up in Jesus' response to the Pharisee
who asked Him to tell which commandment was greatest. That's
simple. Our purpose and mission in life is this: love God and love
others.

The scripture goes on to say that the entire "Law and the
Prophets hang on these two commandments" (Matthew 22:40 NIV). If
you're obeying God's command to love Him above all else and to love
others, then you are fulfilling all the rest.

How can you live a life of love? Ask God to be the very center of
your life. Get to know Him on a moment-by-moment basis. Both His
power and presence are constantly available to you. As you relate to
others, remember the preciousness of each person. Even the difficult
ones. They are created and loved by God.

*Jesus, thank You for summing up Your Word for me so simply. Expand
my love for You and allow me to love others like You want me to.
Amen.*

The Higher Road

*"In this world you will have trouble. But take heart!
I have overcome the world."*
JOHN 16:33 NIV

During World War II, the Nazis imprisoned author Dr. Victor Frankl. As the Gestapo stripped him and cut away his wedding band, Frankl thought, *You can take away my wife, my children, and strip me of my clothes and freedom, but there is one thing you cannot take—my freedom to choose how I react to whatever happens to me.*

John 16:33 acknowledges that Jesus overcame the world on our behalf, so we are fully equipped to do the same.

It's difficult to trust God against all odds when problems slash us like a paper shredder. Yet it is during those times that God gives us a clear choice: choose faith or break under the harsh realities of life.

Dr. Frankl had learned somewhere in his life's journey to take the higher road. He knew that faith and how we react to people or problems is a choice, not a feeling. We can respond in the flesh or submit to the Holy Spirit whatever happens to us. Often that means asking for forgiveness though you've done nothing wrong, encouraging someone despite their negative attitude, or extending a hand and risking rejection.

Mature believers know that hardships are a part of life, but Jesus has paved the pathway to overcome. And although taking "the higher road" is less traveled, it's worth the trek.

*Lord, whatever I face, may I act, not react,
with Your overcoming power. Amen.*

Much, Much More

*With God's power working in us, God can do much, much more
than anything we can ask or imagine. To him be glory in the church
and in Christ Jesus for all time, forever and ever. Amen.*
EPHESIANS 3:20–21 NCV

Think back to a time when something happened in your life that you
never saw coming. Something that happened out of the blue, was not
on your radar, and absolutely amazed you. When God's power is at
work within you, the possibilities are beyond your imagination

The New International Version of the Bible says that He can
do "immeasurably more" than what you could imagine. Whatever
problem you are facing right now—big or small—God cares. As you
pray about it and seek God's will, don't put Him in a box thinking
that there's no way out or that there is only one right answer. His
response just might be beyond your understanding and your wildest
imagination.

Remember that things aren't always what they seem. When you
feel disappointed in God's answers to your prayers, look outside the
box. God is always, always working everything out for your good. God
sees all. What may feel like the best answer may be totally destructive
to you or someone you love. Trust that God can do much more than
anything you could ever ask or imagine!

*Heavenly Father, help me trust You with my whole heart. When I'm
disappointed, help me to see outside of myself and what I think are
the best answers for my life. Thank You for working everything out
according to Your great plan. Amen.*

God's Promises Bring Hope

*"For I know the plans I have for you. . .plans to prosper you
and not to harm you, plans to give you hope and a future."*
JEREMIAH 29:11 NIV

A despondent elderly man, wracked by years of physical pain and
mental abuse, is shown love and concern for the first time. The
result? Hope. A wayward teenage girl is welcomed back home with a
compassionate, forgiving embrace from her disappointed yet loving
parents. The outcome? Hope. An unappreciated middle-aged woman,
consumed with chores, a career, and caring for her two children and
elderly parent, is lifted from despair when friends pitch in to help her.
Hope.

Hope and encouragement are precious gifts we can give one
another anytime, anywhere. They come in the form of a second chance
clothed in a reassuring word; they thrive in the fertile soil of a loving
gesture or compassionate embrace.

The writer of the well-known hymn, "It Is Well with My Soul,"
penned those words at the most grief-stricken time of his life after his
wife and three children were tragically killed at sea. His undaunted
faith remained because he believed in a God who was bigger than the
tragedy he faced. God's promises gave him hope and encouragement.

Despite your circumstances, God has a plan for you, one that will
give you encouragement and hope and a brighter future.

*Father, may I always say "it is well with my soul," knowing Your
promises are true and I can trust You no matter what. Amen.*

Praying the Mind of Christ

*We demolish arguments and every pretension that sets
itself up against the knowledge of God, and we take captive
every thought to make it obedient to Christ.*
2 CORINTHIANS 10:5 NIV

As Christ-followers, we are learning to become like Him in our
thoughts, words, and deeds. Part of becoming Christlike is also in
mastering our minds. Sometimes it is hard to pray because other
thoughts interfere with our ability to listen closely to what God is
saying. This is a favorite trick of Satan's. . .getting us to think about
our to-do list instead of what God is trying to tell us.

By reading and praying scripture and using positive statements
in our prayers that claim what God has already said He will do for us,
the mind of Christ is being activated in us. By taking captive every
thought, we learn to know what thought is of God, what belongs to
us, and what is of the enemy. Recognize, take captive, and bind up
the thoughts that are of the enemy, and throw them out! The more
we commune with God, fellowship with Him, and learn from Him, the
more we cultivate the mind of Christ.

*Lord, help me identify the thoughts that are not Your thoughts and
purge them. I know that soon Your thoughts will be the ones that
I hear, and not the enemy's. In this way, I will hear You more
clearly so I may be an obedient disciple. Amen!*

The Battle Is His

*"Do not be. . .discouraged. . .the battle is not yours. . . .
Stand firm. . . . The LORD will be with you.'"*
2 CHRONICLES 20:15–17 NIV

Jeannie is a teacher in a very liberal public school system. She knows that her job is a ministry and has seen the school as her mission field. Every day, she feels as if she's girding for battle as she prepares for work. And in some ways, she is. When she receives a paycheck, she wonders if all her effort is worth it.

But Jeannie also knows a retired public school teacher who attends her Wednesday night Bible study at church. Georgia always asks Jeannie how she can pray for her and gives her truth to hold on to. Jeannie leaves feeling reenergized to fulfill her calling.

Joshua was discouraged by the battle he faced. God had called him to fight a seemingly unbeatable enemy with meager resources. The man of God had no idea how his small army would prevail.

Then God said, "This battle isn't yours; it's mine. Don't be afraid. . . just stand still, and see what I will do." God, not Joshua and his men, won the battle that day. And He will win our battles for us, if we will allow it.

God, help me to see my daily struggles as opportunities for You to show Your power, instead of unmovable obstacles. Thank You for promising that You are always with me and will fight for me. Amen.

Hurt Happens—Love Anyway

*"I have loved you even as the Father has loved me.
Remain in my love."*
JOHN 15:9 NLT

Do you ever feel like Jesus overcame life's challenges more easily than
you because He was God? It's important to realize that Jesus lived
His life as a man—empowered just as you are today as a believer. He
relied on His relationship with God and the Holy Spirit working in Him
to do all that He did. He, too, was human. He suffered pain, hurt, and
disappointment just as you do.

Imagine His feelings when brothers, sisters, aunts, uncles, and
cousins refused to believe He was the Messiah or discounted His
words of truth because He was family. How painful it must have been
to have those closest to Him reject Him. Jesus knew that Judas would
betray Him and Peter would deny Him. Jesus must have felt that hurt
deeply—and yet He loved them anyway. In the face of the cross, He
asked God to forgive those who put Him there.

When faced with pain or disappointment, it's easier to become
angry, defend yourself, or even sever the relationship. The same Spirit
that empowered Jesus to live His faith can empower you. When hurt
happens—choose to love anyway!

*Lord, You have shown me how to respond in love. Give me strength
by Your Holy Spirit to love others in the face of pain, disappointment,
and hurt. Comfort me and provide ways for me to show love to others.
Amen.*

Mission Impossible

And he said, The things which are impossible
with men are possible with God.
LUKE 18:27 KJV

As capable as we may be, some things will always remain impossible
for us. No matter how much education we get, how determined we
are, or how much money we have, some things are out of our control.

Yet just because something is impossible for us doesn't mean we
don't have any hope. Where we can't, God can. The God who created
the universe, who set the moon and stars in the sky, who placed the
sun in place, and who brought Lazarus back to life after four days in
the grave is a God who knows no limits.

Whatever we face, we can face with confidence. God, who loves
us more than anything, will move heaven and earth to fulfill His
purpose. And He is a God who likes to show off, who likes to take
things to the limit before acting, just so He can get the glory. He is an
amazing, all-powerful God, and He cares deeply about each and every
one of His children.

It may seem like we are facing the impossible. And left up to
us, it may be impossible. But we must never, ever forget. Nothing is
impossible with God.

Dear Father, thank You for being a God of miracles.
Help me to trust in Your ability to accomplish Your purpose,
even when it seems impossible to me. Amen.

Never Quit

*Let us not become weary in doing good, for at the proper
time we will reap a harvest if we do not give up.*
GALATIANS 6:9 NIV

"They've broken my spirit," the elderly woman said as she assessed
her damaged garden. Slashed cucumber vines and mutilated
vegetables littered the once fruitful plot of land across the street from
her home, alongside abandoned railroad tracks. Night vandals had
ruined Mrs. Conner's labor of love.

For years she planted, cultivated, and watered her garden,
laboriously hauling buckets of water across the street to provide
vegetables for needy families. Although well into her eighties, she
took pride and pleasure in her work.

As she cleared her vandalized garden of debris, she muttered,
"I spent over one hundred dollars on the garden this year, and for
what?" Then God spoke, *"Don't quit. If you quit, they've won."*

Are unexpected circumstances breaking your heart and spirit?
Are vandals destroying your life's garden? The Bible teaches us to
persevere at the exact time the voice within screams, "Give up!"

Difficulties can destroy and sabotage the fruits of our labor,
but they cannot rob us of our faith and the power of prayer. Pray for
the ones who hurt you; pray for strength and courage, and God will
restore your garden in due course.

Mrs. Conner did, and she's still gardening today.

*Jesus, it's hard to keep going when times are hard.
Help me persevere in prayer when I'm tempted to quit. Amen.*

Refreshment in Dry Times

*"The grass withers and the flowers fall,
but the word of our God endures forever."*
ISAIAH 40:8 NIV

The grass was lifeless, crunchy, and brown. The trees had already started to lose their leaves, and it was only August. Flowers wilted, and the ground was nothing but dry dirt. The previous winter was unseasonably warm with very little snow. Spring had been practically nonexistent, and summer was day after day of relentless, scorching heat with very little rain. It was a drought with no change in sight.

Sometimes our lives feel just like the grass—dry and listless. Maybe we're in a season where things seem to stand still, and we've tried everything to change our circumstances for the better to no avail. It is during those times that we need to remember the faithfulness of God and the permanence of His Word. His promises to us are many and true! God will never leave us or forsake us; and He will provide for, love, and protect us. And, just like the drought, eventually our personal dry times will give way to a time of growth, refreshment, and beauty.

Dear Lord, help me to remember Your love during difficult times of dryness. Even though it's sometimes hard to hear Your voice or be patient during hard times, please remind me of Your many promises, and remind me to stand firmly on them. You are everything I need and the refreshment I seek. Praises to my Living Water! Amen.

The End of Your Rope

Do not be far from me, for trouble is near and there is no one to help.
PSALM 22:11 NIV

You can feel the desperation in David's prayer as you read Psalm 22. He feels utterly rejected and alone as he cries out to God.

Have you been there? Have you ever felt so alone and helpless that you are sure no one is there for you? Jesus meets us in those dark places of hopelessness. He calls to us and says, "Don't let your hearts be troubled. Do not be afraid" (John 14:27). "I will never leave you or forsake you" (Hebrews 13:5). You are never alone.

The late youth evangelist Dave Busby said, "The end of your rope is God's permanent address." Jesus reaches down and wraps you in His loving arms when you call to Him for help. The Bible tells us that He is close to the brokenhearted (Psalm 34:18).

We may not have the answers we are looking for here in this life, but we can be sure of this: God sees your pain and loves you desperately. Call to Him in times of trouble. If you feel that you're at the end of your rope, look up! His mighty hand is reaching toward you.

Heavenly Father, I feel alone and afraid.
Surround me with Your love and give me peace. Amen.

Sacrificial Love

For God so loved the world, that he gave. . .
JOHN 3:16 KJV

Every mother understands sacrifice. We sit on dusty bleachers in ninety-five-degree heat in anticipation of our child's moment up to bat. Crammed between screaming parents, we cheer on our homegrown Michael Jordan. We struggle with an unbridled umbrella and flyaway blanket to repel the cold, pelting rain and whipping wind just to watch our soccer star kick a muddy ball downfield.

For some of us, sports are foreign. But as moms, it doesn't matter if we confuse a hole in one with a slam dunk; we support, love, and cheer our kids on. It matters little if we have to rush from job to gym or if we sit for hours on hard benches. Love impels us to do so.

God's love is similar. Today's scripture declares that God loved us so much that He *gave.* That included so much more than weathering the elements or laundering smelly socks and grimy uniforms. He gave more than His time, efforts, and care. He gave His Son's life. And His love continues. He's never too busy to attend to our needs, and He isn't irritated when we absorb hours of His time.

Someone commented, "We are shaped and fashioned by what we love." God's love for us fashioned Him in the shape of a cruel cross. That's sacrificial love.

*Father, amid the daily demands of motherhood,
remind me of what You did for me. Amen.*

Putting God to Work

*Since ancient times no one has heard, no ear has perceived,
no eye has seen any God besides you,
who acts on behalf of those who wait for him.*
ISAIAH 64:4 NIV

Prayer affects the three realms of existence: the divine, the angelic, and the human. God, men, and the angels are subject to the rules of prayer, which God has established. Prayer puts God to work in what is prayed for by His people. Prayer also puts us to work. If we do not pray, then God is not sent into action. Prayerlessness excludes God and leaves us at the mercy of our own circumstances. Understanding this, why would we not pray at all times and about everything?

Prayer puts the power into God's hands and keeps it there. Prayer is a privilege. It gives us the ability to ask the God of the universe for action. We should not hesitate.

Father God, thank You for the beautiful and powerful gift of prayer. Prayer puts us in a divine partnership with You. Please help us to remember that we need one another to make prayer the life- and situation-changer that it is. We love how You continue to involve us in Your work. You are amazing, Lord! Amen and Amen!

God's Rest

For anyone who enters God's rest also rests from their works.
HEBREWS 4:10 NIV

Labor Day ushers in the onset of autumn, the last hoorah of summer. Initially, the holiday was designed to provide a reprieve for and dedication to the American worker. Today it represents parades, picnics, and a final visit to a warm, sandy beach before the cold winds blow. Kids head back to school, and daylight hours shorten, reminding us that winter will soon arrive as we exchange our sand pails for snow shovels.

Similarly, each season has significant purpose and value; the scriptures clearly remind us of that in Ecclesiastes 3. From childhood to senior citizenship, each stage of our lives is an adventure, struggle, victory, and blessing even when we don't recognize it at the time. As Christians, we work to accomplish our workloads, maintain our households, cultivate our relationships, and with God's help, reach our spiritual goals. It's hard work—one requiring God's direction and strength.

One day our labors will end when we reach heaven's shore. Meanwhile, God gives us the strength to work His will on this earth, while giving us rest just when we need it.

Father, I thank You for the reprieve You give me from my labors. You know when I need a rest from life's problems and work. Help me not to strive but to thrive in the power of Your presence. Amen.

Online Encouragement

And now, dear brothers and sisters, one final thing. Fix your thoughts
on what is true, and honorable, and right, and pure, and lovely, and
admirable. Think about things that are excellent and worthy of praise.
PHILIPPIANS 4:8 NLT

Negative and impure thoughts cross our minds on a daily basis. Social
media and TV don't help either. Even Christian friends jump on the
bandwagon and post thoughts and ideas online that make us cringe.

Instead of running away from connecting with people online
because you've had enough, make it your goal to be a light in what
can be a very dark, negative atmosphere. Encourage good and right
thinking. Comment, post, and share God's love with your friends as
much as possible.

For the next thirty days, why not plan to post, text, or write
at least one encouraging comment every day? Post encouraging
scripture; text a friend a note to make her smile; tweet your favorite
quote; share sweet stories about your husband and kids on your blog.

Before you grumble or complain about something online, stop
and fix your thoughts on what is true, right, and pure. Then see if
your comment is still valid.

Father, help me not to run from online interaction but
to see it as a mission field. Help me be an encouragement
to everyone I communicate with online. Amen.

The Power of Prayer

*Confess your sins to each other and pray for each other so
that you may be healed. The earnest prayer of a righteous
person has great power and produces wonderful results.*
JAMES 5:16 NLT

There is power in prayer. Do you question this at times? There are
many times in scripture when the fervent prayer of a believer actually
changes God's mind! In James we read that the earnest prayer of a
righteous person has great power and produces great results. You
may be thinking that you are not righteous. Have you given your
heart to Jesus? If you have accepted Him as your Savior, you have
taken on the *righteousness* of Christ. Certainly you are not perfect. In
your humanity, you still sin and fall short. But God sees you through
a Jesus lens! And so, your prayers reach the ears of your heavenly
Father.

Pray often. Pray earnestly. Pray without ceasing. Pray about
everything. Prayer changes things. Look at Jesus' example of prayer
during His time on earth. He went away to quiet places such as
gardens to pray. He prayed in solitude. He prayed with all His heart. If
anyone was busy, it was the Messiah! But Jesus always made time to
pray. We ought to follow His example. Prayer changes things.

*Lord, help me to believe in the power of prayer
and to make time for it daily. Amen.*

Difficult People

"You have heard that it was said, 'Love your neighbor and hate your enemy.' But I tell you, love your enemies and pray for those who persecute you, that you may be children of your Father in heaven."
MATTHEW 5:43–45 NIV

It's easy to thank God for the people we love, who bring joy and peace and laughter and all sorts of other good things to our lives. We thank God for our husbands, our children, our extended families, and our friends.

But what about those people we don't like? What about the people who are all-stress-and-no-bless? Are we supposed to thank God for the people who put knots in our stomachs, who make us cry, or who leave us fist-clenching, smoke-breathing angry? We know we're supposed to pray for our enemies, but do we really need to thank God for them?

Well, yes. God wants us to love our enemies, and it only stands to reason that we'd thank God for the people we love. It is through the difficult people in our lives that we grow and stretch, for they often test our faith in ways the easier relationships can't. Even though we may not see a lot of good in some people, God looks at every person and sees someone He loved enough to die for. And apart from Christ, we can be difficult people, too.

Dear Father, thank You for the easy, happy relationships in my life. And thank You for the difficult people, too, for they stretch me and push me toward You. Help me to love the way You do. Amen.

Devoted

*Devote yourselves to prayer, being watchful and thankful. And pray
for us, too, that God may open a door for our message, so that we may
proclaim the mystery of Christ, for which I am in chains.*
COLOSSIANS 4:2–3 NIV

Ever since Linda was young in her faith, she had been praying
for God to use her talents. As she grew in her creative talents of
writing, acting, and design, she employed her abilities by writing and
producing plays at church. It seemed this was the direction God was
taking her, and this would be what she would do for many years to
come.

As she continued praying and seeking God, doors opened more
in the direction of serving in women's ministry, so she followed that
leading. Occasionally some speaking engagements came her way, and
then event planning and fund-raising were the leading.

Over a decade later, more writing opportunities came her way,
and she grew more and used those skills for God.

What made Linda smile, looking over the years of pursuing
service for God, was that no matter how it changed, God never
stopped giving her growth and new ways to serve Him. It didn't look
at all how Linda thought it would. It was all much more broad and
beautiful than she had imagined it could be.

*God, lead and grow us in the way You would have us go as we
watchfully pray over the Kingdom work You have for us next. Amen.*

Loving Fully

*Jesus replied: "'Love the Lord your God with all your
heart and with all your soul and with all your mind.'"*
MATTHEW 22:37 NIV

When Jesus commanded His followers to love God with all their
hearts, souls, and minds, He meant that loving God fully means
putting aside everything that gets in the way of a relationship
with Him. Everything. That's no small order in a world filled with
distractions.

So how can today's Christians set aside everything to fully love
God? The answer is to shift their desire from serving themselves to
serving Him. Love requires action, and the Holy Spirit gives believers
power to glorify God with everything they do. Praising Him for His
provisions is one way to love Him. Doing selfless acts of service for
others as if working for Him is another way. So is loving others as He
loves us. Studying the Bible and being intimate with God in prayer
is the ultimate act of love toward Him. When Christians center their
lives on their passion for God, they learn to love Him fully.

Loving God with heart, soul, and mind takes practice. It means
thinking of Him all day and working to glorify Him through every
thought and action. It means putting aside one's own desires to serve
Someone greater.

Is it possible to love God more than you love anyone or anything
else? You can try. That in itself is an act of love.

*Dear God, I love You. Help me to love You
more through everything I do. Amen.*

Jungle of Life

*God's word is alive and working and is sharper than a double-edged
sword. It cuts all the way into us, where the soul and the spirit
are joined, to the center of our joints and bones. And it judges the
thoughts and feelings in our hearts.*
HEBREWS 4:12 NCV

Since the time Adam and Eve disobeyed God, the consequences
of sin have often stood between us and God's best for our lives.
Choosing a life of faith can feel like we are lost in a jungle, tangled
in the underbrush. But God has given us a powerful tool that will cut
through the debris of life in a fallen world.

When you take the Bible and live according to His plans, obeying
Him, God's Word cuts like a machete through the entanglements of
life. When you choose to use the Sword of Truth, it clears a path and
can free you from the weights of the world that try to entrap and
ensnare you.

No matter what the challenges of life are saying to you today,
take His Word and speak His plans into your life. Choose His words
of encouragement and peace instead of the negative things the
circumstances are telling you.

*God, I want to live in Your Truth. I want to believe what You say
about me in the Bible. Help me to speak Your words today instead
of letting the problem speak to me. Help me believe. Amen.*

O the Deep, Deep Love of Jesus

*I pray that out of his glorious riches he may strengthen you with power
through his Spirit in your inner being, so that Christ may dwell in your
hearts through faith. And I pray that you, being rooted and established
in love, may have power, together with all the Lord's holy people, to
grasp how wide and long and high and deep is the love of Christ.*
EPHESIANS 3:16–18 NIV

The apostle Paul encouraged the people in Ephesus with his words in
an effort to explain how far-reaching God's love was. Immeasurable.
Unfathomable.

In the late 1800s, the lyricist Samuel Trevor Francis entertained
the idea of ending his own life. In the midst of despair, he felt God
reach out to him, and he wrote a stirring hymn echoing Paul's words.
"O the deep, deep love of Jesus, vast, unmeasured, boundless, free!
Rolling as a mighty ocean in its fullness over me! Underneath me,
all around me, is the current of Thy love, Leading onward, leading
homeward to Thy glorious rest above!"

What an amazing picture. That He should care for us in such a
way is almost incomprehensible. Despite our shortcomings, our sin,
He loves us. It takes a measure of faith to believe in His love. When
we feel a nagging thought of unworthiness, of being unlovable, trust
in the Word and sing a new song. For His love is deep and wide.

Lord, thank You for loving me, even when I'm unlovable. Amen.

Pray for Others

*I urge, then, first of all, that petitions, prayers, intercession
and thanksgiving be made for all people.*
1 TIMOTHY 2:1 NIV

After Moses received the Ten Commandments from God on Mount
Sinai, he called the Israelites together and said to them, "At the
mountain the LORD spoke to you face to face from the heart of the
fire. I stood as an intermediary between you and the LORD, for you
were afraid of the fire and did not want to approach the mountain"
(Deuteronomy 5:4–5 NLT). Moses often was the intermediary between
God and His people. He interceded on their behalf.

Intercessory prayer is a divine act of love and service. It requires
persistence, patience, and faith in God. Christians should intercede for
family and friends, their country, government leaders, their pastors,
the Church, the poor, the sick, the community in which they live, their
enemies, and especially for those who are not saved. Wherever there
is a need, Christians should pray.

The Bible holds many examples of intercessory prayer. Look for
them as you read the scriptures. Discover how God's people prayed
and the great changes those prayers made.

Intercessory prayer is just as important today as it was in Moses'
time. It draws believers nearer to God and provides them with a
powerful way to help others. Whom will you pray for today?

*Heavenly Father, guide me as I pray for others. Help me to
pray for them faithfully, patiently, and persistently. Amen.*

Pure and Faultless Love

*Religion that God our Father accepts as pure and faultless is this:
to look after orphans and widows in their distress and
to keep oneself from being polluted by the world.*
JAMES 1:27 NIV

Janelle lost her husband two years ago, and no one from the church remembers their anniversary anymore. She's feels left out of church activities, which are geared toward couples and families.

Peter is a prisoner who loves hearing about Jesus from the local musicians and preachers who hold services in the prison. He accepted Christ while incarcerated and is working toward his college degree.

The Bible often links together widows, orphans, and prisoners in a group. In ancient times, those were the most ignored parts of society. Therefore, biblical writers urged the Israelites and Christians to devote time and money to their care. Today, we still have such a mandate.

How can you obey that command? Perhaps your church has a widows' or prison ministry with which you could serve. Maybe you and your family could host a college student or single adult whose parents are deceased for the holidays. You might even sense his call to adopt an orphan from the foster care system.

Heavenly Father, give me courage to reach out to those who are often ignored. Help me to hear Your heartbeat for them and to give of my time and resources to minister love to them. Amen.

Your Refuge and Fortress

*Whoever dwells in the shelter of the Most High will rest
in the shadow of the Almighty. I will say of the LORD,
"He is my refuge and my fortress, my God, in whom I trust."*
PSALM 91:1–2 NIV

On September 11, 2001, life as we knew it in America changed. There was fear in the air. Do you remember the days immediately following the attacks? There was unsettledness among us. We were told to be *vigilant*. This was necessary advice from our leaders, but can we really be vigilant enough to avoid danger? We are only human, and life is fragile.

Fortunately, if you know the Lord, you are in good hands. The Bible tells us that if we dwell with the Sovereign God, He will serve as our refuge and our fortress. We cannot place our trust in towers built by man. They may crumble like sandcastles tomorrow. We cannot rely completely on anything or anyone in this world for our security and our peace. That comes only through a relationship with the living Lord. Rest in Jesus. He is your Protector and your Prince of Peace.

*When storms rage around me and the world seems unstable,
call me unto Yourself, oh Lord. I will rest in You. Amen.*

Lead Us, Lord

*I know, GOD, that mere mortals can't run their own lives,
that men and women don't have what it takes to take charge of life.
So correct us, GOD, as you see best.*
JEREMIAH 10:23 MSG

So many changes would happen in our lives if we lived Jeremiah's
words. If we really believed God was in control. We would be able to
release our worries and problems in a prayer of thanksgiving and then
wait. And that's the difficulty that trips us up. In our frenzied world,
we feel we need immediate answers, and we rush to solve situations
our own way. Sometimes that works; however, often we become
enmeshed in less than desirable circumstances.

The last line of the scripture entreats God to correct us, and that's
certainly not a desirous thought. Not many hope to be straightened
out. But when we yield our lives to Him and trust Him implicitly,
understanding full well that our Creator God wants the best for us,
then our prayers of thanksgiving and trust fall more easily from our
mouths. Adoration and praise should fall from our lips before our
requests.

A prayer of total surrender gives glory to God the Father and
pleases Him. It allows Him to work in our lives in ways we often don't
understand.

*Lord, I bless You and give You my heartfelt praise.
Thank You for all You do to work on my behalf. Amen.*

Now What?

And he will be called Wonderful Counselor.
ISAIAH 9:6 NIV

Lisa had been job-hunting for nearly a year. Her emergency savings had almost run out. So had her patience. As she crossed the last company off her list of possibilities, Lisa said, "Now what?"

Everyone has said it at one time or another. Whether it is something important, like not having a job, or something trivial, like not having the key ingredient for a recipe— "Now what?"

The Bible says, "A wise man will hear, and will increase learning; and a man of understanding shall attain unto wise counsels" (Proverbs 1:5 KJV). Of course, that applies not only to men but also to women. Lisa had already sought wise counsel. She received job counseling, and she asked for advice from friends, family, and former business associates. Still, she had no job. Now what?

Lisa sought comfort by reading the Psalms. In Psalm 33:11 (KJV), she read: "The counsel of the LORD standeth for ever, the thoughts of his heart to all generations." Lisa got on her knees and prayed, "Jesus, now what?"

The prophet Isaiah called Jesus "Wonderful Counselor." Jesus devoted His earthly ministry to sharing His wisdom about God and godly living, and He was wiser than anyone on earth. He still is! When we ask, "Now what?" Jesus already has the answer.

Today Lisa is a successful entrepreneur, working from home and loving it.

Dear Jesus, You know the answers to all of my questions.
I trust You to help me. Amen.

Finding Hope after Rejection

Be joyful in hope, patient in affliction, faithful in prayer.
ROMANS 12:12 NIV

Even though Shawna believed she was called to act and be a light for Jesus in the midst of the film industry, major discouragement set in for her when three of her favorite producers turned her down for plum roles *in one week.* Ouch!

Her friends and church family encouraged her to keep going. And she wanted to—but her "fight" was running out.

Then a friend posted Eugene Peterson's *The Message* paraphrase of 1 Thessalonians 5:9–24 on Facebook, at the precise moment she needed it: "God didn't set us up for an angry rejection but for salvation by our Master, Jesus Christ. . . . So speak encouraging words to one another. Build up hope so you'll all be together in this. . . . Be cheerful no matter what; pray all the time; thank God no matter what happens. . . . The One who called you is completely dependable. If he said it, he'll do it!"

Those verses reminded Shawna that God is up to great things behind the scenes. That truth allowed her to trust in His timing and to thank Him, even for rejection. Trusting in God's timing and faithfulness built up her hope, so that she could pray with certainty that He knew what He was doing—and would ultimately use all her circumstances for His glory.

*God, thank You for reminding us to pray
and praise You in any circumstance. Amen.*

The Ultimate Act of Love

*Bring joy to your servant, Lord, for I put my trust in you. You, Lord,
are forgiving and good, abounding in love to all who call to you.*
PSALM 86:4–5 NIV

The modern theologian Lewis Smedes once said, "You will know that
forgiveness has begun when you recall those who hurt you and feel
the power to wish them well." It seems the most unnatural thing in
the world for us to forgive someone who has hurt us deeply, let alone
hoping good things will happen for them. However, that is really the
only loving thing to do.

Forgiveness doesn't require that the person who did the hurting
apologize or acknowledge what they've done. It's not about making
the score even. It doesn't even require forgetting about the incident.
But it is about admitting that the one who hurt us is human, just like
we are. We surrender our right for revenge and, like God, let go and
give the wrongdoer mercy, therefore blessing them.

*Gracious and loving Father, thank You that You love me and have
forgiven me of my sins. May I be more like You in forgiving others.
Although I may not be able to forgive as easily as You do, please
encourage me to take those small steps. In forgiving others, Father,
I am that much closer to being like You. Amen.*

I Grow Weary

*But those who wait for the Lord [who expect, look for,
and hope in Him] shall change and renew their strength and power;
they shall lift their wings and mount up [close to God] as eagles
[mount up to the sun]; they shall run and not be weary,
they shall walk and not faint or become tired.*
ISAIAH 40:31 AMP

Jesus said come to Him, and He would give us rest. Being in His presence, trusting in Him, brings us the rest He desires for us. We can only find this rest when our spirit is in tune with His Word.

As long as we are warring inside, we will not find rest. We must find out what Jesus wants for our lives and then obey. Feasting on His Word and learning more about Him will give us the direction we need and the ability to trust. It is only when we understand our salvation and surrender that we can come to Him, unencumbered by guilt or fear, and lay our head on His chest. Safe within His embrace, we can rest.

Each new day He will give us the strength we need to fight our battles just as His presence will refresh our spirits. We will be as a well-watered garden, refreshed and blessed by our loving Creator.

*Father, I am weary and need Your refreshing Spirit to guide me.
I trust in You. Amen.*

Speaking the Right Language

*[Love] does not dishonor others, it is not self-seeking,
it is not easily angered, it keeps no record of wrongs.*
1 CORINTHIANS 13:5 NIV

Kim was angry. *He just sits on the couch and watches TV,* she fumed inside. *I cook! I clean! I take care of the baby! And he has the audacity to ask me to come and sit with him on the couch. Doesn't he see all the things that need to be done around here?*

The tears were coming again, and she could feel his eyes on her. She walked back to the bedroom. The book she had been reading nightly lay on the bed. She began to think about the chapter she'd been reading. Could her husband be saying he loved her by wanting to spend time just sitting on the couch? A lightbulb went on. His love language was quality time, and her love language was acts of service. She was showing him love the way she wanted to receive it; and he was showing her love the way he wanted to receive it.

She needed to share this revelation with her husband—at the right time. But for now she would speak his language. She walked into the living room and plopped down on the couch next to him.

*Lord, help me to show love to others in the language
that speaks love to them. Amen.*

Don't Worry!

*Don't worry about anything; instead, pray about everything. Tell
God what you need, and thank him for all he has done. Then you will
experience God's peace, which exceeds anything we can understand.
His peace will guard your hearts and minds as you live in Christ Jesus.*
PHILIPPIANS 4:6–7 NLT

The Bible tells us plainly not to worry. But that can be difficult when
the economy is poor, bills need to be paid, health issues arise, and
families face crisis after crisis. Jesus helps us make sense of this in
Luke 12:25 (NIV): "Who of you by worrying can add a single hour to
your life?" The answer is obvious. It can't be done. So why waste
precious time and energy worrying when it will change nothing?

When you start to worry, pray instead. Tell God how you feel and
what you need. Tell Him that you're struggling with worry and ask
Him to take your fears away. He replies to your heartfelt plea gently
in Luke 12:32: "Do not be afraid, little flock, for your Father has been
pleased to give you the kingdom."

How comforting, those words from the mouth of Jesus! Don't be
afraid! Don't worry! You've got the kingdom of God to look forward to
for all eternity. No need to worry about the rest.

*Dear Jesus, thank You for Your promise of eternal life! Give me peace
that exceeds my understanding when I start to worry. Amen.*

Reap in Joy!

*Remember this: Whoever sows sparingly will also reap sparingly,
and whoever sows generously will also reap generously.*
2 CORINTHIANS 9:6 NIV

The list of requirements for the executive assistant job included more
than technical expertise. "Care enough to greet visitors with a warm
welcome and a million-dollar smile. Be sure that a friendly attitude
radiates from your office setting. Demonstrate your caring attitude
by maximizing efficiency and minimizing mistakes when dealing
with coworkers." Although the job description was for a support staff
position, most of it was just as applicable for the CEO as the storeroom
clerk.

All of us want to feel appreciated, and we like to deal with a
friendly person. Have you ever worked with a person who seemed to
have a perpetually bad attitude? You probably didn't feel particularly
encouraged after an encounter with this coworker. Yes, sometimes
things go wrong, but your attitude in the thick of it is determined
by your expectations. If you expect things to turn out well, you'll
generally have a positive mental attitude. Treat everyone with
genuine kindness, courtesy, and respect, and that is what will be
reflected back to you.

*Heavenly Father, help me plant the seeds of patience, love,
compassion, and courtesy in all those I come in contact with.
Please let me make an eternal difference in these people's lives.
I want to joyfully reap a rich harvest for Your Kingdom. Amen!*

Renew Your Strength

*But those who wait for the Lord [who expect, look for,
and hope in Him] shall change and renew their strength and power;
they shall lift their wings and mount up [close to God] as eagles
[mount up to the sun]; they shall run and not be weary,
they shall walk and not faint or become tired.*
ISAIAH 40:31 AMP

Andrew Murray was a South African writer, teacher, and Christian
pastor in the late 1900s who captured the heart of prayer with these
words about Jesus: "While others still slept, He went away to pray and
to renew His strength in communion with His Father. He had need
of this, otherwise He would not have been ready for the new day.
The holy work of delivering souls demands constant renewal through
fellowship with God."

Each day you give a part of yourself to that day—spiritually,
emotionally, physically, financially, and socially. Within each of those
areas of life, you need to refuel. Spiritually, the only way to recharge
is a renewal that comes from God. Waiting for a fresh outpouring of
His life-giving Spirit brings a newness and a fresh perspective on all
the other areas of your life. Give your best each day by drawing on the
strength of your heavenly Father and spending time with Him.

*Heavenly Father, Your Word and prayer are strength to my soul.
Renew me and pour Your life into me. Fill me with Your power and
give me courage for a new day. Amen.*

Humiliating Moments as Raw Clay

*All the LORD's ways are loving and true for those
who follow the demands of his agreement.*
PSALM 25:10 NCV

Did you know that God wants to use even our humiliating experiences to transform our character?

In *The Message*, the psalmist says, "I learned God-worship when my pride was shattered" (51:16). The Creator is an artist. If He can't redeem our worst moments, there will be a lot of material that goes unused. God wants to take our failures and lovingly, like a potter sculpts raw clay, mold them into something beautiful.

As our sin-bearer, Jesus endured one of the most painful, visible humiliations the world has ever seen. And yet—through His death, eternal life became available to us. And as human beings with many faults, we will experience visible and painful humiliations, either through our own sins, others' poor choices, or our foolish decisions. But whatever the cause of our embarrassment, when we surrender to God, He can turn it into a tool for our transformation.

Beth Moore, in her Bible study *Breaking Free*, writes, "Let God have your failures. Surrender to Him your. . .most humiliating defeats. God and God alone can use them to make you twice the warrior you ever dreamed you'd be."

Lord, help me to see those times I am humiliated (at least in retrospect) as moments You can use to change me into the woman You want me to be. Amen.

His Presence

Even when I walk through the darkest valley,
I will not be afraid, for you are close beside me.
Your rod and your staff protect and comfort me.
PSALM 23:4 NLT

The rain drizzled drearily down the windowpanes of Suzy's kitchen. Unfortunately, it matched her mood that day. She heated some water for tea and put on some tomato soup to go with her standby favorite comfort food, grilled cheese.

The warmth and good smells of cooking should have done more for her. *Why do I get in these places?* she asked herself. While things bubbled on the stove, she reached for her Bible, wearily cracking it open to where she had stuck a bookmark several days back.

There was the twenty-third psalm. It always did lift her spirits. Reminded again that God is always with her, she realized that she hadn't spent much time talking to Him lately.

The kettle whistle blew. Suzy poured the steaming water over the tea that would comfort and warm her chilly self. As she sipped it, she let God comfort and warm the deepest parts of her, the parts that only He can get to.

Lord, thank You for being able to touch the depths
of us and for never leaving our side. Amen.

Stop, Breathe, Pray. . .and Repeat

Do not be anxious about anything, but in every situation,
by prayer and petition, with thanksgiving, present your requests
to God. And the peace of God, which transcends all understanding,
will guard your hearts and your minds in Christ Jesus.
PHILIPPIANS 4:6–7 NIV

Being a woman in these times is challenging. Many of us are working demanding jobs, managing our homes and crazy schedules, and taking care of children or aging parents. Often, we feel we don't have enough time to get everything done, let alone take care of ourselves properly. All of this creates stress and anxiety, which just makes many of these situations worse.

What can you do when it seems the world is falling down around your shoulders? Stop. Take a deep breath, and then settle your mind on Jesus. Give Him the situation, the harried thoughts, the worries. God says that we can take anything to Him in prayer! He will provide whatever we need, even the peace that will get us through the most difficult circumstances.

Father God, we are thankful that we can take any worried thought or
situation to You in prayer. You tell us that You will provide for us and
will even give us Your peace! Help us to trust You in this, Lord, to lay
the situation at Your feet and leave it there. Fill our minds and hearts
with Your peace and remind us of how much You love us. Amen!

True Friendship

Rejoice with those who rejoice; mourn with those who mourn.
ROMANS 12:15 NIV

True Christian friendship has this verse stamped all over it. Do you have a friend who truly finds joy in your successes? When you are on top of the world, this person is genuinely happy for you. When you are sad, you have seen tears come to her eyes. This is not a friendship found every day. It is rare and to be treasured.

As believers in Christ, we have this high call on our lives. Pray that you might truly celebrate with others, not secretly wishing you were the one receiving the blessing. On the other hand, know that at times sorrow and loss are so deep that a hug and an "I love you" will mean the world. Lots of words are not needed in such times. To mourn with the mourner is the greatest gift you can give. Just to show up, to extend help, to show love.

If you have such a friend, you no doubt cherish her. Make it your aim to live out Romans 12:15 in small ways this week. Stand and cheer when others are victorious. Stand close by and be ready to comfort them when they experience disappointment or loss.

*Heavenly Father, help me to rejoice with those who rejoice
and to mourn with those who mourn. Give me a sensitive
heart that is focused on others. Amen.*

Why Praise God?

Though he slay me, yet will I trust in him.
JOB 13:15 KJV

One woman asked an honest question: "How can I praise God when everything in my life is falling apart?" Who hasn't pondered that question in moments of defeat, despair, or grief?

In the book of Acts, Paul and Silas, under Roman law, were publicly stripped and severely beaten for their faith. Afterward, they were jailed. Yet with bloody backs and shackled feet, they sat in a dirty cell undefeated. Rather than question God's intentions or apparent lack of protection, the scriptures state that around midnight, "Paul and Silas were praying and singing hymns to God" (Acts 16:25 NIV).

The power of prayer and praise resulted in complete deliverance. The prison doors flew open, and their chains fell off. What's more, the jailer and his family accepted Christ, and these ardent believers were able to witness to other inmates.

It's difficult to praise God when problems press in harder than a crowd exiting a burning building. But that's the time to praise Him the most. We wait for our circumstances to change, while God desires to change us despite them. Praise coupled with prayer in our darkest moments is what moves the mighty hand of God to work in our hearts and lives.

How can we pray and praise God when everything goes wrong? The bigger question might be: How can we not?

*Jesus, help me to pray and praise You despite my circumstances.
Amen.*

He Plows Our Hearts

*Sow righteousness for yourselves, reap the fruit of unfailing love,
and break up your unplowed ground; for it is time to seek the LORD,
until he comes and showers his righteousness on you.*
HOSEA 10:12 NIV

Has God brought you through a season of growth and you thought you might get a break?

Sheri thought the same thing after losing both her parents within a year's time. She was finally moving through life on an even keel and quite content; then her husband lost his job. They had little in savings, and her job was not enough to pay all the bills.

Her husband was depressed about his prospects for another job and often unmotivated because of it. They quickly fell behind on rent and utilities. Vacations and dinners out became extreme luxuries. Sheri picked up a part-time job on top of her full-time job to help make ends meet. Even still, they began to fall into debt, and before long both of them teetered on the verge of despair.

Yet God gave them the strength they needed to get through each week and month and eventually provided better jobs for both of them. None of it was perfect, by any means. But what Sheri and her husband realized was that God was breaking up some unplowed ground in them that they hadn't known needed to be plowed.

*Father God, bless our unplowed ground with productive work,
that our lives may bring forth a fruitful harvest for You. Amen.*

Choose Love

So brothers and sisters, since God has shown us great mercy,
I beg you to offer your lives as a living sacrifice to him. Your offering
must be only for God and pleasing to him, which is the spiritual
way for you to worship. Do not be shaped by this world; instead be
changed within by a new way of thinking. Then you will be able to
decide what God wants for you; you will know what is good
and pleasing to him and what is perfect.
ROMANS 12:1–2 NCV

Only through the power of Christ at work within us can we choose
to love when we don't feel like it. He changes us from the inside and
gives us a new way of thinking.

First Peter 4:8 (NLT) says, "Most important of all, continue to show
deep love for each other, for love covers a multitude of sins." This
verse tells us to keep choosing love. No matter what. Choose love.

Love is a choice, and your attitude is a choice. Our emotions and
feelings often get the better of us. If you are facing a challenge or a
difficult person and you don't feel like choosing to love, ask God to
transform your heart and mind. Ask Him to go before you and to help
you choose a loving and right attitude.

Dear Lord, change my heart and mind to be in Your will. Give me an
attitude that matches Yours, and help me to choose love. Amen.

Don't Sweat the Small Stuff

*I consider that our present sufferings are not worth comparing
with the glory that will be revealed in us.*
ROMANS 8:18 NIV

When a woman gives birth, the time she spends in pregnancy and
labor can seem like an eternity. She's uncomfortable. She's nauseous.
She's swollen. And it all leads up to hours, maybe even days of painful
labor and suffering.

But then she holds that beautiful son or daughter in her arms,
and the memory of any pain fades so far to the background, it's not
even worth considering. The joy of seeing the one she loves face-
to-face fills up her heart and mind so completely, it wipes away
any shadow of discomfort and suffering. Plus, the years of joy and
fulfillment that child brings are much longer than the months of
pregnancy or the hours of labor.

That's how heaven will be for us. Life is like pregnancy and labor.
This life isn't the completion, it's the preparation! Our years here
are just a moment compared to eternity. When life is difficult, don't
sweat it. It won't last forever. One day we will leave it all behind to
be flooded with His complete, perfect love and acceptance. All the
pain of this life will be lost in comparison to the complete peace we'll
experience, forever and ever.

*Dear Father, thank You for the promise of eternal love and peace.
Help me to keep life's hardships in perspective of that eternity. Amen.*

For Love's Sake

*For I was hungry and you gave Me food, I was thirsty and you gave
Me something to drink, I was a stranger and you brought Me together
with yourselves and welcomed and entertained and lodged Me.*
MATTHEW 25:35 AMP

Marie was a regular at her neighborhood coffee shop. The past several
chilly spring mornings, she had noticed a homeless man sitting in the
courtyard a few feet outside the coffee shop. This morning she walked
up to him and sat down next to him. "Hi!" she started. "I noticed you
seem to like this courtyard as much as I do." She extended her hand
and said, "My name is Marie; what's yours?"

"I'm Jack," he replied after a pause. "Most people act like I'm
invisible, so I was a little startled when you spoke to me."

"Well, Jack," Marie said, "I'm going in to get a cup of coffee.
Would you like a hot cup of coffee this morning?"

Jack nodded his head and smiled.

God is love, and He desires for you to extend His love to others.
It's easy to let the homeless, the less fortunate, or the unlovely remain
invisible. When you take time to smile at a stranger or acknowledge
someone's presence with a hello, you are demonstrating kindness and
extending the heart of God to that person.

*Father, give me Your eyes to see others as You see them.
Help me to demonstrate Your love with a smile or
a simple act of kindness each day. Amen.*

Prayer Changes Things

*One day Jesus told his disciples a story to show that
they should always pray and never give up.*
LUKE 18:1 NLT

Have you ever felt like you don't have enough energy to utter one
more word to anyone, let alone share your feelings with the Lord?
Or maybe you've been asking God for the same thing over and over
again, and you feel like He's either not listening or has decided not to
answer.

Jesus gives us a picture of how He wants us to pray in Luke
18. The persistent widow wears down the judge with her constant
request until he finally gives in. God wants us to come to Him with
everything. He has given us an open door to approach His throne with
confidence at all times (Hebrews 4:16).

If an uncaring judge finally responded to the widow's constant
pleas, how much more will the God who created us and loves us
respond to ours? No matter what you are bringing before the Lord,
don't give up! Keep talking to Him. The process will change your heart
to be more like His. So when you feel all prayed out, remember that
God is listening and working on your behalf.

*Heavenly Father, sometimes I feel like the persistent widow when I
come to You over and over again with the same request. I know You
hear my prayer, and I trust that You will do what is best for me. Help
me not to lose heart but to remember Your love and faithfulness.
Amen.*

Everlasting Light

In him was life, and that life was the light of all mankind. The light shines in the darkness, and the darkness has not overcome it.
JOHN 1:4–5 NIV

We all experience times of darkness in our lives. Depression may seep in through a crack of doubt, fear, or worry; and we spiral downward, focusing on the situation. It's not easy to lift our voices in anything but a moan and a plea for God's help. And He hears those cries; He wants to carry our burdens for us. He listens. It's we who should shift our gaze.

Focus on the fact that Jesus is the Light of the World who holds out wonderful hope for us. Set your prayer life to start with praise and adoration of the King of Kings. Lift your voice in song, or read out loud from the Word. The Light will eliminate the darkness every time. Keep your heart and mind set on Him as you walk through the day. Praise for every little thing; nothing is too small for God. Did you get a great parking spot? Thank Him. A raise at work? Thank Him. A terrible headache? Praise anyway. Concentrate on His goodness instead of your pain.

A grateful heart and constant praise will bring the Light into your day.

Dear Lord, how we love You. We trust in You this day to lead us on the right path lit with Your Light. Amen.

Fellowship

*And let us consider how we may spur one another on. . .
not giving up meeting together. . .but encouraging one another.*
HEBREWS 10:24–25 NIV

Before his conversion, Paul, then known as Saul, was a thug—a
mean-spirited man who hated Christians and wanted them killed.
Isn't it amazing that this same man became a great apostle who wrote
thirteen books of the New Testament?

The Bible says that immediately after his conversion, Paul spent
several days with Jesus' disciples. "At once" he began preaching
that Jesus was the Messiah. The Bible also says that Paul became
increasingly powerful, and he had followers. He traveled with other
Christians, and they encouraged one another in their belief and
commitment. Paul enjoyed being with other believers. When in prison,
he lamented that he couldn't be with them to share encouragement.
Paul understood the importance of fellowship.

Associating with other Christians is more than attending church
on Sundays. It is getting to know them on a personal level and
discovering what their faith has to offer in fellowship and learning.
Paul sought after people whose own gifts would help build his faith.
In Romans 1:11–12, he writes, "I long to see you so that I may impart
to you some spiritual gift to make you strong—that is, that you and I
may be mutually encouraged by each other's faith" (NIV).

Do you have friends who encourage your faith?

*Dear God, thank You for sweet fellowship with Christian friends.
Amen.*

My Strength

I love you, Lord, my strength.
PSALM 18:1 NIV

Ever feel like you want to crawl in a hole and pull the earth in around you? Most of us have felt that way at some point. Sometimes life overwhelms us, and we feel like we will drown at any moment.

At times like that, we often don't have the strength to even pray. We don't know what to say to God, and we don't have the energy to form the correct words or thoughts. That's when we need to keep it simple. "I love You, Lord," is all we need to say.

When we utter those three little words to God, we bend His ear to us. We bend His heart to us. When we whisper our love for Him, though we don't have strength to say another word, He shows up and becomes our strength. He wraps His mighty arms around us, pulls us into His lap of love and comfort, and pours His life and love into our spirits.

Truly, it is in those moments of weakness, when we have nothing else to offer God, that He is made strong in us. He longs for our love above all else. When we give it, as weak as we may feel, He becomes strength for us.

Dear Father, sometimes I feel weak, like I can't go on. But Lord, I love You, even then. I know in my weak moments, You are my strength.
Amen.

Praise While Waiting!

*God says, "Be still and know that I am God. I will be praised
in all the nations; I will be praised throughout the earth."*
PSALM 46:10 NCV

Jamie found herself in a transitional season. It seemed that *everything*
was up in the air. Rumors at work suggested changes were coming—
there was talk of layoffs and restructure for the organization. God was
doing some things in her family—suddenly her parents, sisters, and
even cousins were all returning to their home state after everyone
being scattered across the nation for more than a decade. On top
of that, her very best friend had been unavailable for most of the
summer dealing with her mother's health.

Her prayers were constant—asking God to reveal His purpose
and plan—but there were no specifics from Him. In her heart she
continued to hear the word *wait*! She hated to wait. She planned
everything. So she stayed busy doing what she knew to do and kept
asking God for more guidance. Jamie knew it was the season she
was in, and she had no choice but to embrace it. She determined in
her heart to praise Him for what He was about to do—while she was
waiting.

Are you in a season of waiting? God is working behind the scenes,
preparing His big reveal. Like Jamie, move into a season of praise
while waiting.

*God, help me to rest in You—and wait patiently
for Your timing of Your big reveal. Amen.*

God's Love Song

The LORD your God is with you, the Mighty Warrior who saves.
He will take great delight in you; in his love he will no longer
rebuke you, but will rejoice over you with singing.
ZEPHANIAH 3:17 NIV

Read Zephaniah 3:17, and you will find a verse packed with God's love. First, this verse reminds God's children that He is always with them. Wherever they go, whatever they do, in every situation, God watches over them with Fatherly love. Next, it says that God's love is not just ever-present but also all-powerful. When bad things happen, God's children needn't ask, "Where is God?" They can be confident that their Father is present with a mighty plan to save them. The verse continues on, conveying God's gentleness in love. He quiets His children. His love is like a soft, soothing lullaby sung by a mother to her child. It brings His children comfort and peace. The verse ends with God singing. Yes, God sings! The Bible says in Zephaniah 3:17 that God rejoices over His children with singing. Isn't that amazing? God takes such delight in His children that He cannot contain His love for them. His love bursts forth in joyous song.

From beginning to end, this little piece of scripture is God's love song to His children. You are His child. Read it often, and know that He loves you.

Dear God, thank You for loving me fully,
unconditionally, and always. Amen.

Pray through Loneliness

*The widow who is really in need and left all alone puts her hope in
God and continues night and day to pray and to ask God for help.*
1 TIMOTHY 5:5 NIV

Susan's loneliness ended when she married Frank. They had met
and married in their fifties. The couple had no children or siblings,
and their parents had all passed away. It was loneliness that brought
them together, but their strong love for each other soon filled the
emptiness that had been in their hearts. Then, sadly, after only three
years together, tragedy struck. Frank became ill with leukemia and died
several months later. Once more, Susan faced life on her own. But this
time she faced it differently.

When they began dating, Susan hadn't been a believer. It
was Frank who led her to the Lord, and together, throughout their
marriage, they relied on their heavenly Father for help. They turned
all of their hopes and problems over to God in prayer and trusted in
His wisdom. Following her husband's death, instead of becoming lost
in loneliness and grief, Susan turned to the One who would never
leave her, the One who would comfort her and lead her forward. She
turned to God to fill up her heart with His love.

Do you feel alone sometimes? Then, like Susan, give it to God in
prayer. He will lift you up and lead you on.

Come to me, Lord Jesus. Comfort me and give me hope. Amen.

His Steady Hand

*The LORD makes firm the steps of the one who delights in him;
though he may stumble, he will not fall, for the LORD
upholds him with his hand.*
PSALM 37:23–24 NIV

The wonderful thing about our mighty God is He knows our hearts. There are days when we succumb to responding or acting out in the flesh. But praise God, He loves us so much and is faithful even when we as human beings are unable to be. Just as a parent grasps a child's hand, He will take ours in His and help us along our pathway.

The Lord knows there are times when we will stumble. We may even backslide into the very activity that caused us to call on the Lord for salvation in the first place. But His Word assures us His love is eternal, and when we cry out to Him, He will hear.

Do not be discouraged with those stumbling blocks in your path, because the Lord is with you always. Scripture tells us we are in the palm of His hand. Hope is found in the Lord. He delights in us and wants the very best for us because of His perfect love.

*Lord God, the cross was necessary for sinners like me.
I thank You that You loved me enough to choose me,
and I accepted the free gift of salvation. Amen.*

Focused Prayer

*Pray in the Spirit at all times and on every occasion. Stay alert
and be persistent in your prayers for all believers everywhere.*
EPHESIANS 6:18 NLT

"Turn your eyes upon Jesus. Look full in His wonderful face. And
the things of earth will grow strangely dim in the light of glory and
grace." It is an old hymn that has been sung for years and years, but
its words still ring true today. The Bible warns us to stay alert and to
pray persistently. The key is to focus on Jesus even in the midst of
the storm. If the captain of a ship or the pilot of a plane loses focus in
the middle of a storm, it can be very dangerous for all involved. Our
job as believers is to trust the Lord with the outcome and to remain
deliberate and focused in our prayers.

The Bible does not say to pray when it is convenient or as a last
resort. It does not say to pray just in case prayer might work or to
add prayer to a list of other things we are trying. We are instructed in
Ephesians to pray at *all* times and on *every* occasion. When you pray,
pray in the Spirit. Pray for God's will to be done. Pray in the name of
Jesus. There is great power in focused prayer.

*Jesus, I set my eyes upon You, the Messiah,
my Savior, Redeemer, and Friend. Amen.*

Confidently Go

*In him and through faith in him we may approach
God with freedom and confidence.*
EPHESIANS 3:12 NIV

There was a town meeting being held by one of the state representatives in a few days. Sally had some true concerns that she wanted to voice, but thoughts like, *Who am I that this man in power would listen to me?* ran through her head. What if he refuted and discounted everything she said? She thought through her valid concerns and how she might convey her message with integrity. Her case had merit, and she knew others saw it, too. And when else would she be able to accomplish this? She wouldn't be able to take a day off to travel to the state capital for a meeting. Still, she wondered how her little voice could be heard.

She considered the power that her vote had granted this leader. He affected laws that directly impacted her life. Then Sally thought about her One, true, perfect Leader and smiled. It occurred to her how God invites us to approach Him with confidence. The King of Kings *wants* us to approach the *throne.* Furthermore, He is available anytime, anywhere, no travel or days off required.

Sally decided she would go to the town meeting and respectfully voice her concerns. But first she would pay a visit to the King of kings.

*God, thank You that we can come confidently to You at any time.
Amen.*

Discipline Equals Love

"The Lord disciplines the one he loves,
and he chastens everyone he accepts as his son."
HEBREWS 12:6 NIV

"Mom, it's not fair!" Delia yelled. "I hate you!" The teen stomped up the stairs, ran to her room, and slammed her door—hard.

Delia's mother, Faith, sighed. She knew she was doing the right thing by telling her daughter she couldn't attend an unsupervised party, but it wasn't easy to hear venomous words from the girl who once called her "Mommy."

As she prayed for Delia and herself, Faith felt God remind her that He often felt hated by the ones He birthed, too. The truth drove her to her knees. "Lord," Faith prayed quietly, "I'm sorry for the times I've thrown tantrums when You told me no. I believe You always have my best interests at heart."

Love takes many forms, and sometimes it looks like discipline. God disciplines His children in order to get them back on the right track or teach them that His plans are always better than the world's path.

Have you felt the Lord's discipline and taken it as rejection? Remember, He will never leave or forsake us—no matter how we act.

Heavenly Father, thank You for the times You discipline us in love.
Help us to submit to You out of reverence and fear,
instead of turning away from You. Amen.

Strength in our Weakness

He is your Father and Maker, who made you and formed you.
DEUTERONOMY 32:6 NCV

Marita suffers from an autoimmune disease. Some days she feels okay, but other days test her reserves. The disease is incurable, chronic, and maddening. Marita often finds herself unable to attend functions or church events because she is too worn out from her part-time job.

She's often begged for healing and continues to pray for a cure. Marita knows God is with her through her struggles, but it's hard for her not to feel frustrated and lonely. She has family who love her unconditionally, but they can't really understand what she goes through on a daily basis.

However, last year, Marita found a lifeline—an Internet-based Christian support group that provides a chat room, online articles, and daily devotionals for people with "invisible illnesses." Through networking with other people who deal with debilitating conditions, Marita has found friendship, support—and hope.

Each day when she logs onto the site, Marita hears scripture-based advice, stories, and music that encourage her to keep on keeping on. The site has been a true gift from God, and Marita is thankful.

How could you encourage those with chronic illness? Perhaps you could offer to run errands, babysit their children, or just listen. You might just become a lifeline for someone who feels desperate.

God, thank You for Your compassion and love, especially when I am weak. Help me trust in Your goodness, even when I feel terrible.
Amen.

The Word for Every Day

*As for God, his way is perfect; the word of the LORD is tried:
he is a buckler to all them that trust in him.*
2 SAMUEL 22:31 KJV

A few years ago, Jenna followed the advice of a mentor and began praying for God to give her one special word for the year. Two years ago, He impressed upon Jenna the word *refuge*, and it was perfect, because her family moved and experienced a lot of stress during the next year. It comforted her over those hectic and emotionally draining months to meditate on *refuge*.

Last December, God led her to ruminate on the word *delight* for the year. And what an interesting—and yes, delightful—few months it was. Over and over, He brought the word to her attention, sometimes in surprising places. Often, meditation on delight turned to prayer, as Jenna praised and thanked God for His provision and peace.

God's Word is such an incredible gift, one that goes hand in hand with prayer. It's amazing, really, that the Creator of the universe gave us the scriptures as His personal Word to us. When we're faithful to pick up the Word, He is faithful to use it to encourage us. Reading and praying through scripture is one of the keys to finding and keeping our sanity, peace, and joy.

*God, thank You for Your gifts of the holy scriptures and sweet
communion with You through prayer. Amen.*

A Way Out

*The temptations in your life are no different from what others
experience. And God is faithful. He will not allow the temptation
to be more than you can stand. When you are tempted,
he will show you a way out so that you can endure.*
1 CORINTHIANS 10:13 NLT

Is there a hang-up in your life that is hard to get over or get rid of?
Temptation comes in all shapes and sizes, so what might be tempting
to you isn't a problem for someone else. The opposite is also true.
The comforting thing is that everyone has been there. We all make
mistakes, and whatever is tempting you, you can bet that it has also
tripped up many others, too.

It's so easy to get discouraged when we mess up. Especially
when we mess up in the same area over and over again. Christopher
Columbus said this: "I am a most noteworthy sinner, but I have
cried out to the Lord for grace and mercy, and they have covered me
completely. I have found the sweetest consolation since I made it my
whole purpose to enjoy His marvelous presence."

Here's the encouraging thing: whenever you face temptation, God
promises to provide a way out. Look for it! In every moment that you
are tempted, look for it! Pay attention to the interruptions that occur
during temptation and grasp hold of them. They may just be "divine
appointments" there to lead the way out!

*Dear Jesus, I cry out for grace and mercy and praise You
that Your love has covered my sin completely. Help me
find the way out in every temptation. Amen.*

The Winning Team

If God is for us, who can be against us?
ROMANS 8:31 NIV

We always *know* God is for us, but it doesn't always *feel* that way. Even though we know the end of the story, even though we know we are on the winning team, sometimes it feels like we're losing battle after battle.

It can feel like cancer is winning. Or the chemo or radiation that goes along with cancer feels like it's whipping us. Sometimes our relationships are difficult, and we feel like we're on the losing team.

We can make sure God really is on our team, in the little battles, when we conduct ourselves in a way that honors Him. If we've been in the wrong, we can't claim that God is on our side in that battle. But when we love God with all our hearts, when we serve Him and serve others, when we keep our promises and make the people around us feel loved and valued and cherished, we can know God is pleased. We can know that He will stand behind us, defend us, and support us.

And ultimately, no matter how many battles we may feel like we're losing, if we stand with God, we will stand victorious. The other team may score a few points here and there. But when we're on God's team, we know we're the winners.

Dear Father, thank You for being on my team. Help me to live in a way that represents Your team well. Amen.

Only Love Remains

Hatred stirreth up strifes: but love covereth all sins.
Proverbs 10:12 kjv

Marla had a beautiful childhood. She grew up in a home of consistent discipline and love, but she always felt like something was missing. She was captivated by the wonderful stories people shared of how bad their lives were—and how God miraculously intervened. She began to believe she didn't have a story—a *good* story—and she needed to get one.

At nineteen years old, she stepped away from those who loved her, and the enemy opened his mouth and swallowed her up. Years later she found herself using drugs, selling drugs, homeless or with a gang at times, and eventually in jail for possession. She had a story now—what would her parents say? Could God really love her again?

Peter and Greta visited their daughter in jail and discovered she was ready to turn her life around. Marla confessed her sins to God and to her parents, served her time in jail, and came home. She thought it would be different—that her parents would resent her for what she'd done—but consistently they loved her. They showed her the true picture of God's forgiveness. They allowed the past to be the past—and only love remained.

Father, I know Your love is real. There is nothing I can do to make You stop loving me. Help me to show Your love to others as well. Amen.

I Give Up

*God so loved the world that he gave his one and only Son, that
whoever believes in him shall not perish but have eternal life.*
JOHN 3:16 NIV

God encourages us to surrender to Him. How does God expect us
to do that? *Merriam-Webster* defines *surrender* as "to give (oneself)
over to something (as an influence)." God has given us freewill, so the
choice becomes ours: to surrender or maintain total control.

When we make the decision to surrender, we give ourselves over
to God and allow His authority in our lives. We place our hope in the
God who runs the universe. Oswald Chambers said, "The choice is
either to say, 'I will not surrender,' or to surrender, breaking the hard
shell of individuality, which allows the spiritual life to emerge."

Isn't that an amazing thought? Our Creator God cares enough
about us to delve into our everyday lives and help us. Through the
Holy Spirit within, God's gentle hand of direction will sustain each of
us, enabling us to grow closer to our Father. The closer we grow, the
more like Him we desire to be. Then His influence spreads through us
to others. When we surrender, He is able to use our lives and enrich
others. What a powerful message: Give up and give more!

*Lord, thank You for loving us despite our frailties.
What an encouragement to me today. Amen.*

A Mother's Love

Above all, love each other deeply,
because love covers over a multitude of sins.
1 PETER 4:8 NIV

As any new mother will attest, the first few nights at home with a newborn can be scary. A new little person, whose only communication is a cry when wet, hungry, or uncomfortable, can keep a sleep-deprived mom wondering if she will ever survive the first six months.

"Mom, can you come over?" Elizabeth was tired, tearful, and frantic about her two-day-old daughter. "I've burped, diapered, and rocked her, and she won't stop fussing."

"I'll be right there." Diane smiled as she remembered her first few nights with a new baby. Her own mom wasn't available to help, as she lived several hours away.

Once in Grandma's arms, the baby began to settle down. The older woman's familiarity with infants was evidenced in the secure way she held her granddaughter. She put the calmed baby back in her daughter's arms.

"You won't break her. That's right; hold her with confidence. Let her know that you love her and she can always trust you for that. A mother's love is deep and endless."

Heavenly Father, we can't be a perfect parent, but You are.
Please teach us how to love our families with a love that comes
from You, so that it covers our many imperfections. Continue
to bless us and our homes. In Christ's name, amen.

Love Anyway

*"The LORD, the LORD, the compassionate and gracious God,
slow to anger, abounding in love and faithfulness."*
EXODUS 34:6 NIV

Sheila was running errands on a Saturday to get caught up after a long workweek. At the paint store, she was waiting for her color match when a woman walked in abruptly and stood at the counter, nearly pushing Sheila aside. The woman proceeded to be unclear with her request and then quite arrogant when not understood by the knowledgeable associate. When the associate walked away, the woman tried to complain to Sheila; but Sheila just smiled kindly at her.

At the gas station, a rude man spoke harshly to his wife. Sheila later passed this couple several times in the aisles at the grocery store and was as pleasant as she could muster.

At the pharmacy, several people crowded the aisles and acted as if those trying to walk through needed lessons in manners. It was quite the opposite.

Sheila thought how interesting it was to experience so many situations that afternoon. She could truly thank God for giving her an attitude of kindness that could only come from Him.

*Father God, thank You for the way You love us and enable us
to love others who are just as undeserving as we are. Amen.*

Open the Book

For everything that was written in the past was written to teach us, so that through the endurance taught in the Scriptures and the encouragement they provide we might have hope.
ROMANS 15:4 NIV

"Out with the old and in with the new!" is unfortunately some Christians' philosophy about the Bible. Yet the Old Testament scriptures are vital to every believer. We cannot understand the power of the New Testament until we embrace the teachings, wisdom, and moral laws of God revealed in the Old Testament. After all, the Old Testament points directly to the coming of the Messiah, Jesus, and our salvation.

The apostle Paul reminds us that everything in the Bible was written with purpose—to teach us that through our trials and the encouragement of God's Word we might have hope.

Life is tough, after all. We get discouraged and, at times, disheartened to the point of such despair it's hard to recover. Yet the Word of God ignites the power of a positive, godly fire within.

Reading *all* of God's Word is paramount. It is the source of hope, peace, encouragement, salvation, and so much more. It moves people to take action while diminishing depression and discouragement. As the writer of Hebrews put it, "For the word of God is alive and active. Sharper than any double-edged sword. . ." (Hebrews 4:12).

Need some encouragement? Open the Book.

Lord, help me read Your Word consistently to empower me with the hope and encouragement I need. Amen.

Encouraging Words

*Let no foul or polluting language, nor evil word nor unwholesome or
worthless talk [ever] come out of your mouth, but only such [speech]
as is good and beneficial to the spiritual progress of others, as is
fitting to the need and the occasion, that it may be a blessing
and give grace (God's favor) to those who hear it.*
EPHESIANS 4:29 AMP

A talented puppeteer performs at elementary school campuses. His
presentation is meant to decrease bullying. His simple message is
taught through rainbow-haired puppets with silly voices. "Build others
up! Don't tear others down!" It sounds easy, but is it?

Do you find yourself gossiping about coworkers or authority
figures? This is, as the apostle Paul calls it in Ephesians, "worthless
talk." It does nothing to build up but only to tear down. Imagine a
young child playing with blocks. Such joy as the tower grows, block
by block, taller and taller. But then, with a wrong placement, the
whole thing comes crashing down! Are you a builder or a destroyer?
Do your words add to others' welfare or are they destructive of it? As
believers, our conversation should be wholesome and encouraging.
Pray that God will remind you of this at the right moments so that you
will not carelessly corrupt instead of intentionally encouraging.

*Heavenly Father, use me to encourage and to build up. Set a guard
over my lips that I might not use my words to tear others down.
Amen.*

Love Unveils Understanding

*My goal is that they may be encouraged in heart and united in love, so
that they may have the full riches of complete understanding, in order
that they may know the mystery of God, namely, Christ.*
COLOSSIANS 2:2 NIV

Paul had a specific purpose in writing this letter to the Colossian
church. Threatening the spiritual future of the church, a dangerous
false teaching undermined the church's faith in Christ. From his
Roman prison cell, Paul quickly responded.

He appealed to the church for a life grounded in the complete
knowledge and sufficiency of Christ as the only way to advance their
Christian walk. His goal? To not only combat the false teaching but
to underscore Jesus' true nature and the need to become complete in
Him as well.

Paul attempted to encourage believers to unite in God's love.
Why? So that they might experience the *full* riches of *complete*
understanding to know the mystery of the Gospel of Christ and pass
that message on to others.

The Christian walk is a lifelong journey. From "glory to glory"
Christ changes us daily as we read His Word, pray, and know Him
better. In doing so, we practice His teachings. When we are "united in
love" we gain full understanding of Christ and what He desires for our
lives.

*Lord, I often fail to understand what knowing You really means.
Give me encouragement and a heart of love so that I might
spread that understanding to others. Amen.*

Listen Well

*We have heard it with our ears, O God; our ancestors have
told us what you did in their days, in days long ago.*
PSALM 44:1 NIV

It was a busy morning with the family heading off in different
directions. Rachel had a half day of work to get in. On her way out the
door, she said good-bye to her college-age son, who would be back
from class in a few hours—and then the two of them would go to get
his wisdom teeth extracted.

In the garage she reminded her other son, Jon, who was heading
out to work, that David was getting his teeth pulled. "Remember,
David, one o'clock," she said.

Jon paused with a look of confusion. "David won. . .a clock?"

Rachel burst into laughter, and Jon, too, when he figured out the
misunderstanding.

Rachel smiled over that throughout the morning and thought
how easy it was to hear something wrong. She realized afresh how
important it is to listen well. She also gained a fresh appreciation
for God's written Word that is clear and so rich with the powerful
recorded story of God.

*Lord God, thank You for Your Word that helps us know You better
with each recorded passage. Enable us, Lord, by the power of Your
Holy Spirit, to see You living today in the stories of our lives. Amen.*

Triumphant Trust

*If anyone, then, knows the good they ought to do
and doesn't do it, it is sin for them.*
JAMES 4:17 NIV

Jennifer had been with the company for almost ten years. She had worked loyally and conscientiously under several different managers. As a single parent, she was grateful for her job; although at times, providing for herself and her small family on her salary was challenging.

One day she was called into the new branch manager's office.

"Jennifer, I know you don't make a lot of money here. How much is the repair on your car?"

"The mechanic said the estimate for a blown engine is around eight hundred dollars."

"Why don't you take it to where the company takes its vehicles? We can look the other way when the bill comes. Or we can divert some cash from the sale of scrap materials. No one will ever be the wiser."

Jennifer told her boss that she would not accept his offer, even though she was afraid that he might now label her as a difficult employee. She believed that she needed to do the right thing, and God would take care of providing for her.

Thank You, Father, for being my provider in all things. Even when I am afraid or tempted, I want to trust in You for everything. Help me keep my eyes on You and not my circumstances. I love You, Lord.
Amen.

The Right Focus

*Turning your ear to wisdom and applying your heart to
understanding—indeed, if you call out for insight and cry aloud
for understanding, and if you look for it as for silver and search
for it as for hidden treasure, then you will understand the
fear of the LORD and find the knowledge of God.*
PROVERBS 2:2–5 NIV

If you've ever lost something—your keys, your glasses, or an
important document—you've no doubt searched everywhere.
Sometimes when you finally find it, you realize that, in your haste, you
simply overlooked the very thing you were frantically searching for.

It's all about focus! Even when you're looking in the right
direction, you can still miss something because your focus is slightly
off. This can be the challenge in our relationship with God. We can ask
God a question and be really intent in getting the answer, only to find
that His response to us was there all along—just not the answer we
expected or wanted.

Frustration and stress can keep us from clearly seeing the things
that God puts before us. Time spent in prayer and meditation on
God's Word can often wash away the dirt and grime of the day-to-
day and provide a clear picture of God's intentions for our lives. Step
outside the pressure and into His presence, and get the right focus for
whatever you're facing today.

Lord, help me to avoid distractions and keep my eyes on You. Amen.

His Hand on Everything

"For I know the plans I have for you," declares the LORD, "plans to prosper you and not to harm you, plans to give you hope and a future."
JEREMIAH 29:11 NIV

One Saturday, Sara had been talking to her dear friend Mara, who was still recovering from a broken engagement a few months before her wedding. The split had halted Mara's professional life and severed many friendships. Sara's life was affected, too. As she supported Mara, there were people whom she just wouldn't or shouldn't see regularly.

That night for dinner, Sara and her husband tried out a new restaurant in town and ran into some of those lost friends. It was bittersweet to see them. Sara hugged them tightly and shared heartfelt conversation in the brief time they had. That was the sweet part.

When they parted, Sara broke down and cried. The loss from one broken relationship ran so deep, and the fallout from it saddened her immensely.

A wise friend reminded Sara the next day, "God has His hand on all of it. That doesn't take the pain away, but He knew what was best for Mara."

God has His hand on all of it.

Lord, thank You for being the Sovereign God we can trust, even when things are sad and we don't like it. Thank You for Your promise of hope and a future. Amen.

Prayer: The Stress Reliever

*Do not be anxious about anything, but in every situation, by prayer
and petition, with thanksgiving, present your requests to God.*
PHILIPPIANS 4:6 NIV

Kim was overwhelmed. She started a new job, moved into a new
house, and endeavored to prepare her three kids to go back to school.
Plus, that morning she backed out of the garage for work and caught
the side-view mirror on the garage door. It pulled off, dangling by its
wires. Frantically, she duct-taped the mirror together and raced to her
new job in a panic. Anxiety and stress hit with brute force.

After an exhausting day, she cooked a quick dinner, unpacked a
few boxes, and headed to the store to shop for school supplies. "Lord,
I can't do all of this without You," she whispered in desperation. Then
scripture silenced her harried thoughts: "Do not be anxious about
anything. . .present your requests to God."

Kim realized that because she failed to seek God with the smaller
requests, her needs morphed into giant bouts of stress. "In every
situation" the scriptures instruct us to pray. No problem or concern is
too big or too little for God. And although our circumstances may not
change, God changes us to handle life's frustrations with grace and
peace.

*Father, forgive me for thinking that I can do things on my own.
Only You can relieve my anxiety and prepare me for each day
and whatever that day brings. Thank You for hearing and
answering even my smallest requests. Amen.*

Full Redemption and Love

*Israel, put your hope in the LORD, for with the LORD
is unfailing love and with him is full redemption.*
PSALM 130:7 NIV

Jesus offers each of us full redemption: complete freedom from sin because of His great love for us. God doesn't want us to carry around our list of sins, being burdened by our past mistakes. He wants us to have a clear conscience, a joy-filled life!

The Bible tells us at that God removes our sins as far as the east is from the west (Psalm 103:12) and that He remembers our sin no more (Isaiah 43:25, Hebrews 8:12). It's so important to confess your sins to the Lord as soon as you feel convicted and then turn from them and move in a right direction. There is no reason to hang your head in shame over sins of the past.

Turning from sin is tough. Especially when it has become a bad habit. Find an accountability partner to pray for you and check in with you about your struggles, but don't allow the devil to speak lies into your life. You have full redemption through Jesus Christ!

Dear Jesus, I confess my sin to You. Thank You for blotting out each mistake and not holding anything against me. Help me to make right choices through the power of Your Spirit inside me. Amen.

Pass It On!

*After the usual readings from the books of Moses and the prophets,
those in charge of the service sent them this message: "Brothers, if you
have any word of encouragement for the people, come and give it."*
ACTS 13:15 NLT

Who doesn't need encouragement? After the reading in the temple,
the rulers asked Paul and his companions if they had a word of
encouragement to share. Paul immediately stood up and proclaimed
how the fulfillment of God's promise came through Jesus; and
whoever believed—whether Jew or Gentile—would receive
forgiveness and salvation (Acts 13:16–41).

The scriptures state that as Paul and Barnabas left the synagogue,
the people invited them to speak again the following Sabbath. And as
a result of Paul's testimony, many devout Jews came to Christ. Not
only that, on the next Sabbath, nearly the entire town—Jews and
Gentiles alike—gathered to hear God's Word (Acts 13:42–44).

Encouragement brings hope. Have you ever received a word
from someone that instantly lifted your spirit? Did you receive a bit
of good news or something that diminished your negative outlook?
Perhaps a particular conversation helped to bring your problems into
perspective. Paul passed on encouragement and many benefited. So
the next time you're encouraged, pass it on! You may never know how
your words or actions benefited someone else.

*Lord, thank You for the wellspring of encouragement
through Your Holy Word. Amen.*

Hang in There

*Let perseverance finish its work so that you may
be mature and complete, not lacking anything.*
JAMES 1:4 NIV

Perseverance can't be rushed. The only way to develop perseverance is to endure pressure, over a long period of time. A weight lifter must gradually add more weight if he wants to build up his muscles. A runner must run farther and farther, pushing past what is comfortable. If these athletes want to grow and improve, they must persevere through pressure, over time.

The same is true for our faith. If we want to grow as Christians, we have to endure pressure. God allows difficult things into our lives to help build our strength and endurance. Just as the athlete who gives up at the first sign of hardship will never improve at her sport, the Christian who abandons her faith during times of distress will never reach maturity.

No one ever said the Christian life was an easy one. In fact, Christ told us we'd endure hardships of many kinds. But He also said not to get discouraged. When we stick it out and follow Him no matter what, we will become mature and complete, perfectly fulfilling God's plan for our lives.

Dear Father, help me to persevere when life gets hard. Help me cling to You and do things Your way, even when it feels like I can't go on. I trust that You won't give me more than I can handle and You're working to make me mature. Amen.

Seek God

"I love all who love me. Those who search will surely find me."
PROVERBS 8:17 NLT

Did you ever play hide-and-seek as a child? Sometimes it was easy to find your sibling or friend. A foot sticking out from behind the couch or chair was a dead giveaway! Other times, a playmate may have selected a better hiding place. He was harder to find. You searched high and low. You looked behind doors and beneath beds. You lifted quilts and moved aside piles of pillows. But you didn't give up. Not until you found him!

Scripture tells us that God loves those who love Him and that if we search for Him, we will surely find Him. One translation of the Bible says it this way: "Those who seek me early and diligently shall find me" (AMP).

Seek God in all things and in all ways. Search for Him in each moment of every day you are blessed to walk on this earth. He is found easily in His creation and in His Word. He is with you. Just look for Him. He wants to be found!

Father in heaven, thank You for Your unfailing love for me. Help me to search for You diligently. I know that when I seek, I will find You. Amen.

Teach Me Your Paths

Show me your ways, LORD, teach me your paths.
Guide me in your truth and teach me, for you are God my Savior,
and my hope is in you all day long.
PSALM 25:4–5 NIV

This psalm is a great prayer to memorize and keep close in your mind each day. The Bible tells us that God's Word is a lamp for our feet (Psalm 119:105). As we read, study, and hide God's Word in our hearts, the Holy Spirit will bring those Words to mind to guide us and show us the way that God wants us to go. If you want to hear God's voice and know His will for your life, get into His Word.

Hebrews 4:12 tells us that the scriptures are living and active. Just think about that for a moment. God's Word is alive! As busy women, it can be difficult to find the time to open the Bible and meditate on the message—but it's *necessary* if you want God to teach you His path for your life.

Instead of giving up on finding time for Bible reading, get creative. Download a free Bible application on your phone. Have a daily scripture reading and devotion e-mailed to you from heartlight. org. Jot down a few verses on a note card to memorize. There are many ways to get in the Word of God and be trained by it. Start today!

Lord, I believe Your Word is living and active.
I want to know Your will for my life. Help me get in Your
Word more and understand Your plan for me. Amen.

True Love

*Love is patient, love is kind. It does not envy, it does not boast, it is
not proud. It does not dishonor others, it is not self-seeking, it is not
easily angered, it keeps no record of wrongs. Love does not delight
in evil but rejoices with the truth. It always protects, always trusts,
always hopes, always perseveres. Love never fails.*
1 CORINTHIANS 13:4–8 NIV

Imagine the daunting task of accurately defining *love*. Most
dictionaries rely on synonymous phrases: Love is "a strong affection,"
"a warm attachment," "a benevolent concern for others." Dictionaries
define love through the language of emotion.

The apostle Paul understood that love is more than a feeling.
When he sat down to write his famous description of love in 1
Corinthians 13:4–8, instead of defining the word *love*, he explained
what love is—love is the demonstration of selfless acts toward others.

Paul explained that true love is displayed through the unselfish
behaviors of patience, kindness, humility, forgiveness, protection,
trust, hopefulness, and perseverance. This is the kind of love that
Jesus showed toward others and that God shows toward us every day.
God's kind of love never fails.

The words *I love you* slip easily from the lips and drift away.
The passionate feeling of love sometimes grows cold. But God's love
doesn't change. It is always pure, unconditional, and forever.

*Heavenly Father, remind me of Paul's words today. Help me to love
others not only through my words but also through my actions. Amen.*

Prayer and the Word Unlock the Door

I pray that your hearts will be flooded with light so that you can understand the confident hope he has given to those he called—his holy people who are his rich and glorious inheritance.
EPHESIANS 1:18 NLT

Math is a language all its own. Unfortunately, many students struggle to learn that language. Sometimes they never understand it completely but retain just enough of the language to make it through required courses. In many cases it requires another person who speaks "math" to help struggling students unlock the door to the language barrier.

Your spiritual life is also a different language. God's ways are not the ways of this world. Often His ways of doing things are similar to learning a new language. Prayer can unlock the door to understanding God's Word and His design for your life. As you spend time with God in prayer asking for understanding of His Word, His truth will speak to you in a brand-new way. The Holy Spirit will help you unlock the secrets of His purpose and plan for your life.

Discovering His purpose for your life can be exciting, if you're willing to open the door to a new adventure with Him.

Heavenly Father, thank You for the Bible. Help me to read it with understanding and come to know You in a whole new way. Amen.

Keeping Quiet

Hatred stirs up conflict, but love covers over all wrongs.
PROVERBS 10:12 NIV

Let's face it. We all enjoy a juicy bit of gossip now and then. As wrong as that seems, most of us are guilty of stirring the pot, at one time or another. It's not the worst thing we can do, right?

But God's Word tells us that gossip is more indicative of hatred than love. Words can do more damage than any amount of physical harm. Gossip hurts. It tears down and wounds our spirits. It causes deep pain, which can take years to heal. And sometimes its wounds never heal, this side of eternity.

Love always protects, always heals, always builds up. Sometimes, it's necessary to reveal hurtful information. But more often, we can just let things go and protect those around us from hurtful comments. We can keep our mouths shut, quit stirring the pot, and let conflicts die before they begin. Or at least, we can choose not to contribute to the conflict.

Hatred fans the flames of controversy and dissension without concern for who is hurt. Love, on the other hand, covers over wrongs. When love is exercised, conflict can be smothered before the damage gets out of control.

Dear Father, I want to build others up, not tear them down. Forgive me for stirring up conflict. Help me to show wisdom and love by refusing to contribute to gossip, controversy, and dissension. Amen.

Absolutely Nothing

For I am convinced that neither death nor life, neither angels nor demons, neither the present nor the future, nor any powers, neither height nor depth, nor anything else in all creation, will be able to separate us from the love of God that is in Christ Jesus our Lord.
ROMANS 8:38–39 NIV

Sometimes, when our circumstances spiral downward and we feel like we're living a nightmare, we wonder where God went. His love, which is supposed to be never-ending, seems out of reach. We pray, but our words seem to bounce off the ceiling and fall flat on the floor.

But it doesn't matter how we feel. God promised that nothing can separate us from His overwhelming, magnificent, powerful love. And though our circumstances may numb our sensors, making it seem like His love is absent, we can fall back on faith in God's promises. His love is there, enveloping us, whether we feel it or not. Nothing in this world can keep His love from us. Absolutely nothing.

Cancer may destroy our flesh, but it won't destroy God's love. Bills may deplete our finances, but they can't deplete His love. Relationships may break our hearts, but they will never break His love. We don't have to face any of life's difficulties alone, for our Creator loves us. He will hold our hands through it all. And when we are too weak to face another day, His love will carry us.

Dear Father, help me to rest in Your constant, steadfast love. Amen.

He Collects Them

The prayers of all God's people, on the golden altar
in front of the throne.
REVELATION 8:3 NIV

Suzy thought how impossible it seemed to count prayers. There were a lot of answered ones that she could recall and that really bolstered her faith. There were many more unanswered, which challenged her faith but kept her relying on God. In all, she knew she had forgotten probably thousands of prayers that she had uttered to God over the years—answered or not.

There were childhood prayers about fears, squabbles, and Christmas gifts. There were teenage prayers over boys, girlfriend drama, and school. There were young adult prayers over pregnant friends, relationships, and career decisions. As an over-thirty adult, there were prayers about abused friends, broken marriages, and ailing churches.

It was astounding to Suzy to think about how God heard every single prayer she ever said or thought. More astounding is that He will never forget a single one, not in all of forever.

And the way He answers those prayers has changed what forever looks like.

Father God, remind us afresh of the power of prayer.
It's so important—our communication with You—that You
will remember every prayer for eternity. Amen.

Love without Limits

*Your love, Lord, reaches to the heavens,
your faithfulness to the skies.*
PSALM 36:5 NIV

God's love and faithfulness have no bounds. They reach to the heavens. They stretch to the skies and beyond. This is hard for us to understand. As humans, even our very best attempts at love and faithfulness are limited. God's love is limitless. When God created you, knit you together in your mother's womb, and brought you into this world, He loved you. He loves you just as much today as He did when you were an innocent babe. He is incapable of loving you any less or any more than He already does. His love is not based on what you do or don't do. It is not here today and gone tomorrow due to any mistake or failure in your life. He is faithful even when we are faithless. If it seems that you are not close to God as you once were, He is not the one who moved. Draw close to your heavenly Father. You will find that He is there, faithful and true, ready to receive you back unto Himself. Thank the Lord today for an unfailing, unfathomable sort of love. What a blessing is the love of our faithful God!

Thank you, God, for loving me with a love that reaches to the heavens. You are faithful even when I am not. I love You, Lord. Amen.

Pray for His Return

*The end of all things is near. Therefore be alert
and of sober mind so that you may pray.*
1 PETER 4:7 NIV

World peace is an ever-present concern and likely one that God's people take to Him in prayer. It seems overwhelming to pray for something that appears impossible, but when Christians pray for peace, they pray knowing that Jesus will fulfill His promise of coming back. How long will it take for Him to return? No human knows. In the meantime, Christians persistently pray for His return and try to live peacefully in a chaotic world.

Around A.D. 600, Jerusalem fell to the Babylonians. The Jews were exiled to Babylonia and held captive for seventy years. God told the prophet Jeremiah to tell His people to settle there and live normally. He said they should seek peace in the place in which they lived until He came back to get them (Jeremiah 29:4–7).

Today's Christians are similar to those Jews. They live normally in an evil world seeking peace on earth while holding on to the promise of Jesus' return.

Paul wrote, "Brothers and sisters, whatever is true, whatever is noble, whatever is right, whatever is pure, whatever is lovely, whatever is admirable. . .think about such things. . . . And the God of peace will be with you" (Philippians 4:8–9 NIV).

May God's peace be with you today and every day until Jesus comes.

*Lord, may Your kingdom come and the earth be filled with Your glory.
Amen.*

Falling Out of Love

And so we know and rely on the love God has for us. God is love.
Whoever lives in love lives in God, and God in them.
1 JOHN 4:16 NIV

"Mom," Zola said, "Ken and I are getting a divorce."

Her mother sat silently at the kitchen table letting the words slowly sink in. Divorce was against everything she believed in. "Why?" she asked.

"No *one* reason," Zola answered. "We just fell out of love."

It happens often—life gets in the way, hearts fall out of love. Human love fails, and people get divorced.

In Malachi 2:16, God says that He hates divorce. He compares it to violence. Those are strong words. But does that mean that God hates divorced people? No. God loves them.

Human relationships are vastly different from God's relationship with humans. Unlike divorce, the God-human relationship cannot fail. God never falls out of love with His people. He can't. He loves not because He feels love but because He *is* Love.

When couples grow apart, they should be encouraged to work through their difficulties and try to salvage their marriage. But when all else fails, God does not. He loves them through their brokenheartedness and helps them to move on: "For I know the plans I have for you," declares the LORD, "plans to prosper you and not to harm you, plans to give you hope and a future" (Jeremiah 29:11 NIV).

Dear God, when human love fails me,
remind me that Yours will not. Amen.

Pray Regularly

*Evening, and morning, and at noon, will I pray,
and cry aloud: and he shall hear my voice.*
PSALM 55:17 KJV

Jenn and her mom had a close relationship. Whenever something exciting happened, they e-mailed or called each other immediately. Throughout the day, they often communicated by texting on their cell phones. If Jenn was having a hard day at work or her mom was facing a medical test, they would encourage each other.

God wants our prayer life to be like Jenn and her mother's relationship. He wants us to call upon Him morning, noon, and night—and many times in between. It may seem like your heavenly Father is far away, but in reality, He is just a prayer away at any given time. He is always eager to help you when you feel your strength is failing. He loves to rejoice over you in your victories, and He will provide a calm in the midst of the storm when you need to be comforted.

Before you run to someone else, run to God. He is your Creator, Redeemer, and Friend. He knows you better than anyone else, and He is never too busy to hear your prayers.

Lord, before I turn to family and friends, remind me to share my victories and burdens with You. Make prayer as natural as breathing for me, I ask in Jesus' name. Amen.

He Won't Let You Down

*I tell you that Christ has become a servant of the Jews
on behalf of God's truth, so that the promises made
to the patriarchs might be confirmed.*
ROMANS 15:8 NIV

Everyone has been hurt at one time or another by a broken promise. When that happens, it is best to forgive and go on. People are just people. They mess up. But there is One who will never break His promises to us—our heavenly Father. We can safely place our hope in Him.

Hebrews chapter 11 lists biblical characters who placed their trust and hope in God and weren't let down. Do you think Noah was excited about building an ark? Surely Sarah and Abraham hadn't planned on parenting at their ages. Daniel faced the lion's den knowing his God would care for him. We can find encouragement from their examples, knowing that their faith in the God who'd come through for them time and again wasn't misplaced. They did not grow weary and lose heart. They knew He was always faithful.

Today we choose to place our hope in God's promises. We won't be discouraged by time—God's timing is always perfect. We won't be discouraged by circumstances—God can change everything in a heartbeat. We will keep our hearts in God's hand. For we know He is faithful.

*Lord, I choose this day to place my trust in You,
for I know You're the one, true constant. Amen.*

For Freedom

He is so rich in kindness and grace that he purchased our freedom
with the blood of his Son and forgave our sins.
EPHESIANS 1:7 NLT

Freedom always comes with a price. For our US troops, they know
it could be their lives, and they willingly lay them down for their
country. Their sacrifices always include the price of leaving behind
their loved ones for many months or even a year.

In Danny's case it meant leaving his new bride, just days after
their wedding, to be deployed to Afghanistan. The heartache he felt
from missing her seemed nearly unbearable at times. Yet greater was
his sense of duty to his country and the freedom he defended for us all.

That freedom includes the right for citizens to say hurtful things
against military personnel, which happened on occasion to Danny.
But he knew the comments were based on misunderstandings, and he
absolutely knew he was doing the right thing. He responded to them
with graciousness.

Willing to lay his life down. Responding to critics with love.
Offering freedom at the cost of rejection. Seems like Danny is in pretty
good company. Christ did those very things for us, too.

Lord Jesus, thank You for the many Americans who sacrifice for our
freedom, reflecting in many ways Your much greater sacrifice. Amen.

The Perfect Audience

Listen to my words, LORD, consider my lament.
Hear my cry for help, my King and my God, for to you I pray.
In the morning, LORD, you hear my voice; in the morning
I lay my requests before you and wait expectantly.
PSALM 51:1–3 NIV

Greta felt the tug of a small hand on her pant leg.

"Mommy," her toddler, Justin, cried, trying to get her attention.

Her hands were full, putting together peanut butter and jelly sandwiches.

Her oldest daughter gave a shout from the living room, "Mom, the last good strap on my backpack just busted!"

If only I could give each child my undivided attention, she thought. Half an hour later she shut the door behind her school-age children. "Mommy," Justin called again, "you're not a very good listener." He was right. She leaned down to him. "I'm ready to listen, now," she said.

Sometimes it's hard to be the perfect audience for everyone who needs our attention. Thankfully God is never too busy. He is the perfect audience. He may not reply in your time frame, but He promises to be there every time.

God, thank You for always being there when I need You. You are
never too busy to hear me. You have the answers I need for my life.
Help me to give You my full attention when You answer.

Bringing Us to Completion

*Being confident of this, that he who began a good work in you
will carry it on to completion until the day of Christ Jesus.*
PHILIPPIANS 1:6 NIV

Remember the old saying, "If at first you don't succeed, try, try
again"? That's an encouraging statement. But it doesn't tell us how
many times we should try. It doesn't tell us when we should throw in
the towel and give up.

While there may be an appropriate time to give up on a certain
skill or project, we should never give up on people. We should
continue to hope, continue to pray, continue to love them. After all,
that's what God does for us.

No matter how many times we fail, no matter how many times
we mess up, we know God hasn't written us off. He's still working on
us. He still loves us. He knows our potential, because He created us,
and He won't stop moving us forward until His plan is completed.

Those of us who have been adopted into God's family through
believing in His Son, Jesus Christ, can be confident that God won't
give up on us. No matter how messed up our lives may seem, He will
continue working in us until His plan is fulfilled, and we stand before
Him, perfect and complete.

*Dear Father, thank You for not giving up on me. Help me to cooperate
with Your process of fulfilling Your purpose in me. Amen.*

My Child

After this manner therefore pray ye:
Our Father which art in heaven. . .
MATTHEW 6:9 KJV

The famous theologian Charles Spurgeon said, "[The Lord's] prayer begins where all true prayer must commence, with the spirit of adoption, 'Our Father.' There is no acceptable prayer until we can say, 'I will arise, and go unto my Father.'"

What a beautiful word picture this paints: a child in supplication before his heavenly Father. Not a stranger before an unknown god but a child of the King. Yet it takes faith to receive and believe that picture. Our lives on this earth burden us with negative thought patterns, ripping us from the arms of Jesus into self-condemnation and guilt. To absolve ourselves from this recurring problem seems impossible. "No one else has ___." We can fill in the blank with feelings of unworthiness and doubt.

Know this: The enemy loves to divide and destroy by isolating us and making us feel rejected. What a liar he is. We are loved with a great love by the Creator and must allow that thought to permeate our souls. God loves us so much He sent His Son to teach a pattern of prayer. And that pattern begins with the words that give us heart-knowledge: We are His children.

Dear heavenly Father, teach us to accept Your grace and mercy
and understand who You really are in our lives. Amen.

Hope in Hopeless Times

Let us hold unswervingly to the hope we profess,
for he who promised is faithful.
HEBREWS 10:23 NIV

The news on television each morning is filled with reports of the world gone awry. The newspaper requires a search and rescue to find clippings of good news. Far too many friends are dying, diagnosed to die, or are divorcing. Kids in the neighborhood are left alone to care for themselves and resort, all too often, to illegal activities.

In a world deeply steeped with sin, we can look at it two ways: We can feel hopeless to make a difference and do nothing, feeling all is futility. Or we can see that there is endless opportunity to impact the hurting world around us with the love of Christ and the hope He offers.

One church in Ohio sends a group of people to downtown Toledo to sit and talk with people in need on the streets. Tutoring volunteers in a nearby city encourage children in multiple ways with schoolwork and life. A college ministry in another local city makes pancakes in a yard near downtown bars to care for people and invite them to church. One woman takes cookies to her neighbors just for a chance to know them better.

What might you do to make a difference in your neighborhood and town?

God, help us to not lose hope; rather, enable us to love people
and seek to make a difference for You. Amen.

Continue in His Love

I have loved you, [just] as the Father has loved Me;
abide in My love [continue in His love with Me].
JOHN 15:9 AMP

What does it mean to "continue" or "remain" in Christ's love? Since His love is perfect, and was shown in the flesh, remaining in His love means staying connected to the person of Jesus Christ through the priceless gift of His Spirit.

Throughout your day, ask God to give you creative ways to stay connected to Jesus. Here are a few examples:

- When you get up and walk to the coffeepot to turn it on, pray that God will pour His love into You so that you can pour it into others.
- During your shower, ask God to cleanse you of your sins.
- As you put on your makeup or brush your hair, meditate on His beauty and goodness. Ask Him to make you aware of the beauty He gives through creation and other people throughout the day.
- As you eat meals, praise God for the food He gives us in His Word. Take time to meditate on scripture, even if it's just for a few moments, as you eat. If you eat with others, pray for opportunities to talk about Him.

Jehovah God, I praise You for being my Creator, Redeemer,
and Friend. Thank You for giving me the love of Jesus,
and help me to remain in that love every day. Amen.

Prayer—in Real Life

*And when he had taken it, the four living creatures and
the twenty-four elders fell down before the Lamb.
Each one had a harp and they were holding golden bowls
full of incense, which are the prayers of God's people.*
REVELATION 5:8 NIV

In the movie *Dan in Real Life*, actor Steve Carrell plays Dan, a widower whose personal and professional lives become complicated when he falls for Marie, his brother's girlfriend.

At one point in the film, Dan's father encourages him to begin dating again—not realizing that Dan is pining for someone. "You always said that with Suzanne, you won the lottery, and to try again would feel greedy," the dad says. "But it's been four years."

Over the course of the movie, Dan realizes he has fallen in love with Marie because of her zeal for life, her intelligence, and her beauty. Eventually, they begin a relationship. Dan can't believe his luck; lightning has, indeed, struck twice.

Prayer is a similar scenario. Prayer gives us vitality and wisdom and makes us open to God's beauty. The gifts we find through answered prayer are so rich that we can almost feel guilty asking for more. Prayer is more powerful than lightning and holds riches far beyond a winning lottery ticket. And when life gets complicated, we can hold on to the One who adores us more than we can imagine—through prayer.

*Lord, we thank You for the gift of prayer, which is
more valuable than a million dollars. Amen.*

Three Strings

*Two people are better than one, because they get more done by
working together. If one falls down, the other can help him up. But it
is bad for the person who is alone and falls, because no one is there to
help. . .a rope that is woven of three strings is hard to break.*
ECCLESIASTES 4:9–10, 12 NCV

God uses His people to encourage and strengthen one another. As
iron sharpens iron, so a friend sharpens a friend (Proverbs 27:17). We
get more accomplished in our own lives—and in the grand scheme of
things—when we are open to the help and encouragement of others.

If you see a friend in need of physical, emotional, or spiritual
help—ask the Lord to give you the wisdom and understanding to be
used in helpful ways. And when a friend offers similar help to you,
don't be too proud to accept it.

Ask the Lord to guide you in finding a "three-string"
accountability partner. Look for a Christian woman with a strong
faith in the Lord who is willing to pray with you, encourage you in
your faith, and be honest about your strengths and weaknesses. Meet
together several times a month and ask each other the hard questions:
Were you faithful to the Lord this week? Did you gossip? Is there
anything you're struggling with right now? How can I pray for you?

With God, you, and a trusted Christian friend working together,
you become a rope of three strings that is hard to break!

*Father, thank You for using Your people to encourage and sharpen
me. Guide me as I seek an accountability partner who will help me
grow in my relationship with You. Amen.*

Strength in the Lord

The LORD is my light and my salvation—whom shall I fear?
The LORD is the stronghold of my life—of whom shall I be afraid?
PSALM 27:1 NIV

Even when it seems that everything is piling up around you, Christ is there for you. Take heart! He is your stronghold, a very present help right in the midst of your trial. Regardless of what comes against you in this life, you have the Lord on your side. He is your light in the darkness and your salvation from eternal separation from God. You have nothing to fear.

At times, this world can be a tough, unfair, lonely place. Since the fall of man in the garden, things have not been as God originally intended. The Bible assures us that we will face trials in this life, but it also exclaims that we are more than conquerors through Christ who is in us! When you find yourself up against a tribulation that seems insurmountable, *look up*. Christ is there. He goes before you, stands with you, and is backing you up in your time of need. You may lose everyone and everything else in this life, but nothing has the power to separate you from the love of Christ. Nothing.

Jesus, I cling to the hope I have in You. You are my rock, my
stronghold, my defense. I will not fear, for You are with me always.
Amen.

When You Give Your Life Away

*Which of you, intending to build a tower, sitteth not down first,
and counteth the cost, whether he have sufficient to finish it?*
LUKE 14:28 KJV

Henry David Thoreau once said, "The price of anything is the amount of life you exchange for it." Busy lives often dictate that there is no time for the important things. People say, "Oh, I don't have time for this or that," or, "I wish I had the time. . ." The truth is you make the time for what you value most.

Every person has the same amount of life each day. What matters is how you spend it. It's easy to waste your day doing insignificant things—what many call time wasters—leaving little time for God. The most important things in life are eternal endeavors. Spending time in prayer to God for others. Giving your life to building a relationship with God by reading His Word and growing in faith. Sharing Christ with others and giving them the opportunity to know Him. These are the things that will last.

What are you spending your life on? What are you getting out of what you give yourself to each day?

Heavenly Father, my life is full. I ask that You give me wisdom and instruction to give my life to the things that matter most. The time I have is precious and valuable. Help me to invest it wisely in eternal things. Amen.

The Light of His Word

[God] has redeemed my life from going down to the pit [of destruction], and my life shall see the light!
JOB 33:28 AMP

Natasha hung up the phone in shock. The doctor had just called, confirming her worst nightmare: Natasha's mammogram had come back positive for cancer.

Her mind and heart raced. She shook uncontrollably and broke down in sobs. After several minutes, she took a deep breath and sighed, her energy spent.

What now? she thought. She sat, numb, for several minutes. Natasha knew she needed to call her parents, siblings, and friends, but she wasn't ready to do that yet.

And then a voice in her head whispered, *"Read the Bible."*

Natasha shakily stood up, walked over to her bookshelf, and took out her well-loved and well-worn Bible. She turned hungrily to the Psalms and read several out loud, as if to convince herself of the truth they held. Slowly, her heart rate returned to normal, and her thoughts slowed.

Then, Natasha turned to the book of Job in the Old Testament. This servant of God had suffered terribly, yet he never cursed God. Natasha read several passages, and when she came to Job 33:28, she underlined it.

I will hold on to this verse, she thought. It became her lifeline throughout her ordeal with cancer.

Lord, thank You that You are with us and won't ever leave us. Thank You that You redeem our lives and save us from death's destruction.
Amen.

A Forever Love

But I trust in your unfailing love; my heart rejoices in your salvation.
PSALM 13:5 NIV

The Bible tells us that God's love for us is unfailing. The dictionary defines unfailing as "completely dependable, inexhaustible, endless." Our hearts can truly rejoice knowing that we can never exhaust God's love. It won't run out. We can completely depend on God and His love for us at all times and in all situations.

Many people—even Christians—go through life believing that God is just a grumpy old man at the edge of heaven looking down on us with disappointment and disgust. That couldn't be further from the truth! Through Jesus Christ and His power at work within us, God sees us as *holy* and *dearly loved* (Colossians 3:12 NIV) children. His love is unfailing, and that can never change! Check out the following verses:

- In your unfailing love you will lead the people you have redeemed. In your strength you will guide them to your holy dwelling. EXODUS 15:13 NIV

- Many are the woes of the wicked, but the LORD's unfailing love surrounds the man who trusts in him. PSALM 32:10 NIV

- How priceless is your unfailing love, O God! People take refuge in the shadow of your wings. PSALM 36:7 NIV

The next time you start to think that God is upset with you, remember His unfailing and unchanging love.

*Father in heaven, Your unfailing love surrounds me as I trust in You.
Thank You for Your amazing promise! Amen.*

How to Be a Natural Beauty

*Your beauty should not come from outward adornment, such as
elaborate hairstyles and the wearing of gold jewelry or fine clothes.
Rather, it should be that of your inner self, the unfading beauty of a
gentle and quiet spirit, which is of great worth in God's sight.*
1 PETER 3:3–4 NIV

Are you one of those who love clothes, shoes, jewelry, and current
hairstyles? Many of us are! We like looking put together when we go
to work or church. Who doesn't feel wonderful when wearing a great
outfit we know complements us? Or maybe you're one who hits the
gym more than most in pursuit of that perfect swimsuit body?

While there is nothing wrong with wanting to look nice or fit,
outward looks will eventually fade. The beauty that will never fade
comes from the inside. When we know that the Master Creator made
us, we can go into any situation with confidence knowing God wants
us the way He made us and that He has a plan for our lives. What
adornments are you investing in?

*Father God, thank You for making me. Thank You also for loving me
just as I am. Help me to look at myself the way You look at me
and to love myself for who You made me to be—a beautiful
child of the Most High God. Amen.*

Please God

For God is pleased with you when you do what you know is right.
1 PETER 2:19 NLT

Few moms hear comments from their children or husband like, "Hey, thanks for washing my basketball uniform," or "I appreciate the way you remind me to do my homework," or "Wow, the toilet bowl is sparkling clean!" Face it. Women just don't receive that kind of encouragement; yet we do those things anyway, with no thought of receiving credit. It's simply what we do for our families.

The same is true as believers. It's always right to do right. Christians serve, give, pray, encourage, and bless others because it is the right thing to do. These actions are as natural to the true believer as escorting a five-year-old across the street is to a mother.

Are you discouraged when no one notices how well you conducted a Bible study or served a church dinner? Does it bother you if your good deeds go unnoticed? Then it's time for a motive-check. God, who knows the thoughts and intents of our hearts, is well pleased when we do what is right, whether or not anyone notices.

We serve without applause because we love God, not because we desire to please men. Besides, the only One we should strive to satisfy is our God, who sees what we do in secret and is well pleased.

Dear Lord, thank You for the encouragement You give me daily. Although I don't deserve it, I appreciate Your appreciation! Amen.

A Powerful Weapon

*He urged them to plead for mercy from the God of heaven
concerning this mystery, so that he and his friends might
not be executed with the rest of the wise men of Babylon.*
DANIEL 2:18 NIV

Nina accepted a part-time position with her church as a children's
midweek Bible study coordinator. She loved the children and parents
she served, but every Wednesday something happened to threaten her
sanity.

One week, the church's computer crashed, sending all her
files—including copies of that evening's lessons—into oblivion. The
next Wednesday, not one but two bathrooms on the children's wing
flooded.

Finally, a wise woman on the church's senior staff mentioned that
her difficulties might have something to do with spiritual warfare.
After all, the woman asked, aren't children learning about loving and
living for Jesus? Doesn't the devil hate that?

Nina nodded and marveled that she had missed such an obvious
aspect of ministry. That day, she began to form a team of individuals
who vowed to pray daily for Bible study teachers, students, facilities—
and Nina. Though her difficulties didn't cease, Nina noticed that she
felt less anxiety and more peace as she planned each week's lessons.
She also saw an increase in children's attendance and teachers'
faithfulness.

The Bible says it, and Nina saw it: prayer works.

*Heavenly Father and Creator of all things, thank You
for giving me the gift of prayer. Help me seek and find
people who will covenant to pray for me. Amen.*

A True Heart

*Jesus answered, "Isaiah was right when he spoke about you
hypocrites. He wrote, 'These people show honor to me with words,
but their hearts are far from me. Their worship of me is worthless.
The things they teach are nothing but human rules.'"*
MARK 7:6–7 NCV

Jesus considered the Pharisees hypocrites because they were
pretending to honor the Lord so that others would think they were
holy and hold them in high regard. But their hearts weren't in it.

God wants our hearts *and* our words. The Bible says in Luke 6:45
(AMP) that "out of the abundance (overflow) of the heart his mouth
speaks." What you think and feel inside is eventually what will come
out. If your heart isn't really set on the Lord, people will see that your
actions don't match up with what you're saying.

When you pray, always be honest with God and with yourself.
When asked to pray in public, there is no need to use large, flowery
words to impress others. God is the only One who matters.

A man was asked to pray a blessing before a big holiday dinner.
He complied but spoke so softly that not many could hear him at all.
When he said "amen," the family looked up to see if he was really
finished.

"We couldn't hear you!" the family said.

"Well, I wasn't praying to you!" replied the man.

*Dear Jesus, let my heart, my words,
and my actions always be true to You. Amen.*

Homegrown Blessings

*Then God said, "I give you every seed-bearing plant
on the face of the whole earth and every tree that has
fruit with seed in it. They will be yours for food."*
GENESIS 1:29 NIV

One young girl was a notoriously picky eater, especially when it came to fruits and vegetables. One spring her mother got the idea of planting a garden as a family project, hoping that her daughter's involvement would help change her opinion.

"Mom, look! Corn!"

A few ears had managed to pollinate correctly in the summer sun with well-developed kernels, which were a shiny, variegated yellow color.

"Can we keep these for Thanksgiving, Mom? Have them for dinner just like the pilgrims did?"

"If we freeze them," the mother said as they removed the ears from the stalks. She was excited that the little girl actually wanted to eat what they'd grown.

That Thanksgiving, they did take the corn out of the freezer and prepare it. They also opened several jars of homegrown vegetables that had been canned. Before them was a bountiful feast, most of which came from the labor of their own hands and the blessings of enough rain and sunshine. God had provided in much the same way as He had for our forefathers that first Thanksgiving Day.

*Thank You, Lord, for Your abundance in so many ways—Your love,
Your provision, and the ultimate sacrifice of Your Son. I am so
thankful that You have provided for my every need. Amen.*

Live in Unity

*May God, who gives this patience and encouragement,
help you live in complete harmony with each other,
as is fitting for followers of Christ Jesus.*
ROMANS 15:5 NLT

How does one live in unity with so many different types of people?
One woman prefers vibrant, bold colors and has a personality to
match. Another woman prefers muted tones, and her demure attitude
fits accordingly. One church member might gravitate toward the
classical, traditional hymns, while another prefers more contemporary
music.

Christians disagree on a lot of issues, and conflicts often result—
in and out of the Church. Yet we are to exercise the patience and
encouragement God provides to help us live in harmony with one
another.

One quotation says it well: "God prizes Christian unity above
doctrinal exactitude." Our salvation is based on whom we worship,
not where or how we worship. Quibbling over the cut, style, or color
of our spiritual clothing causes us to succumb to our fleshly nature
rather than God's will for us.

Personal preferences and heartfelt opinions are what make us
individuals. Every believer has a gift to share within the Body of
Christ. If we were all the same, how could we grow and learn? Jesus
prayed for unity among the believers. God encourages us to do the
same.

*Father, thank You that You give me the ability and power to walk in
unity with my brothers and sisters in Christ. I pray for Christian unity.
Let it begin with me. Amen.*

Thankful, Thankful Heart

I will praise you, LORD, with all my heart.
I will tell all the miracles you have done.
PSALM 9:1 NCV

If you live from the perspective that 10 percent of life is what happens to you and the rest is how you respond, then every situation has a side—positive or negative. Say you're late to work; every stoplight on your way is a red one; and you feel like you just can't make up the time. Instead of complaining, consider the delay was one that God appointed to keep you safe.

When you choose to approach life from the positive side, you can find thankfulness in most of life's circumstances. It completely changes your outlook, your attitude, and your countenance. God wants to bless you. When you are tempted to feel sorry for yourself or to blame others or God for difficulties, push PAUSE. Take a moment and rewind your life. Look back and count the blessings that God has given you. As you remind yourself of all He has done for you and in you, it will bring change to your attitude and give you hope in the situation you're facing. Count your blessings today.

Lord, I am thankful for my life and all You have done for me.
When life happens, help me to respond to it in a healthy, positive way.
Remind me to look to You and trust You to carry me through
life's challenges. Amen.

Keep Praying

Pray without ceasing.
1 THESSALONIANS 5:17 KJV

"Talking to men for God is a great thing, but talking to God for men is greater still" (E. M. Bounds). Did you realize that we can witness all day to someone and never reach that person for Christ until prayer energizes our words?

Perhaps you have a wayward son or daughter, or an unsaved husband. You're heartbroken and have tried to share the message of salvation repeatedly to no avail. You've prayed, but nothing changes. Hoping to open their eyes, you continue to "preach," but soon your preaching becomes nagging and they resist your words all the more. So what should you do? Stop sharing the truth that you know will set them free? Keep silent and hope for the best?

Jesus said, "No one is able to come to Me unless the Father Who sent Me attracts and draws him and gives him the desire to come to Me. . ." (John 6:44 AMP). Prayer is a prerequisite to salvation. Consistent and passionate prayer for others moves God to draw them through the power of the Holy Spirit. Our prayers soften hardened hearts and prepare the heart's soil to receive God's Word.

It's our job to pray specifically for the needs of a person, and it's God's job to change that person's heart to receive the Gospel message.

So don't despair. Just keep praying.

Lord, when I get frustrated and fail to see the results of my prayers, encourage me to keep praying. Amen.

Kindness

*"Here is my servant, whom I uphold,
my chosen one in whom I delight."*
ISAIAH 42:1 NIV

Jackie and her daughters celebrated Advent in a unique way. They decided that every day they would perform little acts of kindness. They wrote their ideas down, and with much excitement they planned to surprise friends, family, and strangers with unexpected blessings. They paid parking meters that were about to expire, sang carols at nursing homes, gave hot chocolate to the mail carrier, babysat for free, and did many other things anonymously or expecting nothing in return. The result? They were blessed with smiles, thank-yous, and even a few happy tears; and they hoped that their acts of kindness would prompt others to do the same.

In 1 Peter 5:2, the Bible says, "Be shepherds of God's flock that is under your care, watching over them—not because you must, but because you are willing, as God wants you to be; not pursuing dishonest gain, but eager to serve. . ." (NIV).

God calls His people to serve, and service comes in many forms. Some work actively in the church as ministers and missionaries. Others volunteer in their communities through homeless shelters, fund-raising projects, food banks, and other causes. And every day, Christians like Jackie and her girls work silently in the background performing little acts of kindness.

Can you encourage someone today through a little act of kindness?

*Dear God, how can I serve You today?
What can I do to show kindness to others? Amen.*

Smile, Someone Needs It

A merry heart maketh a cheerful countenance.
PROVERBS 15:13 KJV

The gas station attendant whistled and smiled as Phyllis paid for a purchase.

"Nice to hear someone so cheerful this early in the morning," Phyllis said.

"Well, my Christian dad always said that no matter how bad you feel inside, keep a cheerful attitude," the man replied. "People think I'm always happy, but my heart is breaking," he confessed as he bagged her items. "As we speak, my twenty-three-year-old son is standing in a courtroom for sentencing. I bailed him out many times, so I told him that this time he'd have to face it alone. But it hurts."

Touched, Phyllis encouraged the man, saying, "No matter what, know that God's hand is on your son's life."

The man smiled and said, "Thank you. That's why I can smile."

One quote reads, "Some pursue happiness, others create it." Everyone has a story, and often it's a sad one. Who knows what the store clerk is facing, or the person sitting alongside you in the church pew? A smile or kind word can diminish their sorrow even for a split second. It may be the only "hug" they receive all day.

Phyllis prayed for the father who whistled despite his pain—the man who had learned that no matter what happened, God would encourage him to smile.

*Lord, create in me a merry heart to offer a smile
in the midst of adversity. Amen.*

God Is in Control

*So do not fear, for I am with you; do not be dismayed,
for I am your God. I will strengthen you and help you;
I will uphold you with my righteous right hand.*
ISAIAH 41:10 NIV

One evening, after yet another chemo treatment, Jim was exhausted
and ready to throw in the towel. Jim's son, a well-known football
coach, came by after a game to check on his dad. He found Jim on the
couch, slumped and defeated. "I can't even sit up straight anymore,"
he told his son. "What's the use? What good am I to anyone? I can't
even feed myself."

The healthy, young coach sat down on the couch by his dad.
"Remember when I was a kid?" he asked. "You used to do everything
for me. You and Mom had to cut up my meat for me! You lifted me
up on your shoulders at ball games so I could see over the crowd.
Remember, Dad?"

Jim smiled at the thought of those long-ago days.

"Well, now it's my turn," Jim's son said. He adjusted his father's
thin, weak body so that pillows helped prop him up straight. He took
the dinner plate that Jim had pushed aside in frustration and began
cutting up the food.

What a blessing that he was there to hold Jim up, physically and
emotionally. Our heavenly Father has it all under control. In your
weakest moment, He holds you up with His righteous right hand. You
have nothing to worry about. He will be your strength.

*Lord, thank You for the assurance that You are my strength.
When I am weak or afraid, You will hold me up with
Your strong, righteous right hand. Amen.*

Love Your Enemies

*"Love your enemies, do good to them, and lend to them without
expecting to get anything back. Then your reward will be great."*
LUKE 6:35 NIV

These words, spoken by Jesus, are some of the hardest words we have
to consider. Love our enemies? Really?

The thought of loving those who do us harm just doesn't sit
right. The thought of giving kindness in return for malicious intent
makes no sense and causes our stomachs to knot up, our shoulders to
tighten. Love our enemies? Please, God, no.

Isn't it enough to avoid our enemies and do them no harm?

Sometimes. Maybe. But most of the time, God calls us to a love
so brave, so intense that it defies logic and turns the world on its side.
He calls us to love like He loves.

That means we must show patience where others have been
short. We must show kindness where others have been cruel. We
must look for ways to bless, when others have cursed.

Something about that just doesn't feel right to our human hearts.

But God promises great rewards for those who do this. Oh,
the rewards may not be immediate. But when God promises great
rewards, we can know without doubt that any present struggle will be
repaid with goodness and blessing, many times over.

*Dear Father, help me to love those who hate me, bless those who
curse me, and show kindness to those who have been cruel.
Help me to love like You love. Amen.*

Be of Good Cheer

*But the LORD said to Samuel, "Do not consider his appearance
or his height, for I have rejected him. The LORD does not look
at the things people look at. People look at the outward appearance,
but the LORD looks at the heart."*
1 SAMUEL 16:7 NIV

Many are waiting to hear from others that they are valuable. They go
from group to group until they settle on the highest bidder. No matter
how badly this group mistreats them they think, *This is what I am
worth.* But that's not truth. Only God knows your potential. Only God
knows the hidden talents He has placed within you. Only God knows
His plan for you. Only God knows your heart. Other people will always
sell you short!

God told the prophet Samuel to pick out the new king of Israel,
for God had revealed he would come from that lineage. God looked
over the ones who arrived and asked Jesse if he had another. God
was after someone whose heart was turned toward Him. When the
youngest, least likely boy arrived, the Lord said, "Rise and anoint him;
this is the one" (1 Samuel 16:12 NIV).

David became the king of Israel because he listened to God and
poured out his heart to Him. God chose David because God looked
at David's heart. And He liked what He saw. Today, turn your heart
toward God so He will be pleased.

Father, I choose You this day. Amen.

Pray for Christian Households

*When she speaks, her words are wise,
and she gives instructions with kindness.*
PROVERBS 31:26 NLT

Is there a Christian woman whom you admire, someone who has helped you grow in your faith? In Paul's second letter to Timothy, he mentioned two special women in Timothy's life: "I am reminded of your sincere faith, which first lived in your grandmother Lois and in your mother Eunice and, I am persuaded, now lives in you also" (2 Timothy 1:5 NIV). How precious it is in God's sight when children are raised in households where He is the foundation and family is the priority.

In Christian households, children learn about God's love and faithfulness. Discipline is administered out of loving-kindness not anger, and love is taught through the parents' example. It is a home in which Christlike wisdom is passed from generation to generation.

In Timothy's household, he learned from his mother and grandmother's faith, and according to Paul, those seeds of faith grew in young Timothy and led him to become a servant of the Lord.

Whether you are married or single, have children or not, you can plant seeds of faith though your own Christian example and prayer. Pray for all children that they will grow up in godly homes, and pray for women everywhere that they will raise their children in Christian households and remain always faithful to God.

*Heavenly Father, shine Your light through me today
that I might be an example to others. Amen.*

Misery Becomes Ministry

There is nothing better for a man than that he should eat
and drink and make himself enjoy good in his labor.
Even this, I have seen, is from the hand of God.
ECCLESIASTES 2:24 AMP

Donna spent her teen years modeling professionally. At first she felt
powerful and beautiful, but over time the glamour of the industry
began to fade. As she ate less and less, Donna's energy flagged, and
she succumbed to the pressure to do drugs. But those substances took
their toll quickly on her mind, body, and spirit.

One night, in desperation, she cried out to God. Minutes later,
a friend from her past messaged her on Facebook. "Can you meet?
Wanna catch up?" said the message. As it turned out, her friend
was now a seminary student as well as a great listener. Over several
conversations, Donna gave her life to Christ. She started turning down
jobs for lingerie and swimsuits (to her agents' consternation), got
involved in a church, and studied the Bible in her free time.

Now, Donna has a worldwide ministry to young women, through
speaking events, books, and online videos. She often gives her
testimony and offers advice on dating, beauty, and peer pressure.
Donna has never been happier. "My misery became my ministry," she
says, beaming.

Lord, You waste nothing. Give me wisdom to trust You
as You lead me to the most fulfilling job, where I can
glorify You and make a difference. Amen.

Love Covers a Multitude

And now these three remain: faith, hope and love.
But the greatest of these is love.
1 CORINTHIANS 13:13 NIV

He leaves the toilet seat up and forgets to shut the drawers on a regular basis. He sometimes uses the wrong toothbrush, leaving dried toothpaste on her brush. He drops coffee grounds in the silverware drawer and leaves all but one pan dirty in the kitchen when he cooks. But he will text to say he loves her.

His balled-up, sweaty socks that need to be unraveled before washing or drying are usually full of grass or dirt. He leaves bikes and things behind parked cars, where he forgets about them. But he keeps working hard to support her and the kids.

He can't remember the dinner event she has told him about three times this week, and he has lost his phone again. . . .

Then she remembers how patient God is with her many shortcomings. God never stops working, and He clearly loves her. God says in His text how He died for her and will never give up on her.

Love covers a multitude. Indeed.

Lord, thank You for the way You love us without fail, even with our many flaws. Thank You for helping us to love others the same way.
Amen.

Thank You

*I have not stopped giving thanks for you,
remembering you in my prayers.*
EPHESIANS 1:16 NIV

After Japan attacked Pearl Harbor, President Franklin Roosevelt
issued an order proclaiming much of the US Pacific Coast as a military
area and excluding people of Japanese ancestry from living there.
In 1942, more than one hundred thousand Japanese were forced to
relocate to "War Relocation Camps." Among them was the Honda
family who lived near Los Angeles.

Young Rose Honda, a seventh grader, had to leave the school
she loved, a place where she excelled both academically and socially.
Relocation affected not only Rose but also her school friends and
teachers. They kept in touch through letters.

Today, the Manzanar National Historic Site marks the location
of one of the camps. On exhibit there is a letter from Rose's school
written to the family. It thanks them for all the gracious things they
did and credits them for building up a fine spirit among Japanese
students who were forced to relocate. The letter goes on to praise
Rose and to encourage her toward coming back soon.

A sincere letter expressing gratitude is one way for Christians
to encourage one another. Paul often wrote letters when he was in
prison, and he relied on his friends' letters for support.

Written words last—so write a letter today. Tell someone thank
you. Encourage them with your words.

*Dear Lord, please provide me with the best words
to sincerely thank and encourage others. Amen.*

Praying for Our Loved Ones

*Therefore I tell you, whatever you ask for in prayer,
believe that you have received it, and it will be yours.*
MARK 11:24 NIV

One of the best things we can do for our friends and family members
is pray for them. And while there isn't one single formula for prayer
in the Bible, we can take cues from the prayers of people in the
scriptures.

Are we pharisaical as we talk to our heavenly Father, asking Him
to change others—but neglecting to ask Him to change us? Do we
take responsibilities for the hurts we have caused, like David did in
the Psalms? Do we pray with thanksgiving, like Mary did after Gabriel
came to her?

Do we beseech God with faith, believing that He can do anything,
as Hannah did? Or do we pray in hesitation, lacking conviction?
We could also learn a lot from the prayers of Paul in his letters to
the churches he ministered to. Many of his prayers can be prayed
verbatim for those we love.

We also find help and hope when we sit in silence, listening in
prayer. God, through His Holy Spirit, can give us wisdom, endurance,
and insight we would never come up with on our own.

Though we can't always see it, He is at work. . .in our loved ones'
hearts—and in ours.

*Lord, thank You for Your concern for those I love.
I know You love them even more than I do. Amen.*

Love's Current

The grace of our Lord was poured out on me abundantly,
along with the faith and love that are in Christ Jesus.
1 TIMOTHY 1:14 NIV

Giving a gift to a loved one often gives us great pleasure. We shop in anticipation of the recipient's excitement in our purchases. When we love that person, our joy can be even greater. So it is with God's love for us. He gave us His Son: a pure and perfect gift, because He loves us in vast measure.

No matter what our attitude may be toward God, we can never forget His precious gift of Jesus Christ. Even if we reflect despair or anger, He loves us. Scripture states grace and love is given abundantly, which means bountifully, plenteously, generously. How can we miss God's love when He is so gracious?

The famous theologian Charles Spurgeon put it this way: "Our God never ceases to shine upon his children with beams of love. Like a river, his lovingkindness is always flowing, with a fullness inexhaustible as his own nature."

This day, rise with the expectation of God's great grace and love. Let your life reflect that love and feel His pleasure. Plunge into the river of His love and feel Him carry you on its current. Relax in His arms in the knowledge that He cares for you.

Lord, carry me along in the current of Your love's stream.
I love You extravagantly. Amen.

Rejoice!

Rejoice in the Lord always. I will say it again: Rejoice!
PHILIPPIANS 4:4 NIV

Paul wrote these words from prison. Considering his circumstances, it doesn't seem like he had much reason to rejoice. Yet, he knew what many of us forget: when we have the Lord on our side, we always have reason to rejoice.

He didn't say, "Rejoice in your circumstances." He told us to rejoice in the Lord. When we're feeling depressed, anxious, or lost in despair, we can think of our Lord. We can remind ourselves that we are so very loved. We are special to God. He adores us, and in His heart, each of us is irreplaceable.

Perhaps the reason we lose our joy sometimes is because we've let the wrong things be the source of our joy. If our joy is in our finances, our jobs, or our relationships, what happens when those things fall through? Our joy is lost.

But when God is the source of our joy, we will never lose that joy. Circumstances may frustrate us and break our hearts. But God is able to supply all our needs. He is able to restore broken relationships. He can give us a new job or help us to succeed at our current job. Through it all, despite it all, we can rejoice in knowing that we are God's, and He loves us.

Dear Father, thank You for loving me.
Help me to make You the source of my joy. Amen.

Pray without Ceasing

*Pray without ceasing. In every thing give thanks:
for this is the will of God in Christ Jesus concerning you.*
1 THESSALONIANS 5: 17–18 KJV

*Pray without ceasing. Pray continually. Never stop praying. Pray all
the time.* Regardless which translation of the Bible you choose, the
command is the same. It seems impossible! How can one pray all
the time? Consider this. You are young and in love. You must go to
school and work. You may be separated by a great distance from your
beloved. And yet, every moment of every day, that person is on your
mind. You talk on the phone and text constantly. His name is always
on your lips. So much so that some of your friends find it annoying! Is
your relationship with Jesus like the one described here? He wants to
be the name on your mind when you are daydreaming. He wants to be
the first one you chat with each morning and the last one you confide
in each night. He wants you to be so utterly absorbed in Him that
it begins to annoy some of your friends! Pray without ceasing. Love
Jesus with all your heart. He is crazy about you.

*Jesus, thank You that even in my sin, You died for me.
May my walk with You be the most important thing in my life.
Amen.*

Snowy Strength

"So be strong and courageous! Do not be afraid and do not panic before them. For the LORD your GOD will personally go ahead of you. He will neither fail you nor abandon you."
DEUTERONOMY 31:6 NLT

Jenna met a good friend for dinner and shopping one winter night. It was a beautiful time together. They enjoyed an Italian dinner at an upscale restaurant that they rarely could afford to bring their families to. They found a few last-minute Christmas gifts at an outdoor shopping center and ended up at a coffee shop, where they lost track of time talking.

When they realized that it was nearly midnight and time to head home, they also realized that six inches of snow had accumulated on the roads. They were both so happy to spend time together that they hadn't noticed.

But when Jenna got behind the wheel to begin the thirty-mile trek home, her concerns grew. The driving wasn't too bad until she reached the unplowed roads, which was most of them. It was especially dark that night, and there was almost no traffic. Her car slid sideways a few times, and Jenna began to feel panicky.

She began praying and thinking on the person God enables her to be. The strong person that she often loses sight of. Singing her way home, she thanked God that she could be the courageous person He made her to be.

Lord God, thank You for helping us to be strong and courageous in the face of fearful or challenging situations. Amen.

Unshakeable Love

*"For even if the mountains walk away and the hills fall to pieces, my
love won't walk away from you, my covenant commitment of peace
won't fall apart." The God who has compassion on you says so.*
ISAIAH 54:10 MSG

As modern women, anxiety seems to stalk us. Our Twitter newsfeeds
mention uprisings, terrorist attacks, market fluctuations, and
hurricanes. Fear is a very common reaction to the world's instability,
and it can easily cloud our mind and turn us into quaking, terrified
children. The question is, do we want to dissolve into frightened,
anxious women who rarely step outside our comfort zones, or do we
desire to be bold, unashamed, fearless women of the Most High King?

God doesn't want us to cower beneath the weight of uncertainty.
Instead, through the scriptures, other believers, and the indwelling
Holy Spirit, He encourages us to be bold, passionate, and faithful. But
how do we bridge the gap between our emotions and His desires for
us?

The answer: love. We must rest in God's wild, unbending love
for us. He promises in Isaiah that no matter what happens, He will
never remove Himself from us. When we believe Him wholeheartedly
and rest in His love, we will be filled with fear-busting peace and
adventurous faith. That faith allows us to dream big dreams and
conquer the worries that keep us chained.

*Lord, thank You for Your love, which never leaves me.
Help me to rest in Your love above all else. Amen.*

Fully Equipped

*His divine power has given us everything we need for a godly
life through our knowledge of him who called us by his own glory
and goodness. Through these he has given us his very great
and precious promises, so that through them you may participate
in the divine nature, having escaped the corruption in the
world caused by evil desires.*
2 PETER 1:3–4 NIV

As Christians, we are fully equipped to live a godly life on earth. We
don't have to live in a state of constant confusion. We don't have to
stress about what to do or how to live. God has given us everything
we need to be able to follow Him daily.

Second Corinthians 1:21–22 (NIV) tells us, "He anointed us, set his
seal of ownership on us, and put his Spirit in our hearts as a deposit,
guaranteeing what is to come." When we accept Christ as our Savior
and Lord of our life, God gives us *His Spirit!* He places *His very own
Spirit* in *our* hearts! Isn't that amazing? Take some time to fully reflect
on that!

John 15:26 calls the Holy Spirit our "Helper." We are never
alone. God's Spirit is right there with us as we make decisions, as we
go about our day, as we face trials, and as we enjoy His blessings. We
have a constant Helper everywhere we go!

*Heavenly Father, I'm amazed at what You've done.
Thank You for placing Your Spirit in my heart.
Help me to listen as You lead and guide me! Amen.*

Knowing God

Whoever does not love does not know God, because God is love.
1 JOHN 4:8 NIV

At first glance, this is one of those sweet, easy verses. God is love. And we like to think about love. It's soft and cushy, like velvet.

Yet, if we want full access to that great love of God, we must love others the way He loves us.

Ouch.

If love is patient, then we must show patience to others, or we don't really know God. If love is kind, we too must be kind, or we can't claim a close relationship with God. If love always hopes, always protects, always endures. . .we must do all those things for others, or we can't know God intimately.

We can't be jealous of others, for love is never jealous.

We can't be easily angered, or brag, or dishonor others, or gossip, or seek to elevate ourselves above those around us, because none of those things are characteristic of God's kind of love.

If we want to know God intimately, if we want to experience the rewards of His great love for us, we must allow Him to live out that love in our lives. When we do, we experience a closeness with God that brings our spirits to that soft, velvety place that can only be found in His love.

Dear Father, I want to know You. I want to love like You love,
so that others can experience Your great love. Amen.

What's Your Gift?

*Yes, my brother, please do me this favor for the Lord's sake.
Give me this encouragement in Christ.*
PHILEMON 1:20 NLT

Encouragement comes in many forms. A standing ovation and generous applause encourage the performer. Sport teams are uplifted through the cheers of loyal fans. For the Christian, nothing compares to the encouragement we receive from one another through God's love.

The world is full of competition; consequently, words of encouragement are few. Sadly, the Body of Christ often does the same, as jealousy blocks the flow of encouragement toward our brothers and sisters in Christ.

Every believer is gifted in different ways. Yet we often covet another's God-given gift. We wish we could sing or recite scriptures or teach like others. Yet God equips every believer with different talents.

Have you found yours? Often the greatest gifts are ones behind the scenes. The intercessors who pray daily for the pastors and leaders are greatly gifted with the power of the Holy Spirit to target and pray for whomever God puts on their hearts. Some possess the gift of giving—not just financially, but of themselves. Others possess God's wisdom and share a word that someone desperately needs. Where would we be without these loving, caring people?

Imprisoned, Paul wrote to Philemon asking him for a favor, indicating it would be of great encouragement to him. Similarly, God encourages us to encourage, too.

Lord, help me encourage others just as You encourage me. Amen.

Unfailing Love

I will instruct you and teach you in the way you should go;
I will counsel you with my loving eye on you. Many are the
woes of the wicked, but the LORD's unfailing love
surrounds the one who trusts in him.
PSALM 32:8, 10 NIV

How awesome and amazing that the God of all creation wants to instruct us and counsel us personally! He loves each of us individually as if there were only one of us to love. He's watching over us and protecting us. Doesn't that make you want to tell the world about God's unfailing love?

God's love surrounds us always—if we trust in Him. Have you put your complete trust in the Lord? If not, open your heart to Him and ask Him to become the Lord of your life. Jesus is standing at the door of your heart, ready to come in when you respond (Revelation 3:20). Or maybe you've already accepted Christ as your Savior, but you're not really sure if He can be trusted. Know that He has been faithful to His children through all generations and that He is working out every circumstance in your life for your own good (Romans 8:28).

Father God, I praise You for Your unfailing love. Continue to counsel
me and lead me in the way I should go. Thank You for watching over
me. Help me trust You completely. Amen.

Prayer Targets Selfishness

*Do nothing out of selfish ambition. . . . Rather, in humility value
others above yourselves, not looking to your own interests
but each of you to the interests of the others.*
PHILIPPIANS 2:3–4 NIV

Every workplace seems to have one. A slacker: the person who sweats
and toils when the boss is present but loafs, chats, and avoids work
when unsupervised. As a result, the workload of truly industrious
people increases.

People who strive to appear better than others give little thought
of how their self-absorption affects their coworkers, friends, or family.
They are difficult to tolerate, let alone pray for.

The above scripture discourages selfish ambition and encourages
us to look to the interests of others. As believers, God expects us to
take the high road. That means, despite someone's behavior, we are
called to pray. Pray for her salvation; pray for God to work on her
heart and mind; pray that when approached with the truth, she will
receive it with a humble, open spirit.

God targets every heart with the arrow of His Word. It travels
as far as the power of the One who thrust it on its course. Prayer,
coupled with God's Word spoken to the unlovable, never misses the
bull's-eye.

But we must first pray to see beyond the selfishness and view the
needs behind it. When we do, God equips us to pray for others. Then
the arrow of transformation is launched.

*Jesus, help me not only to tolerate but
pray for the ones for whom You died.*

How Long Has It Been?

Trust in him at all times, you people;
pour out your hearts to him, for God is our refuge.
PSALM 62:8 NIV

An early twentieth-century hymn goes like this:

Go to the deeps of God's promise;
Ask freely of Him, and receive;
All good may be had for the asking,
If, seeking, you truly believe. . . .

Has it been a long time since you've completely poured out your heart to God? Not just your everyday prayers for family and friends, but a complete and exhaustive outpouring of your heart to the Lord? Oftentimes we run to friends or spiritual counselors in times of heartache and trouble, but God wants us to pour out our hearts to Him first. He is our refuge, and we can trust Him to heal our hearts completely.

The next time you reach for the phone to call up a friend and share all of your feelings, stop and pray first. Share your heart with God and gain His perspective on your troubles. The God who created you knows you better than anyone. Let Him be your first point of contact in any situation.

Heavenly Father, help me to trust that You are here for me—to listen and to guide me. Give me wisdom to make decisions that honor You.
Amen.

Wonderful You

*For you created my inmost being; you knit me together in my mother's
womb. I praise you because I am fearfully and wonderfully made;
your works are wonderful, I know that full well.*
PSALM 139:13–14 NIV

Many of us look at ourselves and find something we want to change:

"I wish I had Julie's figure. I hate my hips."

"I love Marcia's curly hair. Mine is so straight and hard to
manage."

"Maybe I will color my hair auburn. Brown looks mousy."

And yet, many of the very things we may not like are what make
us unique. The psalmist says that we are fearfully and wonderfully
made. That means that we are made in such a way to produce
reverence and inspire awe. Our bodies are complicated and wondrous
in the way they work and heal.

By looking at ourselves the way God looks at us, we can see that
our differences are reason to praise Him and acknowledge that it is
right to honor, love, and be grateful for all of His creation, including
us. Even though we may not understand why He gave us the physical
attributes that He did, we can praise Him since we know He took
great love and pleasure in creating us.

*Loving Father, I praise You for making me the way You did. I am
deeply impressed by how You put me together, making me so unique;
there is no one exactly like me. I love You! Amen.*

Mary's Prayer

*And Mary said, Behold the handmaid of the Lord; be it unto me
according to thy word. And the angel departed from her.*
LUKE 1:38 KJV

Imagine Mary's excitement and delight as she accepted Joseph's
marriage proposal. A young bride-to-be with her entire life before her
is suddenly approached by an angel with a different proposal. Seeing
an angel in the first place was certainly a shocking surprise; then to
be told that she had been chosen to carry God's Son—to become a
mother without ever knowing a man. Imagine the thrill and also the
concern! What would Joseph think, finding her pregnant before their
wedding day? She certainly must have thought about that.

Yet Mary told the angel she would accept God's assignment—"Let
it be done in me as you have said." She was willing to accept God's will
by faith. She had to believe God would take care of all the details. . .
and He did. He took Joseph aside and assured him that Mary had not
been with another man, but the child was God's own Son.

What has God put in your heart? Are you willing to allow His
perfect will to be done in you at the expense of what others might
think?

*Lord, give me a heart for Your purpose and plans. Help me to believe
that You will take care of all the details as I step out in faith. Amen.*

The Christmas Gift

"The second is this: 'Love your neighbor as yourself.'
There is no commandment greater than these."
MARK 12:31 NIV

The neighborhood knew Mary had emigrated from Germany during World War II, but since she kept to herself, that was pretty much all they knew. The other residents witnessed her odd habit of always sweeping the street in front of her house.

Suzanne decided Mary's house should be on the list for Christmas caroling. As the resident activities organizer, Suzanne had already amassed a stack of music and a group of volunteers of all ages.

"We'll learn 'O Tanenbaum' in German," she explained to the group of volunteers. "I'll even provide phonetic spellings."

As the group gathered around Mary's front door on Christmas Eve, the first tentative strains of the carol were sung. The carolers had only rehearsed a few times, and the German sounded pretty rough. However, they continued to sing on the dark front porch. Soon the light snapped on and the door swung open, revealing an old woman with tears streaming down her wrinkled face.

"That was the most beautiful song I've ever heard," she exclaimed, wiping the tears from her cheeks. "It was the best gift ever."

Thank You, Father, for leading us to show Your love in many ways—
the touch of a hand, a smile, or even sharing a simple song.
We are all valuable in Your sight, no matter our age or our
circumstances. Your love is amazing! Amen.

Perfect Love

*And there were shepherds living out in the fields nearby, keeping
watch over their flocks at night. An angel of the Lord appeared to
them, and the glory of the Lord shone around them, and they were
terrified. But the angel said to them, "Do not be afraid. I bring you
good news that will cause great joy for all the people. Today in the
town of David a Savior has been born to you; he is the Messiah,
the Lord. This will be a sign to you: You will find a baby wrapped
in cloths and lying in a manger."*
LUKE 2:8–12 NIV

The holidays can be a time when fear creeps up on us unexpectedly.
We can fear for our country, fear the family conflicts that may surface
over holiday dinners, fear the state of our finances and relationships. . .
the fear list can be long.

What the angel said to the shepherds applies to us now and
always. "Do not be afraid. I bring you good news that will cause great
joy for all the people." This Christmas, let your focus be on that joyful
news. Jesus' birth gives us hope. We don't have to fear.

First John 4:18 tells us that perfect love casts out fear. Perfect
love was born on Christmas Day. Let that perfect love fill your heart
with joy, hope, and peace. Then there will be no room in your heart
for fear.

*Dear Jesus, fill my heart with Your unfailing love this Christmas
and always. Thank You that I never have to be afraid. Amen.*

Look Up!

*"Your love, LORD, reaches to the heavens,
your faithfulness to the skies."*
PSALM 36:5 NIV

In Bible times, people often studied the sky. Looking up at the heavens reminded them of God and His mighty wonders. A rainbow was God's sign to Noah that a flood would never again destroy the earth. God used a myriad of stars to foretell Abraham's abundant family, and a single star heralded Christ's birth.

The theme of the heavens traverses the scriptures from beginning to end. The Bible's first words say: "In the beginning God created the heavens." The psalmist David shows God's greatness in comparison to them: "the heavens declare the glory of God." And in the New Testament, Jesus describes the end times saying, "There will be signs in the sun, moon and stars. . . At that time [people] will see the Son of Man coming in a cloud with power and great glory."

Some of God's greatest works have happened in the sky.

This immense space that we call "sky" is a reflection of God's infinite love and faithfulness. It reaches far beyond what one can see or imagine, all the way to heaven. Too often jobs, maintaining households, parenting, and other tasks keep us from looking up. So take time today. Look up at the heavens, and thank God for His endless love.

Heavenly Father, remind me to stop and appreciate Your wonderful creations. And as I look upward, fill me with Your infinite love. Amen.

Unconditional Love

*Neither height nor depth, nor anything else in all creation, will be able
to separate us from the love of God that is in Christ Jesus our Lord.*
ROMANS 8:39 NIV

To try to compare God's love with human love is nearly impossible.
We love our families and our closest friends. But is our love
unconditional? Families have divided for incidents as minor as a lack
of understanding or an unexpected flare-up. Disagreements, hurt
feelings, or built-up anger have caused many people to sever precious
ties.

God's love, however, is unconditional. His love isn't based on our
good deeds. It isn't grounded in our personal goodness or faithfulness.
When we sin, He forgives. If we fall, He lifts us up and helps us go
forward. He isn't easily angered, and He doesn't turn His back when
we do or say something disapproving.

What would happen if we exercised God's love toward others?
If we didn't take offense when someone was offensive, if we forgave
when wronged, if we prayed instead of accused, if we loved even
when someone failed to love us?

As Christians, nothing can separate us from God's unconditional
love that is rooted in a personal relationship with Jesus. God loves you
no matter what. Go and do the same.

*Father, thank You for the unconditional love You show me every day.
Help me to extend that love to others. Amen.*

A Day Like That

When you were dead in your sins and in the uncircumcision of
your flesh, God made you alive with Christ. He forgave us all our
sins, having canceled the charge of our legal indebtedness,
which stood against us and condemned us;
he has taken it away, nailing it to the cross.
COLOSSIANS 2:13–14 NIV

Have you ever had a day that felt doomed for dismal right out of the
gate? No, forget the gate; you didn't make it that far. It was right out
of the warm blankets that you didn't want to leave.

The demands of the day were firmly in place, and they beckoned
you out into a much colder space, sometimes quite literally. You took
no time to pause with God. "Took time?" you say. There was no time.
Your attitude suffered miserably in the trenches of your duties. Yes,
now you are in the trenches.

There (in the trenches), other people are quite miserable as well,
and you all say and do miserable things. You offend people. They
offend you. You forgot for a while what God did for you—redeeming
you on the cross.

Now you come to God asking again for His forgiveness, and you
forgive the other people from that miserable day.

Have you ever had a day like that?

Lord, thank You for placing our sins on the cross and redeeming us.
Thank You for your forgiveness and love. Amen.

Love Leads the Way

*You yourselves have seen what I did to Egypt, and how I
carried you on eagles' wings and brought you to myself.*
EXODUS 19:4 AMP

When Moses led the children of Israel out of Egypt toward the
Promised Land, he did not take them on the shortest route. God
directed him to go the long way lest the people turn back quickly
when things became difficult. God led them by day with a pillar of
clouds and by night with a pillar of fire. How clearly He showed
Himself. The people placed their hope in an almighty God and
followed His lead. When they thirsted, God gave water. When they
hungered, He sent manna. No need was unmet.

The amount of food and water required for the group is
unimaginable. Moses depended upon God. He believed God would
care for them. Because he knew of God's great love and trusted in the
Creator.

If God can do this for so many, do you not think He will care
for you? He knows your needs before you even ask. Place your hope
and trust in Him. He is able. He's proven himself over and over. By
reading the scriptures and praying to the One who loves you, you can
feel His care is infinite. His word is final. God loves you.

*Lord, help me see You gave Your life for me.
Teach me to trust in You. Amen.*

Open the Eyes of Faith

Therefore I tell you, whatever you ask for in prayer,
believe that you have received it, and it will be yours.
MARK 11:24 NIV

At the conclusion of World War II and the end of the Holocaust, these words were found scratched on the wall of an abandoned farmhouse: "I believe in the sun even when it does not shine. I believe in love, even when it is not shown. I believe in God, even when He is silent." Sketched alongside the time-worn prose was the Star of David.

Have you ever prayed for something or someone, and God seemed to turn a deaf ear? One woman prayed for her son's salvation for seven years. Each day she knelt at the foot of her tear-stained bed, pleading for her child. But God seemed silent. Yet, what she failed to understand was that the Lord had been working all along to reach her son in ways unknown to her. And finally her son embraced the Gospel through a series of life-changing circumstances.

The world says, "I'll believe it when I see it," while God's Word promises, "Believe then see."

Someone once said, "The way to see by faith is to shut the eye of reason." When we pray, rather than ask God why our prayers remain unanswered, perhaps we should ask the Lord to close our eyes so that we might see.

Lord, I believe, even when my prayers go unanswered.
Instead, I know You are at work on my behalf. Amen.

What If?

The LORD will keep you from all harm—
he will watch over your life.
PSALM 121:7 NIV

"Mommy, what if the sun falls down? What if an earthquake swallows our house? What if. . .?" When the world appears scary to children, they run to their parents with questions. They look to their mothers and fathers for comfort, reassurance, and peace.

Grown-ups are no different. They run to Father God with their what-ifs. "What if I have cancer? What if I lose my job? What if there is a terrorist attack? What if. . .?"

Psalm 46 provides the answer to all these questions. It says, "God is our refuge and strength, an ever-present help in trouble. Therefore we will not fear, though the earth give way and the mountains fall into the heart of the sea, though its waters roar and foam and the mountains quake with their surging. . . . The LORD Almighty is with us; the God of Jacob is our fortress" (NIV).

Feeling safe and secure rests not in the world or in other human beings but with God alone. He is a Christian's help and hope in every frightening situation. He promises to provide peace to all who put their faith and trust in Him.

What are you afraid of today? Allow God to encourage you. Trust Him to bring you through it and to give you peace.

Dear Lord, hear my prayers, soothe me with Your Words,
and give me peace. Amen.

Contributors

Emily Biggers is an Advanced Academics Specialist in Texas. She enjoys writing, traveling, and decorating. Emily is in the process of adopting a little girl from the country of Honduras.
Find Emily's devotional contributions on: January 1, 5, 14, 28; February 14, 21; March 1, 7, 18; April 4, 10, 18, 20, 27; May 3, 11, 21, 29; June 15, 26; July 10, 15, 25; August 2, 3; September 3, 11, 24; October 8, 20, 30; November 6, 9, 19; December 3, 13.

Renae Brumbaugh is a bestselling author, freelance writer, and award-winning humor columnist. She lives in Texas with her handsome husband and two nearly perfect, overactive children.
Find Renae's devotional contributions on: January 3, 6, 11, 27, 31; February 6, 15, 25; March 2, 8, 19, 26; April 6, 19, 24; May 8, 22, 28; June 3, 11, 27; July 7, 19; August 4, 12, 26; September 4, 28; October 3, 14, 29; November 3, 4, 13; December 4, 12, 17.

As a busy mom and minister's wife, **Dena Dyer** constantly loses things—but she's holding on to her sanity (barely). Her favorite forms of therapy? Talking and laughing with her sons, date nights with her hubby, reading, cooking, and watching movies. Dena is thankful for her creative life, which is varied and full. That doesn't mean it's easy, though. . . .
Find Dena's devotional contributions on: January 9, 15; February 4, 8, 20; March 14, 16, 21; April 12, 21, 22, 28; May 13, 14; June 7, 8, 13; July 3, 16, 26; August 8, 10, 24; September 10, 14, 21; October 10, 11, 12; November 16, 17, 21, 25; December 7, 10, 15.

Jean Fischer writes Christian literature for adults and children. A nature lover, she enjoys living in Wisconsin within walking distance of the Lake Michigan shore.

Find Jean's devotional contributions on: January 7, 25; February 3, 7, 10, 13; March 4, 9, 11; April 2, 13, 17; May 2, 6, 10; June 5, 19; July 2, 6, 11; August 1, 6, 16; September 6, 9, 13; October 5, 6; November 1, 7, 8; December 1, 6, 9, 26, 31.

Shanna D. Gregor is a freelance writer, editor, and product developer who has served various ministries and publishers since 1996 to develop more than sixty books that express God's voice for today. With a passion to see the truth of God's Word touch lives through the written word, she continues to serve through the open doors God sets before her. The mother of two young men, Shanna resides with her husband in Tucson, Arizona.

Find Shanna's devotional contributions on: January 2, 10, 22; February 1, 9; March 6, 10, 15; April 5, 9, 11, 14, 23, 26; May 7, 17; June 2, 12; July 4, 12, 18, 21; August 11, 18, 25; September 7, 17, 20, 29; October 4, 15, 24; November 2, 12, 20, 29; December 23.

Eileen Key retired after teaching school for thirty years. A freelance writer and editor, mother of three, and grandmother of three, Eileen resides in San Antonio, Texas, where she is an active member of Grace Community Church.

Find Eileen's devotional contributions on: January 8, 12, 17; February 2, 11; March 3, 5, 13; April 1, 8, 16; May 1, 4, 9, 16; June 4, 10, 16; July 1, 9, 13, 17; August 5, 7, 17; September 8, 12, 16; October 1, 7, 16; November 10, 14; December 5, 11, 29.

Tina Krause is the author of *Laughter Therapy*, Barbour's *Grand Moments for Grandmothers*, *The Bible Promise Book for Women*, *Life Is Sweet*, and *God's Answers for Your Life—Parents' Edition*. She is a contributor to over twenty-three book compilations and has nine hundred published writing credits. A freelance writer and award-winning newspaper columnist, Tina lives with her husband, Jim, in Valparaiso, Indiana, where they enjoy spoiling their five grandchildren.

Find Tina's devotional contributions on: January 16, 21; February 5, 24, 27; March 17, 27, 31; April 3; May 5, 19; June 9, 22, 25, 28, 30; July 24, 29; August 20, 22, 27, 30; September 1, 25; October 19, 21, 26, 28; November 24, 28, 30; December 2, 18, 20, 27, 30.

Shelley R. Lee has authored the books *Before I Knew You* and *Mat Madness*. Her byline has appeared in numerous magazines and newspapers, as well as Barbour's Heavenly Humor series. She resides in northwest Ohio with her husband of twenty-eight years, David, and their four grown sons.

Find Shelley's devotional contributions on: January 4, 18, 24; February 12, 19, 23; March 12, 22, 30; April 7, 15, 29; May 12, 15, 18, 24; June 1, 6, 18; July 23, 28, 31; August 9, 14; September 5, 22, 26; October 9, 18, 22, 25; November 5, 11, 15; December 8, 14, 28.

Betty Ost-Everley is an internationally published author living in Kansas City, Missouri. She presently works as an executive assistant. Out of the office, Ost-Everley is active in her church and advocates for her neighborhood. She is also a member of the Heart of America Christian Writers' Network.

Find Betty's devotional contributions on: January 20, 23, 26; February 16, 18, 22, 28; March 24, 25, 29; May 25, 26, 30, 31; June 14, 21, 24; July 5, 8, 20, 22, 27; August 13, 15, 23, 28, 31; September 15, 19, 23; October 17, 23; November 23, 27; December 22, 24.

MariLee Parrish lives in Ohio with her husband, Eric, and young children. She's a speaker, musician, and writer who desires to paint a picture of God with her life, talents, and ministries. Visit her website at www.marileeparrish.com for more info.

Find MariLee's devotional contributions on: January 13, 19, 29, 30; February 17, 26; March 20, 23, 28; April 25, 30; May 20, 23, 27; June 17, 20, 23, 29; July 14, 30; August 19, 12, 29; September 2, 18, 27, 30; October 13, 27, 31; November 18, 22, 26; December 16, 19, 21, 25.

Scripture Index